Complete Guide to Houseplants

Meredith® Books
Des Moines, Iowa

Complete
Guide to
Houseplants

At Home with Houseplants 6

The Basics of Plant Care 20

Special Care Concerns 68

Troubleshooting 88

Houseplants bring the popular pastime of gardening indoors, where their colors and textures add beauty and tranquility to any decor.

AT HOME WITH
Houseplants

Houseplants have been a part of indoor decor since Victorian times, when a few brave gardeners discovered they could grow plants on a window ledge. Soon the Victorians were putting ferns on pedestals and palms in parlors and adding heated conservatories to their homes so they could grow even more plants.

Houseplants have been thriving ever since. In fact, the modern home, with its larger windows and skylights and better climate control, makes an even better environment for indoor plants. Given the wide availability of artificial lighting and humidifiers, homeowners can now supply plants with absolutely optimal conditions for healthy growth. Indoor gardening is no longer just an effort to keep plants alive but an opportunity to grow them to perfection.

Gardening indoors does require some careful thought, but as long as you choose plants according to your home's conditions and the amount of care you're willing to give, you can grow them successfully. If you're willing to spend as little as a few minutes per week, there are at least a few houseplants out there that you can manage. If you're passionate about plants and have more time to spend on their care, you'll find a wide variety of choices. Whether you opt for tough foliage plants that can live for decades on little more than the occasional watering or the more delicate bloomers that

really do need specific care on an almost daily basis, you can succeed with houseplants. This book will show you how.

An overview

This introductory chapter shows you how to fit indoor plants into your home and lifestyle. You'll learn about designing with plants and why having them indoors is important for your physical and psychological health. You'll find out where and how to purchase plants and how to acclimatize them to your home. You'll also discover which tools and supplies to have on hand to guarantee success.

In "The Basics of Plant Care" you'll learn all you need to know about growing plants indoors, from meeting their lighting needs to watering and nourishing them. You'll also find information on controlling your indoor environment's humidity, temperature, and air circulation in order to give plants the best possible conditions for growth. If you're interested, you can read about growing plants in hydroculture, without soil, as well as how to pot plants in more traditional containers with potting mix and drainage holes. You'll also find information on how to propagate and fertilize your plants, and tips on proper grooming, pruning, staking, and training. A list of seasonal chores reminds you what to do and when.

A chapter on "Special Care Concerns" goes beyond the usual indoor gardening tips and into the realm of specialty plants. Here you'll discover the pros and cons of moving plants outdoors for the summer, and you'll find ideas for container gardening, both outdoors and in. You'll learn about the particular needs of bonsai and terrariums, as well as techniques for growing plants in greenhouses and solariums. You'll find information on forcing bulbs, such as crocuses and tulips, and ways to grow herbs indoors for kitchen use all year long. A section that covers three groups of plants that have unique needs helps you provide special care for orchids, bromeliads, and cacti and succulents.

Turn to "Troubleshooting" if you need help diagnosing and treating a specific plant problem. This chapter discusses insect pests and diseases as well as the symptoms of poor culture and how to alleviate them.

You may be tempted to jump straight into the largest chapter in this book, "Gallery of Houseplants," where you'll find more than 200 different foliage and flowering plants, table and floor plants, and climbing and trailing plants. The colorful photos and easy-to-read descriptions help you choose the best plants for your home and understand how to keep them healthy.

So read on! Soon you'll be at home with houseplants.

Making the Match

Clivia miniata **is especially easy to grow and care for inside the home, even in less than ideal conditions.**

An expanse of sunny window lets English ivy climb and trail to best effect. If your window receives direct sunlight in summer, protect tender plants from the heat with a sheer curtain.

While beautiful plants make tempting impulse purchases, you'll have longer-lasting success when you plan ahead and buy only those that you easily can make permanent additions to your home. Keep the following points in mind as you shop.

Location, location, location

First assess the growing conditions in your home. Your ability to supply the environment indoor plants require is one of the most important aspects to ensuring their long-term health. You will only be frustrated if you try to grow a plant in an unsuitable spot.

If you want a houseplant for a south window that receives hot sun all day all year long, for example, buy a cactus, euphorbia, or other sun-loving plant instead of a more delicate, shade-loving fern. If you've chosen a spot that receives only indirect or medium light, on the other hand, you will have poor luck with bright-light plants such

as cactus and hibiscus. In an area with little light, you can create an arresting display of foliage and flowers using plants such as philodendron, peace lily, and pothos.

If you love the exhilaration of an open bedroom window at night and want to keep houseplants nearby, choose a Japanese aralia or a Norfolk Island pine; both tolerate cooler temperatures. Some plants, such as prayer plant or anthurium, do poorly in drafty areas. If you have an enclosed porch or cellar that doesn't freeze even though you don't heat it in winter, take advantage of it by selecting houseplants, such as cacti or succulents, that need to be moved into a cold area for their dormant period.

Whatever the conditions in your home, the "Gallery of Houseplants" (starting on page 100) will help you identify and select the best plants for your specific growing environment.

African violets bloom for months when they receive plenty of bright, indirect light. Their small size makes them perfect for windowsills and tabletops.

Complement your style

You'll need to consider how much room you have for houseplants. Perhaps you have seen a striking plant in a hotel lobby, office building, or conservatory and vowed to get one for your home, but when you visited the plant store and saw the same kind of plant in a different context, you realized its size would dwarf everything else in your house. A simple solution to this problem is to look for substitutions that provide the same effect yet fit the space you have available. For example, if you want the look of a kentia palm but can't accommodate the 10-foot fronds, a parlor palm with only 1-foot fronds produces a proportional effect. An 8-foot-tall weeping fig is a dramatic plant, but if you don't have the room for its 6-foot canopy spread, you can select a 3-foot-tall specimen and place it on a pedestal to achieve a similar look.

Also take into consideration your decorating scheme. Although you may have many reasons for acquiring houseplants, one of the best is to complement a home's decor. Some plants naturally fit well with a particular style of decoration—a cactus or an agave used to highlight southwestern-style furnishings, for instance.

You can also complement the features of a room by emphasizing houseplant shape, size, and color. A towering palm makes a powerful accent in the archway of an older home with high ceilings, a fluffy fern is a good accent plant for a soft floral decor, and a spiky dracaena provides contrast in a country style. You may choose a white African violet to emphasize an all-white color scheme or use a scarlet hibiscus as a contrasting focal point. By taking into account these design factors, the houseplants you choose create a real statement about you and your house.

Choose plants that complement the scale of your home.

HARD-TO-KILL PLANTS

These plants may not live forever, but most will grow for at least a year or more even in very poor conditions. Give them moderate care, and they may well be with you for decades!

Agave (*Agave* spp.)
Alii fig (*Ficus maclellandii* 'Alii')
Angelwing begonia (*Begonia* 'Lucerna')
Aroid palm (*Zamioculcas zamiifolia*)
Arrowhead vine (*Syngonium podophyllum*)
Artillery plant (*Pilea microphylla*)
Asparagus fern (*Asparagus densiflorus*)
Bamboo palm (*Chamaedorea seifrizii*)
Cast-iron plant (*Aspidistra elatior*)
China doll (*Radermachera sinica*)
Chinese evergreen (*Aglaonema commutatum*)
Cissus (*Cissus* spp.)
Clivia (*Clivia miniata*)
Cow's-horn cuphorbia (*Euphorbia grandicornis*)
Dallas fern (*Nephrolepis exaltata* 'Dallasii')
Dieffenbachia (*Dieffenbachia* spp.)
Dracaena (*Dracaena* spp.)
Dwarf schefflera (*Schefflera arboricola*)
English ivy (*Hedera helix*)
Fiddle-leaf fig (*Ficus lyrata*)
Heart-leaf homalomena (*Homalomena rubescens*)
Jade plant (*Crassula ovata*)
Japanese aralia (*Fatsia japonica*)
Lady palm (*Rhapis excelsa*)
Medicine plant (*Aloe vera*)
Norfolk Island pine (*Araucaria heterophylla*)
Parlor palm (*Chamaedorea elegans*)
Peace lily (*Spathiphyllum wallisii*)
Peperomia (*Peperomia obtusifolia*)
Peruvian apple (*Cereus* spp.)
Philodendron (*Philodendron* spp.)
Ponytail palm (*Nolina recurvata*)
Pothos (*Epipremnum aureum*)
Screwpine (*Pandanus* spp.)
Silver vase plant (*Aechmea fasciata*)
Snake plant (*Sansevieria trifasciata*)
Spider plant (*Chlorophytum comosum*)
Swedish ivy (*Plectranthus australis*)
Sweet bay (*Laurus nobilis*)
Umbrella plant (*Cyperus alternifolius*)
Wandering Jew (*Tradescantia* spp.)
Wax plant (*Hoya carnosa*)
Yucca (*Yucca elephantipes*)

Designing with Houseplants

Tuck plants among your favorite art objects to create an eye-catching indoor garden.

Group together plants of different heights, shapes, and textures for the most pleasing effect.

As beautiful as plants are in their own right, a mere grouping of them may not always produce the most pleasing indoor garden. Choose and arrange your plants according to some simple design principles that take advantage of your personal style, your home's decor, and the plants' natural aesthetic qualities. There is almost no limit to the looks you can achieve, and the result can be a stunning place to work or play. Keep in mind your plants' various characteristics as you design, and feel free to experiment in search of the effect you want.

Style basics

What kind of houseplants do you want? Do you envision only blooming plants—a temporary arrangement that you will need to change often—or a more permanent display of foliage plants? Will you have many plants or just a few? In a large grouping, the focus becomes the plants themselves. On the other hand, one plant displayed by itself has another focal point: its container. Choose the container as carefully as you selected the plant.

POINT OF VIEW: Once you've decided what type of display you want, determine the point or points from which it will be viewed. You may want to back your plants against a wall where you view them from only one or two sides. If so, pay attention to the backdrop. Remember to leave room behind the plants for air circulation as well as access for routine watering and grooming. Also leave space between plants and wallpaper or artwork. Blooming plants in particular may leave behind traces of pollen or stains from flower petals.

An island grouping of plants is designed to be appreciated from any direction. It requires a fairly large, open area that is accessible from all sides.

FORMAL OR INFORMAL: Is your home's decor formal or informal? Create your indoor garden to blend with it. Formal style tends to be symmetrical and typically uses complementary shades of one color. Everything is neat and tight, the kind of look you get with topiary plants or cacti. Informal style is asymmetrical and freely uses contrasting colors, textures, and shapes including loose, trailing plants such as grape ivy and asparagus fern.

COMBINING PLANTS: The plants chosen for a display must be able to grow together. Mixing full-sun plants with shade-lovers may look good when you first put them on display, but they can't last. Take into consideration all your environmental conditions.

Make a list of plants you want to use that are adaptable to your home's conditions.

Take into account the space you have available and each plant's mature size, texture, form, and color. Large plants make good anchors in a multiple-plant display, much the same way shrubs and trees are used in an outdoor garden. Small plants create an intimate effect and bridge the space between larger specimens. The most effective look comes from combining plants of varying heights, forms, and textures that share similar culture needs.

FORM: Plants come in a variety of shapes, from a vertically trained pothos or spiky dracaena to a horizontal Christmas cactus or sword fern. They may be softly rounded like a polka-dot plant or peperomia or trailing like a Swedish ivy or philodendron. Dramatically different heights and shapes add excitement to your houseplant display and keep the viewer intrigued.

HEIGHT: It is common to place shorter plants in front, medium in the center, and tall in the back. There are ways to break with this tradition, however, that result in a more interesting display. Keep plant sizes in mind as you experiment with different combinations so large species do not overwhelm smaller ones. Try placing small plants on inverted pots or pedestals to increase their height among larger plants.

TEXTURE: A grouping of similar plants is striking in its simplicity, but plants with a variety of leaf textures add depth and energy to a display. Texture refers more to the appearance of a plant's foliage than to the actual feel of its leaves. The large, smooth leaves of a peace lily evoke calm while the smaller, perkier leaves of a ming aralia seem more energetic. A combination of many types of leaf shapes and sizes adds interest and diversity.

The spiky leaves of a Madagascar dragontree juxtaposed with the billowing foliage of a Japanese aralia or Balfour aralia shows off the individual plants and also draws attention to their differences. Large, coarse textures are more obvious, so place them farther from the viewer. The fine textures of small leaves tend to recede, so use them close up, where viewers can see them easily.

COLOR: Flowering houseplants come in every color of the rainbow. Selecting the ones you'll display at home is part of the fun of indoor gardening.

Bold colors make wonderful focal points. Bright scarlet hibiscus blooms or rich red anthurium spathes add impact to a houseplant grouping. White and silver blend well with other colors

An Asian-style cachepot complements the jade plant it holds.

and lighten the design. Use silver-leaved peperomia or silver-variegated nerve plant as a filler for a bright effect.

Even if the plants you choose don't have flowers, you'll have many shades and hues of green to choose from. Foliage plants are particularly easy to design with because green is soothing to the eyes.

If you pick plants and containers you like and use them in a decor that includes your favorite colors, you can't go wrong!

A giant euphorbia naturally enhances the southwestern decor of this sitting room.

Improving Health with Houseplants

Studies show that exposure to plants indoors relieves stress and increases productivity.

Plants are used in therapy for elderly or disabled people, bringing nature indoors to those who can't go out.

Plants make people happy. Their colors add cheer to life, and the smell and feel of greenery help soften some of the harsh elements in everyday routines.

Research shows that working with or handling plants lowers blood pressure, eases stress, and generally makes people feel better. Growing plants, whether vegetables for the table or flowers for their beauty, appeals to almost everyone and can bring a moment of peace or a few minutes of joy to an otherwise dreary day. Indoor plants provide a chance to interact with nature without leaving the house. People care for them and derive pleasure from their well-being, a relationship that fulfills a basic human emotional need.

Members of the American Horticultural Therapy Association (AHTA) use plant growing as a fundamental part of their therapy plans. They develop horticulture programs for the elderly and disabled in nursing homes and for surgery and chemotherapy patients in hospitals. They also create gardening plans for the residents of group homes and prisons.

The AHTA philosophy relies on the fact that plants appeal to human beings' senses, even when those senses are somewhat diminished. The sight of richly colored plants may be exciting or soothing to the eyes. The smells of foliage, humus, moisture, and fragrant flowers can elicit a peaceful and serene feeling or even evoke pleasant memories. AHTA members also make frequent use of plant textures in their therapy. Touching plants calms humans, whether they are wiping dust from a snake plant's leaves, pinching out the tips of a wayward grape ivy, or merely stroking the soft, fuzzy leaves of a panda plant.

Exposure to plants has been shown to improve health in many ways. It can minimize the time spent in a hospital after surgery, as well as reduce the amount and potency of painkillers requested by patients. In a study at the Sloan-Kettering Institute, postoperative breast cancer patients recovered their strength faster, increased their ability to focus attention, and reduced their depression by taking walks regularly in a landscaped garden.

These positive effects are evident in the business world as well. A study reported in the *Journal of the Mississippi Academy of Sciences* in 1996 showed that plants not only raise humidity levels, making the workplace more comfortable, but the moisture they release into the air seems to suppress airborne microbes. A Washington State University study showed that people with plants in their

COMMON SOURCES OF INDOOR AIR POLLUTION

FORMALDEHYDE: Carpeting, pressed wood, fiberboard, foam insulation, paper products
HYDROCARBONS: Vinyl furniture, detergents, fabric softeners
NITROGEN DIOXIDE: Malfunctioning furnaces, water heaters, leaking chimneys
BENZENE: Glue, spot remover, paint, varnish, paint stripper
METHYLENE CHLORIDE: Paint stripper, aerosols
TRICHLOROETHYLENE: Ink, paint, lacquer, varnish, adhesive

work environment were 12 percent more productive and had lower blood pressure than those without plants. Numerous studies continue to provide evidence that adding plants to indoor environments improves people's lives.

Pollution fighters

In this world of energy-efficient houses and office buildings sealed against the elements, it is alarming to learn just how many pollutants inhabit indoor spaces. Copy machines and printers, rug pads and carpeting, insulation and other synthetic materials, veneer furniture, products made of pressed wood and plywood, smoke, and detergents all give off volatile organic chemicals, such as xylene, benzene, trichloroethylene, ammonia, and formaldehyde. Studies conducted by the U.S. Environmental Protection Agency indicate that indoor air pollution is one of the fastest growing environmental problems.

You can reduce these toxic substances by growing plants indoors. Plants improve air quality by absorbing pollutants through their leaves, where naturally occurring microorganisms break down the chemicals. Some absorption and breakdown also occurs in potting soil.

The original research on plant filtering began when NASA recognized a need to find ways to reduce the large amount of pollutants emitted by equipment on the space shuttle. Researchers at the National Space Technology Lab found that houseplants reduced pollutants, particularly nitrogen and formaldehyde. In fact, just a single spider plant in an enclosed chamber filled with formaldehyde removed 85 percent of the pollutant in a day. As few as 15 plants can significantly reduce the pollutants in an average household. The study suggests using one potted plant for every 100 square feet of floor space for pollution control.

BEST AIR POLLUTION ABSORBERS

BENZENE: Florist's mum, peace lily, 'Warneckei' dracaena, Madagascar dragontree
FORMALDEHYDE: Bamboo palm, 'Janet Craig' dracaena, snake plant, peace lily
TRICHLOROETHYLENE: Madagascar dragontree, peace lily, 'Janet Craig' dracaena, bamboo palm

Besides breaking down toxic chemicals in the atmosphere, plant leaves clean the air by trapping particulate matter. And, in their natural process of respiration, plants absorb our respiratory waste product—carbon dioxide—and give us oxygen and moisture in return.

Spider plants improve air quality by absorbing pollutants.

THE BEST OF THE BEST

The following 12 houseplants, in approximate order of efficiency, are generally considered the best plants for reducing pollutants in the air.

Boston fern
Florist's mum
Pygmy date palm
'Janet Craig' dracaena
'Kimberley Queen' fern
Bamboo palm

Rubber plant
English ivy
Weeping fig
Peace lily
Areca palm
Corn plant

Buying Houseplants

Some houseplants are inherited from relatives or received as gifts. Others are potted and salvaged from outdoor gardens, especially if you live in a mild climate. Mostly, though, you'll select and purchase the plants you want to add to your home. When it's time to go shopping, a few tips will help you make the best choices.

Look closely

You can expect all plants in a retail display to be healthy. Be wary if some are and some are not. Pick the healthiest plants you can find and look them over carefully. Plants should have few brown-edged leaves, and they should show few or no signs of having been trimmed, particularly on new growth. The foliage should be full and bushy, with little space between the leaves. Large gaps between new leaves suggest that the plant has been overfertilized and crowded to induce rapid growth or that it has spent a long period under inadequate light. Healthy leaves should be free from dust and grime but should not look unnaturally shiny.

Always examine the soil or potting mix. Avoid plants with algae, slime, or a dry white chalky crust or powder on the growing medium or the pot. Sniff the soil. A sour smell, like a rotting potato, may indicate root or crown rot or overwatering. A strong pesticide smell could mean that the plant has been treated recently for insects—not a good sign! Make sure the plant fits comfortably in its container. If the roots are showing through the drainage hole, the plant is pot-bound; choose another plant.

Inspect the leaves and stems for any sign of insects or disease. Undersized or yellowing leaves sometimes indicate stress or a hidden insect problem. Insects tend to gather underneath leaves and at leaf axils. Even if you don't see any insects, look for the sooty mold or sticky

Plant specialists offer the widest— and healthiest— selection of houseplants.

honeydew they leave behind: either may indicate a hidden problem. Check carefully for webbing on the foliage, and then tap a leaf over a piece of white paper to check for spider mites.

If you see insects you don't recognize, check with the sales personnel. Commercial greenhouses often use predatory insects to keep pests under control. Such beneficial insects are good!

Flowering plants should have many buds that are just beginning to open. Plants in full bloom may already have exhausted much of their beauty. (Chrysanthemums are an exception: Buy them in full bloom, as buds often won't open under average home conditions.) Buying budded specimens is particularly important with those plants that will be discarded after the blooms fade.

Plants should be properly wrapped or sleeved by the nursery or retailer to protect them during transportation from the store to their new home. This is doubly important in winter: Even a few seconds of exposure to cold air can do damage. In summer, a wrapper protects from the sun's burning rays.

Keep newly purchased plants in sleeves to protect them from sun and drafts on the trip home.

Shop carefully

Houseplants are available almost everywhere. You'll find them in booths at flower and gardening shows, county fairs, and farmer's markets; in hardware and grocery stores; under tents at busy intersections; and even in cafes and drug stores.

While you may find attractive plants at all of these places, you may not be able to obtain reliable information about caring for the ones you purchase. Plants sold by anyone other than a plant specialist might be mislabeled, mishandled, or unhealthy. Some sellers may not allow you to return or exchange unsatisfactory plants.

For the best selection and the best access to information, go to plant specialists: a commercial greenhouse that specializes in houseplants, a garden center or nursery with a houseplant department, a home supply store with a greenhouse section, a florist's shop, or a botanic garden that sells plants.

Most of these stores employ knowledgeable people who can help you make good choices. And most are careful about the quality of their plants: Those with pest or disease problems are quickly culled, and declining plants are removed from sale. That means the plants you buy from them are less likely to have pest or disease problems. Plant specialists also know how to pack plants properly for the trip home.

Specialty sources, such as orchid or bonsai suppliers, are an invaluable source of plants not available elsewhere and also a good place to look for tools and information. Stores that cater to hydroponic growers are a good source of houseplant supplies such as lights, fertilizers, and sprayers.

Buying Houseplants
(continued)

You can find healthy, bargain-priced houseplants in supermarkets and other nonspecialist stores if you know how to choose.

Houseplants are sometimes sold in small pots. Be sure to find out how large a plant will be when it matures.

Look for rare plants in specialty stores or mail-order nurseries, which usually offer a printed or online catalog. Some mail-order nurseries are specialist growers, dealing only in one or a few plant types, such as orchids, African violets, ferns, geraniums, or cacti and succulents. Others have a wide range of both flowering plants and foliage plants. See the "Resources" listings on page 215 for information on some of these plant suppliers.

While the choice of plants offered by mail-order nurseries is often impressive, mature specimens can be costly. Full-size plants are difficult to pack and ship, elements that add to their cost. Some specialist growers sell rooted cuttings instead, and the price is unbeatable: You can buy half a dozen for the cost of one adult plant.

You can order by mail, phone, or e-mail. Most companies add shipping charges to your order that can make the price of one plant seem prohibitive, so order several plants or place a group order with a few plant-loving friends to minimize shipping costs. If your new plants are coming from another country, you'll also be charged fees for inspection and a phytosanitary certificate. Again, the larger your order, the lower your total cost per plant.

Be prepared

If you plan to be away at any time during shipping season, let the supplier know. If you're never home during the day, arrange to have the package delivered to a neighbor who is. A box of tender houseplants will bake in the sun or freeze on a doorstep in cold weather.

When the box arrives, open it and take out the plants as soon as possible. Water them immediately if they look parched. Don't water cacti and succulents, though; their roots heal better from shipping trauma when they're kept on the dry side for a few days. Pot bare-root plants without delay. Even potted plants are often shipped in small containers. You'll probably want to repot them into larger pots within a few weeks. If you have purchased cuttings, insert them into rooting mixes according to the instructions on page 53.

Protect freshly unpacked plants from full sun at first. Put them in a bright spot with little or no direct sun for a few days, then gradually acclimatize them to their permanent display location in your home.

The condition your plants arrive in depends as much on the shipper as on the quality of the nursery that shipped them. Be prepared for the occasional disappointment. Contact the seller immediately if there are serious problems.

Examine new plants for signs of damage or infestation, and report any problems to the seller immediately.

them home because of the shock of yet another new environment. Such major changes in only a few weeks' time can simply be too much for the plants to withstand.

You can profit from the inexpensive, freshly shipped plants in stores and supermarkets if you know when a delivery is due and you can be on hand the same day. Pick the healthiest plants you can find and acclimatize them to your home's growing conditions. You'll find that young plants acclimatize better than mature ones, making them the best buy.

High-quality plant sources remove weak or sick specimens from sale; supermarkets may not. So resist the urge to purchase marked-down or sick-looking plants—they are unlikely to recuperate and may introduce insects or diseases to other plants in your home.

Most will reimburse you or give credit toward future purchases only if you call about problems immediately.

Trust your instincts

Although specialty plant stores are usually the surest source of healthy new plants, there's no reason you can't pick up a plant at the grocery store or from some other nonspecialist source when you see an especially nice one. Such plants are often reasonably priced; if you know how to pick them carefully, you may end up with some real bargains.

Trust your instincts. If the store is clean and smells good and the plants look healthy at first glance, chances are you've found a good supplier. However, most plants sold come from businesses that operate in the full sun and high humidity of Florida, Texas, or California. The plants are shipped quickly for rapid sale before they start to decline. They've

been through a lot during shipping, and conditions only got worse when they reached the vegetable aisle of the local supermarket. As a result, these plants often lose leaves or even die when you bring

Some nurseries ship by mail. For plants you can't find locally, shop the Internet.

Buying Houseplants
(continued)

Plant costs

Several factors—besides the obvious ones such as rarity and availability—affect the price of a plant. But the major factor is the cost of producing the plant. Species vary greatly when it comes to how long it takes or how easy it is to grow them. A kentia palm *(Howea forsteriana),* for instance, takes twice as long to grow 5 feet tall as a parlor palm *(Chamaedorea elegans)* does; because it needs twice the labor and care to grow to its mature height, the kentia palm costs more.

Some plants are hardier than others and grow well in open fields rather than requiring more expensive conditions, so they cost less than greenhouse plants. Two seemingly identical plants of the same species may vary in cost because one was shipped directly from the field for immediate sale while the other was shade-grown or held in lower light levels for a period to acclimatize it to home growing conditions.

Just a few simple tools and supplies will help you grow healthy plants. Keep on hand some houseplant potting mix; a watering can with a long spout; a pump mister; a hand trowel; pruners; and sharp scissors.

Acclimatization

Get your plant home as quickly as you reasonably can: Don't leave it in a hot car while you do more shopping. Ask for double wrapping if the weather is below freezing, and put the plant on carpeting or towels or another nonmetal surface for the trip home. (You may even want to warm up your car before leaving the store during winter months.) Be sure to remove the wrapping once the plant is inside your house.

Although you carefully inspected your plant before purchase, a few pests still could be hiding on it. Insects or diseases brought into the home on a new plant can infect every other plant in your collection. Therefore, it is always best to keep a newly purchased plant in isolation for a few weeks, in a room away from other plants if possible. This is true even for gift or florist plants bought in full bud. Pretty as they might look among your foliage plants, you should keep them separate.

Plants need time to adjust to new surroundings; they may even go into shock when you first bring them home. Over a short period of time, they have traveled from the hot, humid field or the meticulously controlled environment of the commercial greenhouse to a different environment at the retailer's and finally to a home with yet another set of light, humidity, and temperature conditions.

Acclimatization takes several weeks. At first, leaves may turn yellow and blossoms may drop. Pay special attention to plant care during this time. A plant that will eventually tolerate dim lighting may have been grown under strong light and will need time to adjust to the change. Ease the plant through the transition by moving it to interim locations with decreasing light intensity for periods of several weeks or more before placing it in its final site.

Keep plants moderately moist during this adjustment period; never allow them to dry out. Water thoroughly each time and discard excess water from the drainage saucer. Some plants, such as croton and weeping fig, are so sensitive to change that even when they are acclimatized to their permanent surroundings, it's best not to move them to other spots. You can move tougher plants, such as dracaenas and philodendrons, once they have acclimatized to the general conditions of your home.

PLASTIC BAG ACCLIMATIZING

One way to acclimate a plant while keeping it isolated is to place it in a large, transparent plastic bag (a dry-cleaning bag, for example) and set it in the brightest light possible, but not direct sun. The high humidity inside the bag is just what the plant needs to help it adapt to the lower light of the average home, and the plastic keeps any insects trapped. After two weeks, if no insects are discovered, move the plant to a light level closer to what it will ultimately require and punch holes in the bag, one or two per day, so the plant can slowly adjust to the lower humidity of your home. When the bag is in tatters, remove it. You'll find your plant is now thoroughly acclimated to its new growing conditions. Even if you move it into lower light, it probably won't drop a leaf.

THE BASICS OF
Plant Care

Houseplants are domesticated wild plants. Over the years, naturally occurring plants have been cultivated and bred to flourish in an indoor environment. The selected plants have one essential feature in common with their wild cousins: adaptability. They can endure filtered light, widely varying temperatures, and the low humidity found in most offices, stores, and homes. Those that can't adapt to indoor growing were long ago eliminated as suitable houseplant choices.

Today you can select from a wide range of houseplants, from familiar favorites to the countless new hybrids specifically adapted to the modern interior. Whatever your tastes, choose plants not only for their shape and appeal but also with an eye to where you will place them and how much maintenance they will require.

Providing the right amount of light is the key to success. Most homes, even the smallest apartments, offer a wide variety of light conditions. You can find plants in this book to suit almost any indoor environment.

While light comes primarily from natural sources, watering is your responsibility. It's the only task you'll need to repeat with any regularity. With just a little practice, you'll learn how to read a plant's watering needs and quickly discover how meeting them can become a natural part of your regular routine.

This chapter also helps you understand the importance of proper temperature, air circulation, and humidity. In most cases, you can easily meet the requirements by locating your plants in a specific part of your home. In some special situations, you can grow healthy plants by making a few simple adjustments, such as running a humidifier when the indoor air is exceptionally dry.

Most plants are already in pots and thriving when you buy them, but all will eventually outgrow their original containers. These pages show you how to repot and when, as well as how to choose the correct size and type of pot and the best potting medium. The tips on plant division and propagation help you share your favorite specimens with friends and family. You'll also learn how to fertilize according to your plants' needs and how to prune, stake, or train them for optimum growth and attractive appearance.

Growing houseplants is surprisingly simple, as their needs are few and usually easy to meet with a moderate amount of care. You'll find all the basics here.

Most houseplants need only minimal care beyond adequate light, water, and humidity.

How Plants Survive

Caring for houseplants may seem complicated to a beginning indoor gardener. The to-do list of watering, lighting, fertilizing, grooming, propagating, and seasonal care may be bewildering at first, but these tasks become easy and natural once you understand the basic processes of plant growth.

PLANT PARTS: There are four parts to most plants: roots, stems, leaves, and flowers. All are crucial to plant growth and health.

Roots anchor the plant and absorb the water and minerals

Chlorophyll absorbs primarily violet, blue, and red light wavelengths. Green light is reflected, giving plants their green appearance.

that nourish it. Most of the absorption occurs through the root tips and the tiny hairs on young roots. These tender tissues are easily injured. Transplanting often destroys

them, causing the top of the plant to wilt, but under the proper conditions, new root tips will grow within a few days. Roots send water and nutrients to the stem, which carries the nourishment to other parts of the plant. The thickened roots of some plants also store food.

The stem transports water, minerals, and manufactured food to the leaves, buds, and flowers. It also physically supports the plant. In some cases, stems store food during a plant's dormant period; in others, the stem manufactures food. In some plants, stems grow as rhizomes that creep above or underground, but most plants have obvious, aboveground stems, with or without branches, at least on mature specimens.

The leaf manufactures food for the plant through photosynthesis, absorbing light over its thin surface area. Its pores absorb and diffuse gases and water vapor during photosynthesis, respiration, and transpiration. A few plants have learned to live without leaves; they use their stems to carry out photosynthesis, respiration, and transpiration. The vast majority of plants do, however, have clearly defined leaves.

Tropical plants, such as this Boston fern, thrive in the steamy air of a warm, moist bathroom if light levels are adequate.

Cacti's succulent stems store water to survive dry conditions.

The flower is the sexual reproductive organ of the plant. Most plants flower in their natural environments, but fewer bloom indoors. At home, plants are mostly grown for enjoyment, and only rarely to produce attractive fruits or viable seed for propagation.

PHOTOSYNTHESIS: Like all other living things, plants need food for energy. The basic food element for all living things is sugar or other carbohydrates. Unlike animals, however, plants are able to harness the energy of the sun to manufacture their own sugar. They do this through the process of photosynthesis.

In photosynthesis, light energy, carbon dioxide, and water interact with the green plant pigment chlorophyll to produce plant sugars and oxygen, which is released into the atmosphere. (Houseplants get light from the sun, filtered in through windows, or from electric lights.) The carbon dioxide is drawn in from the atmosphere by the leaves, and the roots supply the water. Plant photosynthesis supplies most of the oxygen in the atmosphere of the earth.

Photosynthesis requires an environment that provides adequate light, warmth, and humidity. No amount of fertilizer can compensate for an unfavorable environment because fertilizer provides only nutritional building materials, not the plant's real food, which is the sugar the plant manufactures through photosynthesis.

RESPIRATION: The sugar created by photosynthesis combines with oxygen to release energy. This respiration energy is used for growth and survival and enables the plant to convert the building materials provided by nutrients in the soil into plant tissues. Respiration produces carbon dioxide, water, and a small amount of heat as byproducts, which are released into the atmosphere.

TRANSPIRATION: Sunlight falling on a leaf can heat it well above the temperature of the surrounding air. Transpiration, the movement of water vapor from a leaf into the atmosphere, is important in stabilizing leaf temperatures (keeping them cool), in much the same way human perspiration has a cooling effect.

As water vapor leaves the plant through leaf pores (stomata), the leaf cools. The higher the temperature and the lower the humidity, the faster a plant transpires. If it loses more water than it can absorb through its roots, it wilts, which is why proper watering is so essential to the survival of a houseplant.

Light

Light is the most crucial element to consider when choosing a location for a plant. Plants need light for photosynthesis, which produces the food and energy necessary to keep them alive, as well as for hormone production, which induces flowering. If a plant enjoys perfect conditions yet is in more or less light than required for optimum growth, it will be stressed. And a stressed plant is an invitation to trouble.

The subject of light covers much more than just the amount of sun passing through a window during the day. Plants are affected by the amount of light (its intensity), the color of light (its quality), how long it lasts (its duration), and the direction it comes from (phototropism).

All about light

INTENSITY: Depending on geographic location and time of year, east and west windows receive a few hours of direct sun each day, the west sun being the hotter of the two. South windows can receive five or more hours of direct sun even in winter, yet sometimes only indirect (but intense) light in summer. North windows typically receive minimal direct light in northern regions and none in

Intensity, quality, and duration of sunlight change with the seasons. Plants may need periodic relocation to maintain good health.

southern ones. The amount of indirect light received depends on any reflective surfaces nearby.

However, other factors also affect how much light a room actually receives. For example, as the seasons change, so does the angle at which the sun hits a window. In summer, the sun is high in the sky and an overhanging roof may block its rays. In winter, when the sun is lower in the sky, its rays may directly enter most windows. Outdoor elements, such as awnings, neighboring buildings, and trees, reduce light coming in; reflective surfaces (indoors and out) increase it.

The amount of light a plant receives varies widely

depending on its distance from the primary light source. For instance, a much greater amount of light will fall on a plant placed 6 inches from a window than on a plant 2 feet away from the same window. For that reason, a plant that requires moderate light will do well close to an east window or a few feet away from a hotter west window.

QUALITY: Natural sunlight is the best source of light because it has the greatest range of colors from the spectrum and the greatest intensity. Although reflected light adds light to a room, its intensity is reduced and therefore less beneficial to plants. You may need to add supplemental lighting to

HINT

Phototropism is the natural tendency of plants to grow toward a light source. Indoor plants will usually bend toward a window. Rotate plants periodically to avoid excessive growth on the side nearest the light.

Blooming plants must have a cycle of day and night in order to produce flowers. Christmas cactus blooms are formed in response to long nights and short day lengths.

provide plants with the type of light they need to thrive.

DURATION: The length of time that houseplants receive light is important because plants need a certain length of light period for adequate photosynthesis. Most require 8 to 16 hours of light every day. Plants given too many hours of light each day tend to have elongated or curled leaves that may eventually drop off. Too few hours of light causes elongated shoots and thin, easily damaged leaves. You can control this ratio by adding supplemental light to lengthen the day or by turning off the lights to give more hours of darkness.

PHOTOPERIODISM: The cycle of light and dark is particularly important for blooming plants because it helps trigger flower production. Some plants flower when the days are long (14 hours or more). Other plants, known as short-day plants, flower when they receive at least 14 hours of darkness while their flower

buds are forming. Most plants, however, bloom regardless of day length as long as there is a cycle of day and night.

Consider your home's specific conditions when deciding where to place your plants for best lighting. The intensity, quality, and duration must be in balance. For example, if you have a west window suitable for growing a plant that needs bright light but a nearby building blocks the sun's rays after only an hour, you have the intensity but not the duration required.

If your south windows are shaded in summer by deciduous trees, the light intensity will be reduced. Bright-light plants that thrive in that window in winter may languish in summer. A north window that looks out on a tall white building may provide a considerable amount of reflected light. While reflected light is not of sufficient quality to grow a bright-light plant, a plant that tolerates medium light may do well in that window.

HELPING SHORT-DAY PLANTS BLOOM

Several popular short-day houseplants exist, but the best known are holiday cacti and poinsettias. In the average home, which is illuminated at night, these plants may never bloom. Even a streetlight or garden lamp shining down on them is enough to prevent flowering. You can help them to bloom in time for the holidays by taking a few easy steps.

■ If your climate is frost-free, simply put short-day plants outdoors in the fall, in a spot where they won't receive any light other than daylight. Make sure they are protected from streetlights and even car headlights.

■ Indoors, starting about October 1, put short-day plants in a dark closet or cover them with a cardboard box in the evening, then expose them to bright light again in the morning. They need a full 14 hours of uninterrupted darkness.

Light

(continued)

Light requirements

Levels of light needed for plants to grow, as opposed to merely survive, vary widely. Lower light may be sufficient to maintain a plant and keep it looking good, but not enough to get it to bloom.

Generally plants are categorized as low-, medium-, bright-, or intense-light plants. These categories indicate the optimum conditions for growing specific plants, although some plants thrive in a variety of light levels. Plants may tolerate slightly more or less light than is optimal; however, drastically different amounts of light cause a plant to fail. Too much light or direct sun causes damage, and too little light causes plants to become spindly.

Light categories

Because plants need light to grow, it makes sense to define light in categories that correspond to the needs

Light closest to the window is the most intense and long-lasting, and contains the broadest spectrum of color wavelengths.

of most plants. Following are descriptions of the light categories used in the "Gallery of Houseplants," which begins on page 100.

LOW LIGHT: This is light shade, a position well back from the nearest window. It provides enough light to read by without too much strain but little or no direct sunlight. Some plants can survive for a while at even lower levels than this, but they will not grow. Few plants thrive in low light; at best they can be said to tolerate it.

MEDIUM LIGHT: Medium light is an all-purpose level at which both foliage and flowering plants thrive, although flowering plants will bloom more profusely with bright light. Medium light is found in a northeast or west window that receives a few hours of early morning or late afternoon sun and is well lit the rest of the day. You can obtain the same effect in sunnier windows by moving plants back from the light or drawing sheer curtains during the hottest part of the day.

A FEW GUIDELINES ABOUT LIGHT

■ A sheer curtain lessens the light intensity and heat in a south or west window, making the conditions appropriate for a medium- or bright-light plant.

■ Flowering plants usually need bright to intense light, but some fare well in medium light.

■ A south window provides direct light farther into the room in winter than in summer, but heat build up is greater in summer.

■ The intensity of direct light varies according to the season. When the sun is higher in the sky (in the summer in the Northern Hemisphere), the light is hotter and more intense, but reaches less distance into the room. In winter, the sun is lower in the sky, providing direct light farther into the room but with less intensity.

■ Low-light plants usually do well in east, northeast, or north windows, where they get mostly indirect light.

■ A west window is usually hotter than a south window because of the concentrated quality of the sunlight in the late afternoon.

■ An east window strikes a nice compromise between heat and intensity. It receives full sun in the morning hours when the temperature is still cool. Most flowering plants thrive under such conditions.

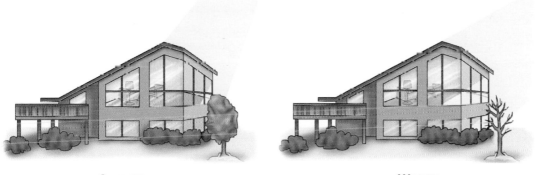

SUMMER

WINTER

Sunlight may reach plants more directly in winter, when the sun is lower in the sky.

Indoor light intensity for plant growth depends on the distance from the window and the direction of exposure.

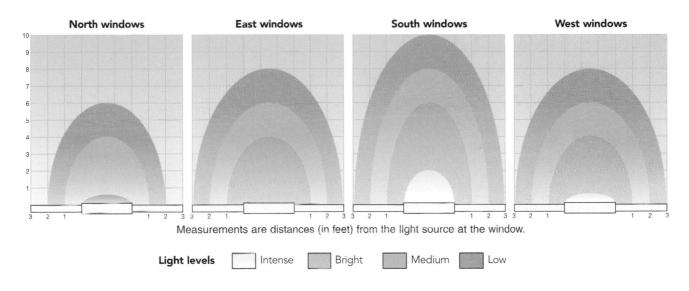

Measurements are distances (in feet) from the light source at the window.

Light levels ☐ Intense ☐ Bright ☐ Medium ☐ Low

BRIGHT LIGHT: Direct sunlight for several hours in the morning or afternoon, but not the full strength of midday sun, qualifies as bright light. Usually this is the light found directly in front of an east or west window or a few feet back from a south window. It is the ideal light for many flowering plants, herbs, and vegetables as well as most cacti and succulents, but too bright for most foliage plants.

INTENSE LIGHT: Four or more hours of direct sunlight daily is intense light. An unshaded window facing due south during the summer months receives intense light. Intense light is usually accompanied by excessive heat, so few plants thrive there, although cacti and succulents tolerate it well. If you can control the heat, many plants that prefer full sun outdoors, such as cacti, succulents, miniature roses, herbs, and some orchids, will thrive here. Install sheer curtains or move plants back several feet from the window to reduce the impact of intense light.

TOO MUCH OR TOO LITTLE LIGHT?

How can you tell whether your plant is getting the right amount of light? If new growth is spindly and pale and seems to stretch toward the light source, the plant is suffering from a lack of light. Move it to a spot where it will receive better illumination. If the plant wilts rapidly or is yellowish or whitish in color, the plant is getting too much light. Move it away from the light source. If the plant looks good but doesn't flower as it should, it is probably getting sufficient light for good foliage growth but not enough for flowering. Move it just a little closer to the light source.

Light
(continued)

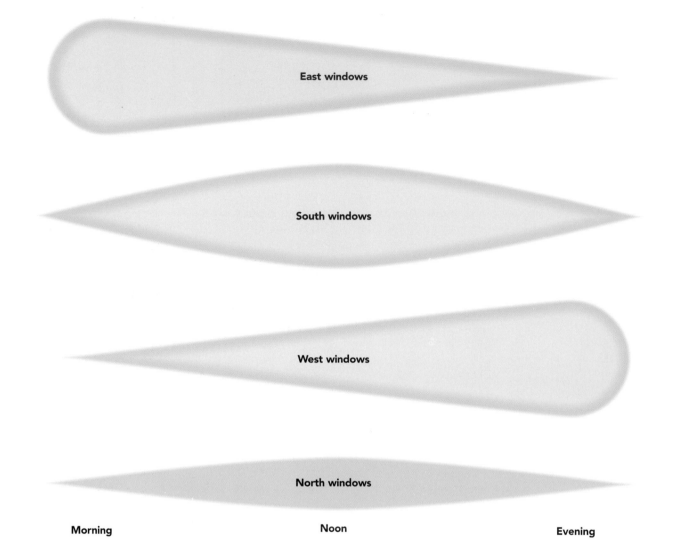

East windows

South windows

West windows

North windows

Morning   Noon   Evening

The amount of available indoor light varies by exposure of the window and the time of day.

PLANTS THAT TOLERATE LOW LIGHT* (DIM READING LEVEL)

BOTANICAL NAME	COMMON NAME	BOTANICAL NAME	COMMON NAME
Aglaonema commutatum	Chinese evergreen	*Homalomena rubescens*	Heart-leaf homalomena
Aspidistra elatior	Cast-iron plant	*Howea forsteriana*	Kentia palm
Beaucarnea recurvata	Ponytail palm	*Philodendron* spp.	Philodendron
Chamaedorea spp.	Parlor palm, Bamboo palm	*Rhapis excelsa*	Lady palm
		Sansevieria trifasciata	Snake plant
Dieffenbachia maculata	Dieffenbachia	*Spathiphyllum wallisii*	Peace lily
Dracaena spp.	Dracaena	*Syngonium podophyllum*	Arrowhead vine
Hedera helix	English ivy	*Zamioculcas zamiifolia*	Aroid palm

*Many florist's plants bought in full bloom can be maintained for a while in low light.

PLANTS THAT NEED MEDIUM LIGHT (GOOD LIGHT BUT LITTLE DIRECT SUN)

BOTANICAL NAME	COMMON NAME	BOTANICAL NAME	COMMON NAME
Adiantum spp.	Maidenhair fern	*Ludisia discolor*	Jewel orchid
Aeschyanthus lobbianus	Lipstick plant	*Maranta leuconeura*	Prayer plant
Alocasia spp.	Alocasia	*Monstera deliciosa*	Swiss-cheese plant
Anthurium spp.	Anthurium	*Neoregelia* spp.	Blushing bromeliad
Araucaria heterophylla	Norfolk Island pine	*Nephrolepis exaltata*	Boston fern
Asparagus spp.	Asparagus fern	'Bostoniensis'	
Asplenium bulbiferum	Mother fern	*Oxalis regnellii*	Oxalis
Asplenium nidus	Bird's-nest fern	*Pandanus* spp.	Screwpine
Beaucarnea recurvata	Ponytail palm	*Paphiopedilum* spp.	Slipper orchid
Begonia spp.	Begonia	*Pellionia* spp.	Pellionia
Caladium spp.	Caladium	*Peperomia* spp.	Peperomia
Calathea spp.	Calathea	*Phalaenopsis* spp.	Moth orchid
Calceolaria spp.	Calceolaria	*Philodendron* spp.	Philodendron
Chirita sinensis	Chirita	*Plectranthus australis*	Swedish ivy
Chlorophytum comosum	Spider plant	*Podocarpus macrophylla*	Buddhist pine
Cissus spp.	Cissus	'Maki'	
Clivia miniata	Clivia	*Polyscias* spp.	Aralia
Columnea spp.	Columnea	*Pteris* spp.	Table fern
Cryptanthus bivittatus	Earth star	*Radermachera sinica*	China doll
Cycas revoluta	Sago palm	*Rhipsalidopsis gaertneri*	Easter cactus
Cyrtomium falcatum	Japanese holly fern	*Rhipsalis* spp.	Mistletoe cactus
Davallia spp.	Deer's-foot fern	*Saintpaulia ionantha*	African violet
Episcia cupreata	Episcia	*Schefflera species*	Schefflera
Ficus spp.	Fig	*Schlumbergera buckleyi*	Christmas cactus
Fittonia spp.	Nerve plant	*Selaginella* spp.	Moss-fern
Hedera helix	English ivy	*Soleirolia soleirolii*	Baby's tears
Hoya carnosa	Wax plant	*Tillandsia*	Air plant
Leea coccinea	West Indian holly	(green-leaved varieties)	

PLANTS THAT NEED INTENSE LIGHT (FOUR OR MORE HOURS OF DIRECT SUNLIGHT)

BOTANICAL NAME	COMMON NAME	BOTANICAL NAME	COMMON NAME
Adenium spp.	Adenium	*Jasminum* spp.	Jasmine
Aeonium spp.	Aeonium	*Kalanchoe* spp.	Kalanchoe
Agave spp.	Agave	*Lantana camara*	Lantana
Arygranthemum	Paris daisy	*Pisonia umbellifera*	Birdcatcher tree
fruticosum		'Variegata'	
Cleistocactus straussi	Silver torch	*Plumbago auriculata*	Cape leadwort
Dyckia spp.	Dyckia	*Punica granatum nana*	Dwarf pomegranate
Echeveria spp.	Echeveria	*Rosa* (miniature species)	Miniature rose
Euphorbia	Euphorbia	*Tillandsia*	Air plant
(succulent species)		(silver-leaved varieties)	
Heliotropium arborescens	Heliotrope		

Light
(continued)

Increasing light

Most indoor settings are far darker than they seem to the human eye. In many homes, it's difficult to read a newspaper even at midday without extra light. The bright light that so many plants require to do well is often attainable only directly in front of windows. Strategies for increasing the amount of light that reaches the interior of a room make it possible to

PLANTS THAT NEED BRIGHT LIGHT (SOME FULL SUN EXCEPT AT MIDDAY)

BOTANICAL NAME	COMMON NAME	BOTANICAL NAME	COMMON NAME
Abutilon spp.	Flowering maple	*Hypoestes phyllostachya*	Polka-dot plant
Acalypha hispida	Chenille plant	*Impatiens walleriana*	Impatiens
Achimenes spp.	Orchid pansy	*Iresine herbstii*	Bloodleaf
Adenium spp.	Adenium	*Justicia brandegeeana*	Shrimp plant
Aechmea spp.	Vase plant	*Kalanchoe* spp.	Kalanchoe
Agave spp.	Agave	*Mandevilla sanderi*	Mandevilla
Aloe spp.	Aloe	*Musa* spp.	Banana
Ananas comosus	Pineapple	*Neomarica gracilis*	Apostle plant
Bambusa spp.	Bamboo	*Nepenthes* spp.	Tropical pitcher plant
Beaucarnea recurvata	Ponytail palm	*Nerium oleander*	Oleander
Browallia spp.	Browallia	*Ornithogalum caudatum*	Pregnant onion
Brunfelsia spp.	Yesterday-today-and-tomorrow	*Osmanthus heterophyllus*	False holly
Capsicum annuum	Ornamental pepper	*Pachypodium* spp.	Madagascar palm
Chrysalidocarpus lutescens	Areca palm	*Pachystachys lutea*	Lollipop-plant
Chrysanthemum ×*morifolium*	Florist's mum	*Pedilanthes tithymaloides* 'Variegatus'	Variegated devil's backbone
Citrus spp.	Citrus	*Persea americana*	Avocado
Clerodendrum thompsoniae	Clerodendrum	*Phoenix roebelenii*	Pygmy date palm
Codiaeum variegatum pictum	Croton	*Pisonia umbellifera* 'Variegata'	Birdcatcher tree
Coffea arabica	Coffee plant	*Platycerium bifurcatum*	Staghorn fern
Crassula ovata (and others)	Jade plant	*Portulacaria* spp.	Elephant bush
Curcuma alismatifolia	Siam tulip	*Primula* spp.	Primrose
Cyperus alternifolius	Umbrella plant	*Pseuderanthemum atropurpureum* 'Tricolor'	Purple false eranthemum
Dionaea muscipula	Venus flytrap	*Rhododendron* spp.	Azalea
×*Epicactus* spp.	Orchid cactus	*Ruellia makoyana*	Monkey plant
Euonymus japonicus	Evergreen euonymus	*Sanchezia speciosa*	Sanchezia
Euphorbia pulcherrima	Poinsettia	*Sedum morganianum*	Donkey's tail
Exacum affine	Persian violet	*Senecio* ×*hybridus*	Florist's cineraria
Fatsia japonica	Japanese aralia	*Serissa foetida*	Serissa
Fuchsia ×*hybrida*	Fuchsia	*Sinningia* spp.	Gloxinia, sinningia
Gardenia augusta	Gardenia	*Solanum pseudocapsicum*	Jerusalem cherry
Gynura aurantiaca	Velvet plant	*Solenostemon scutellarioides*	Coleus
Hedychium coronarium	White ginger lily	*Streptocarpus hybridus*	Cape primrose
Hibiscus rosa-sinensis	Chinese hibiscus	*Tradescantia* spp.	Spiderwort
Hippeastrum spp.	Amaryllis	*Yucca elephantipes*	Yucca
Hydrangea macrophylla	Florist's hydrangea	*Zantedeschia* spp.	Calla lily

use houseplants as part of your decor rather than simply clutter on your windowsills. Here are a few:

■ Keep the windows clean. Dust and grime reduce light considerably.

■ Remove window screens when they're not needed. They cut light by up to 30 percent.

■ Paint walls white or pastel shades and use pale-colored furniture and floor coverings to help reflect light. Dark colors absorb light.

■ Hang mirrors strategically to reflect light.

■ Add a skylight or solar tube to increase light.

■ Replace small windows with larger ones. Better yet, add a greenhouse window, bay window, or solarium.

■ Use artificial lighting when natural light is too weak.

■ Keep foliage clean. Dust and grime blocks light.

A DECORATOR'S SECRET

Does your decor call for a houseplant in a spot that is just too dark for even low-light plants to thrive? Don't let that ruin your design ideas! Purchase two identical low-light-tolerant plants, and keep switching them back and forth. Place one in the desired spot for two weeks while the other basks in bright light and high humidity elsewhere in the house, then switch them around. Most foliage plants will thrive for years if they get enough light for just two weeks out of each month.

Supplemental light

If you don't have the right amount of light for what you want to grow, it's possible to supplement the natural light with artificial lighting. You can combine artificial lights with natural light to provide plants with a longer day, or you can grow plants entirely with artificial light.

Good supplemental light sources provide more light than heat. Plants respond best to the full spectrum of sunlight, and there are several ways to get it.

INCANDESCENT: The bulbs commonly found in lamps and ceiling fixtures are incandescent lights and not appropriate as the sole source of light for houseplants. Not only are they hot, but they also emit only the red-orange part of the spectrum, which is too narrow for plants to thrive. Although they are inefficient, they can be used to supplement natural light in situations where plants get nearly enough light and need only a bit more. In such cases, the lamp must be set far enough away from the plants so it does not heat their leaves. Special incandescent plant lights are available but are not much more effective than ordinary incandescent light bulbs.

HALOGEN: These very intense lights are popular in contemporary interior design. They produce an excellent quality of light with a nearly perfect spectrum for plant growth. However, their narrow beams and the extreme heat they produce make them inappropriate for houseplants.

FLUORESCENT: Fluorescent lights remain cool to the

The lightbulbs in household lamps are too hot to help plants grow. Move lamps a safe distance from tender leaves.

touch, allowing plants to grow much closer to the tubes without damage. They also cost less and use less electricity than other lights.

Three types of fluorescent lights adapted to standard fixtures are commonly used with houseplants. Cool white tubes have an enhanced blue range, and warm white tubes have an enhanced red range. A combination of the two provides a wide, although not full, spectrum that's usually sufficient for most plants' light needs.

Full-spectrum grow lights are the preferred choice for plants that normally require full sun, such as cacti, herbs, miniature roses, some orchids and other flowering plants. Emitting almost 90 percent of the sun's range, full-spectrum grow lights cost considerably more than standard fluorescent bulbs.

To be effective, fluorescents must be close to the plants. A plant whose canopy is 6 inches below a fixture with two 40-watt tubes and a reflector receives 900 foot-candles of light, about the same as it would in an east

Light

(continued)

window in summer. Doubling the light source to include four 40-watt tubes adds about a third more intensity, the extra amount needed for some bright-light plants. This intensity drops by half for each additional 6 inches the plant is away from the tubes.

Note that 40-watt 48-inch tubes are the standard in the industry. You can use shorter lamps and tubes, but they may cost more to buy and replace than standard sizes. It's best to design fluorescent plant lighting to accommodate standard length tubes wherever possible.

HIGH-INTENSITY: By far the most efficient supplemental lighting, high-intensity lamps work best in large areas. They are more expensive than fluorescent lights but are worth it if you need a great deal of supplemental lighting. Several types are available:

■ **Metal halide** lamps offer the best spectrum for the largest number of plants and are intense enough to work in areas with limited or no natural light. The light from metal halide covers much of the spectrum, although it has a greater concentration of blue/violet wavelengths. You can purchase enhanced spectrum halide lamps, which give off much more red light. They offer a spectrum that's complete enough to be used to grow vegetables and fruit. Metal halide lamps give off about 20 percent more light than fluorescent lights and range in wattage from 175 to 1,500. For a typical grouping of houseplants in a living area, 400 watts is adequate.

■ **High-pressure sodium** offers an enhanced red-orange color range that is best for flowering plants, although spectrum-enhanced lamps with more blue light are available. They give off an amber glow, which may distort colors in your decor.

■ **Low-pressure sodium lamps and mercury discharge lamps** are generally used for commercial purposes only and so are not included here.

If you need significant supplemental indoor lighting, use a combination of high-intensity halide and sodium lamps. High-intensity lights come in a range of wattages. In order to figure out how much you need, use the following guidelines: As the sole lighting source, 400 watts effectively lights 25 square

ALL LIGHT IS NOT EQUAL

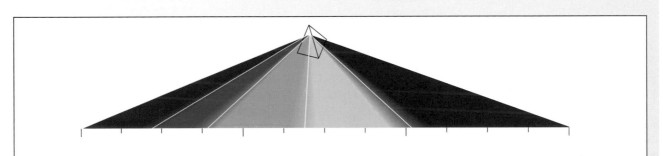

To human eyes, light from most sources may seem about equal, but plants don't "see" things quite that way. Plants have spent millions of years adapting to sunlight, a complete source of light that gives off rays (or wavelengths) over the entire range of the spectrum. When sunlight travels through a prism, as in the illustration, it shows the entire range of light produced. Artificial lights usually have a narrower range, giving off light in only a limited part of the spectrum.

Plants are not efficient users of the light from the middle part of the spectrum, especially green and yellow wavelengths. They use light primarily from the blue/violet and red ends of the spectrum. Blue light alone tends to produce dense, dark green foliage but does not induce bloom. Red rays alone result in long, narrow leaves that seem light-starved, but they also stimulate flowering. Ideal artificial light gives off equal quantities of blue/violet rays and red rays plus a slight amount of ultraviolet light, which human eyes don't see at all. Ultraviolet light is especially useful for plants that normally endure full, blazing sun in the wild: cacti, herbs, miniature roses, and some orchids.

The closer any artificial light source comes to full-spectrum light (all of the colors of the rainbow, plus some ultraviolet rays), the better it is for growing plants.

feet. As a supplement, 400 watts covers 64 square feet. One thousand watts effectively lights 144 square feet. For smaller areas, use lower wattage.

All types of lights lose effectiveness over time, so replace bulbs regularly, especially fluorescent tubes. Follow the manufacturer's recommendations for replacement, but as a general rule, replace bulbs after a year of use. Also, be sure your fixtures have white reflectors to make the best use of the light.

Controlled day length

When houseplants have a fair share of natural light available, turning on supplementary lighting only a few hours each day—often early in the morning or late in the afternoon to extend the day length in northern areas during the winter months—is usually sufficient.

Plants grown under lights alone, though, need 8 to 16 hours of lighting every day. Studies have shown that most plants grow best with 12 to 16 hours of light per day. Put short-day plants (see page 28) under 8- to 10-hour days for a few months each year, though, or they won't bloom.

Using a timer ensures plants get the right amount of light. After setting the timer, watch your plants for the next few weeks and adjust the cycle as needed. Also, adjust it as the sun's intensity and duration changes over the year. Many indoor gardeners, for example, give their plants 14- to 16-hour days during

much of the year, then cut back to 12 hours or less to simulate winter, before moving back up to long days.

Rotate plants regularly if you use fluorescent lights because the ends of the bulbs don't provide as intense a light as the centers. Or put low-light plants toward the ends and bright-light plants in the center.

Fluorescent lighting ideas

The most common lights for houseplants are fluorescents, partly because they are inexpensive to buy and use, but mostly because you can place them almost anywhere—under stairs, in a closet, in an attic, or wherever you have the growing space. You can suspend commercial fluorescent lights, complete with reflectors, from the ceiling on chains, or you can build a "light garden." At the right are two simple light garden models you can build

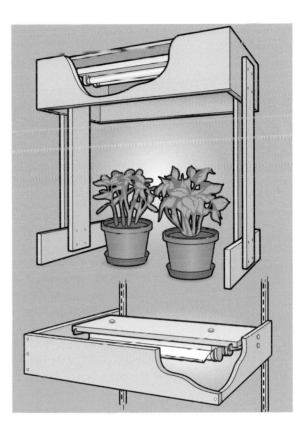

yourself. Note that the lower model is on adjustable shelf brackets. You can move it up or down to give your plants more or less light as needed.

INDOOR LIGHTING COSTS

Light	Fixture Cost (i.e. reflector, ballast)	Bulb Cost	Amount of Light (in lumens)	Life Span (in hours)
HALIDE				
250 watt	$200–$300	$35–50	23,000	10,000
400 watt	$250–$300	$50–60	40,000	20,000
1,000 watt	$350–$400	$55–75	125,000	12,000
SODIUM				
250 watt	$150–$200	$35	28,000	24,000
400 watt	$175–$250	$40	50,000	24,000
1,000 watt	$250–$300	$80	140,000	24,000
FLUORESCENT				
40 watt, cool	$25–$45	$4–6 for 2	3,300	20,000
40 watt, warm	$25–$45	$6–8 for 2	2,180–3,000	20,000
40 watt, full spectrum	$25–$45	$5–7 for 2	2,200	20,000

Water

Find out if your plants need water by feeling the potting mix with your fingers.

High humidity slows transpiration, which reduces moisture uptake by roots. Unless the plant is in a breezy area where wind moves moisture away from the leaves, you'll need to water less often.

Light affects water uptake too. Overcast skies in spring and fall slow plant growth and reduce water requirements. Plants exposed to bright light use more water than those in low light, depending on humidity.

When to water

How do you know when to water? It's simple. Give plants water when they need it. The secret lies in learning to recognize the individual signals each plant gives.

Look at your plant. A well-watered plant looks healthy. Its tissues are firm because all the cells are filled with water, and its leaves are glossy. Many plants show signs of decline before wilting entirely: Their leaves have lost their sheen and are slightly limp and pale. Such flagging is a sure sign that a plant needs water. If you catch a plant at this point, before it actually wilts, you can prevent permanent damage. Once a plant has completely wilted, it seldom fully recovers. It may perk up after being watered, but it will suffer from brown edges and poor growth.

Underwatering and overwatering surprisingly can cause the same symptoms. Consistently overwatering plants saturates the soil, which causes the plant's tiny root hairs to rot and die. And a plant without root hairs can't absorb water, so it wilts even though the soil is saturated.

A plant's water requirements vary as the seasons change. Watering according to a set schedule—for example, once a week—doesn't take into account these variations. Instead, check your houseplants frequently and keep in mind all the factors that affect their watering needs.

Plants absorb more water when humidity is low. If your skin is dry, your plants are probably dry too. However, plants grow more slowly in the cooler, shorter days of winter, a sign that they're using less water. So if you compensate for dry air by watering on a schedule suited to the warm days of summer, you'll end up overwatering.

HINT

Get into the habit of checking your plants not once a week but every four or five days. Then water only those plants whose soil is dry to the touch. Some plants, such as tender ferns or others too large for their pots, may be dry only a few days after a thorough watering, while a cactus or succulent might need watering only once a month or so during winter.

More water will not reverse the wilting or save the plant.

To know when plants are ready for water, check the moisture level of the soil by inserting a finger (down to the second knuckle in the case of plants in large pots) into the mix. If a plant needs moist soil, the surface should be damp. If a plant should dry somewhat between waterings, the top inch or two of soil can be dry, but if it's dry below that point, water the plant. Letting a plant dry out completely damages the roots, sometimes beyond repair.

You may eventually get to a point where you know your plants well enough to lift a pot and judge from its weight whether to water. You will learn which plants dry out most quickly, such as those in clay pots, south windows, or some potting mixes. Over time, adjusting your watering to accommodate your plants will become second nature.

MOISTURE METERS LEND A HAND

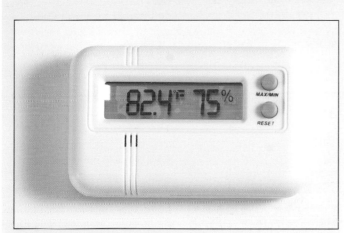

Small pots less than 8 inches in diameter are easy enough to water: When the soil at the top is dry, the rest of the root ball is probably fairly dry as well. In big pots, especially 12-inch standard pots and larger, the same may not hold true. The mix may be dry on the top, yet still soaking wet at the bottom. That bottom layer needs to dry out before you water again, or stagnation, a precursor to rot, can set in. For such pots, it's wise to use an inexpensive water meter, a gadget that's made up of a long metal probe with an easy-to-read gauge on top. Insert the meter deep into the root mass, and water when it reads "dry." Replace the meter once a year, as meters tend to give false readings after a while.

Another type of water meter "sings" when plants need water. Usually shaped like a bird (although you can also find cow meters that moo, frog meters that croak, and green thumbs that sing "How Dry I Am"), it's designed to be inserted permanently into the soil of a plant, rather than being moved from plant to plant as with traditional meters. When the soil dries out too much, its vocal warning reminds you that it's time to water. Most models also have a photoelectric eye so they won't sound off in the middle of the night. Although these meters may seem like a gimmick, many gardeners find them helpful. Use one per room in the plant that always seems to dry out first. When the meter sings, it's time to water that plant and check the others as well.

Water
(continued)

Submerge a plant that has become too dry to water efficiently. Soak for 30 minutes, then drain.

You can water most plants from the top. Make sure the soil is evenly moist.

Let a crowded plant wick up moisture through the holes in the pot's bottom.

The best way to water

For most plants, the best and easiest watering method is to pour water on the soil surface. Pour until water runs out the drainage holes, an action that also leaches excess salts from the soil. The goal is to thoroughly moisten the growing mix.

If dry soil has pulled away from the sides of the pot so that water runs down the sides without wetting the soil, immerse the entire pot in a bucket of tepid water. Let it sit for about 30 minutes, then drain. This technique, called submerging, is also useful for plants that need massive amounts of water, such as blooming plants or florist's hydrangea and other gift plants that dry out quickly.

A few plants, such as African violets, benefit from bottom watering because water droplets mark their leaves. Simply set the pot in a saucer of tepid water and capillary action draws the water into the soil. This method takes longer than top watering, but it keeps water off the leaves. Wick watering systems and self-watering pots (see page 39) are other ways to bottom water.

Whichever way you choose, it is essential that a plant not sit too long in water. After about 20 minutes, empty the saucer. If the plant is too heavy to lift, remove the excess water with an old turkey baster.

On the other hand, semiaquatic plants, such as umbrella plant (*Cyperus alternifolius*), actually prefer to have their pots sitting in water at all times. Place them in a cachepot that's 2 inches wider than their pot and keep adding water as the level drops. You can even submerge the entire root ball under an inch or so of water if you prefer. These plants also put up with regular watering, but only if they're thoroughly watered before their root ball dries out entirely.

An occasional trip to the shower is also an effective way to water plants thoroughly and, at the same time, to rinse dust and dirt from the leaves and leach the soil of excess mineral salts. Use tepid water and a gentle flow so the soil does not wash out of the container. This is usually done in the bathtub or shower, but if weather permits and your water is not too cold, take plants outside and rinse them with a garden hose.

What kind of water?

To avoid shock and possible root damage from extreme temperatures, use tepid water when watering. Many gardeners let water stand overnight to reach "room temperature," but standing water actually can be considerably colder than room temperature.

Tap water is fine for houseplants unless the species you are growing is known to be sensitive to hard or softened water. Unless your municipal water supplier issues a treatment warning, there is no need to let tap water stand for 24 hours before using it. The small

(see page 39)

HINT

The watering can is by far the most popular tool for watering houseplants. However, if you have many plants, you might want to consider watering with a hose and wand. It can save you many trips to the faucet!

amount of chlorine it normally contains is not dangerous to most plants.

If your tap water is hard (alkaline) and you're growing plants that require an acid soil, such as azaleas and hydrangeas, you'll need to amend the soil. For example, regularly repotting in a growing mix with added acid soil amendments, such as peat moss, will provide the acidity needed to release nutrients. You can also use fertilizers designed specifically to retain soil acidity while nourishing the plant.

Alkaline conditions make it difficult for plants to absorb iron and other trace elements. Regular applications of iron chelate, included in some fertilizers, help keep foliage green. When the new foliage on acid-loving plants is yellow, it's a sign that the plant may need extra iron chelate fertilizer.

Softened water contains sodium that may accumulate in the soil and harm plants. If your home has a water softener, use an outdoor tap for plant water or install a bypass tap in the water line before it enters the softener so you'll have a source of hard water for plants. If this is not possible, draw water just before the softener cycle, when sodium is at the lowest level.

Plants benefit from a bath once or twice a year. Spray them gently with tepid water.

When You're Away

If you're going to be away for a few days and can't find someone to care for your plants, you can easily set up a self-watering system. Simply line a sink or bathtub with old towels, newspapers, or any thick, absorbent material. Set pots with drainage holes directly on the matting. Soak the matting well and leave the faucet dripping on it. The plants will draw up moisture as needed.

Another temporary self-watering method: Make a wick out of nylon stocking and put one end into the drainage hole of the plant you want to water, making sure it is in contact with the potting mix. Run the other end into a bowl of water. Water will soak slowly from bowl to plant. Cover the bowl with a plate if you have pets that might drink the water. Several plants can share the same water source this way, but make sure there is enough water in the bowl to last your entire absence.

As an option, you can clean up your plants, removing dead and fading leaves and flowers, water them well, and seal them inside large, transparent plastic bags. Place them well back from full sun or they will cook! Inside the plastic bags air still circulates, yet water can't escape, so your plants can go for months without a drop of added water.

Use a capillary mat to water pots with drainage holes while you're away. Soak the mat well.

Water
(continued)

Special watering needs

Not all plants have the same watering needs, of course. Here are a few that require special attention.

HANGING BASKETS: A hanging container may need more frequent watering than a pot set on the ground or on a windowsill. Exposed to air on all sides, it can quickly lose water to evaporation. Give the soil a thorough soaking whenever you water it, or water it sparingly several times in one day until the mix is evenly moist. Even better, take down the container and submerge it in a bucket or sink of tepid water for half an hour, then drain carefully before hanging it up again. Or use a self-watering hanging container that has a large reservoir.

You can water hanging planters easily using a squeeze-type plastic watering bottle designed especially for the purpose. Gardeners with many plants may prefer to use a hose with a wand to water hanging baskets. A squeeze bottle or water wand acts like

A watering hose that attaches to any indoor faucet is a timesaver for a homeowner who has many houseplants.

an extension to your arm, letting you reach a plant well above your head without having to take it down. You can also find commercial pulley systems that allow you to lower the pot to chest-level for watering, then raise it up again with little effort.

WOOD SLABS: Some plants, notably staghorn ferns, bromeliads, some orchids, and other epiphytic plants, are frequently grown fixed to slabs of wood, cork, or osmunda. This allows them the air circulation they prefer but makes watering more challenging. You can water by spraying the plant, but if so, you may need to do it frequently. It is far easier to soak the slab in tepid water for 20 to 30 minutes. Plants grown on slabs dry out even more quickly than those in

hanging baskets. As with other plants, be sure to soak them as soon as their leaves begin to flag.

ORCHIDS: Most orchids are grown in light mixtures that require special watering. See "Growing Orchids," on pages 84–85, for more information.

BROMELIADS: Most bromeliads have a central cup that you must keep filled with water. Air plants *(Tillandsia)* absorb water only through their leaves. For more information, see "Growing Bromeliads," on pages 82–83.

TERRARIUMS: With their high-sided glass walls, terrariums maintain extremely high humidity and therefore must be watered with utmost care. For more information, see "Maintaining a Terrarium," on page 75.

Watering from the bottom keeps droplets off plants with sensitive leaves, such as this African violet.

Reducing watering needs

If watering every four or five days is too frequent for your schedule, there are a few ways you can keep plants moist a bit longer.

LARGER POTS: Repot plants that dry out too quickly into larger pots. Soil acts as a water reservoir, so a larger pot holds more water than a smaller pot. For information on repotting, see pages 50–51.

DOUBLE POTS: Another easy method of reducing watering needs for plants in clay pots is to double pot. Simply place the pot inside a larger cachepot, adding peat moss, sphagnum moss, Spanish moss, or perlite to fill the void around the inner pot. When you water, moisten the filler material as well as the soil. Water will slowly filter through the porous clay walls into the potting mix. Double potting also reduces the soil temperature, thus further reducing watering needs and humidifying the air. Mulching (see page 65) similarly keeps soil moister and cooler while increasing air humidity.

SELF-WATERING POTS: These special containers have a water reservoir that needs attention only when it gets low, usually every couple of weeks. Since fertilizer is typically added to the water at the same time, feeding and watering become something you do twice a month instead of every few days. Meanwhile the pot automatically delivers water at the rate the plant uses it, adjusting to changes in light, humidity, or temperature. Plants in self-watering pots are usually more evenly watered than plants in conventional pots,

Double-potting reduces the need to water often. Sphagnum moss helps the soil retain moisture.

but since the soil is kept constantly moist, plants that need to dry out between waterings don't perform well in them.

Self-watering pots operate on the principle of capillary action. In the same way water moves upward to moisten an entire towel when just one corner dips into the sink, water moves from the reservoir into the potting mix above. All that's needed is a link—a wick of some sort—between the water and the growing medium.

Many types of self-watering containers are available. Some have built-in reservoirs. Others are actually two pots: a grow pot and an outer pot or cachepot that fits around the grow pot like a reservoir.

Self-watering pots have different ways of indicating when the reservoir is empty. Some pots show the water level with a float, often colored red for maximum visibility. Others have a clear plastic gauge along one side

of the reservoir. In still others, the entire reservoir is made of a transparent material so you can see the water level even from a distance. The disadvantage of the latter is that the water is exposed to light, which encourages the growth of unsightly algae.

Most containers have an opening in the side or on the top into which you can pour the water. Always wait until the reservoir is empty before watering again.

Self-watering containers have built-in reservoirs.

Temperature, Air Circulation, and Humidity

Drafty doors, bright windows, heat registers, and humid spaces all create specific microclimates in your home.

You know your home and its idiosyncrasies better than anyone else. Therefore, you are the perfect person to find the best locations for your houseplants to thrive. Once you learn a plant's origin and under what conditions it grows in the wild, you can map out the areas in your home that are the most appropriate.

When choosing a location, you need to consider humidity, temperature, and air circulation as well as light. As a general rule, immediately eliminate really hot, sunny areas or dark locations. If you have any doubts about a spot's suitability for a particular plant, it's okay to experiment.

Microclimates inside your home change with the season and the weather, so your plants may be in the perfect situation in winter and need to be placed elsewhere for the summer months. Be prepared to relocate them if you see that they aren't thriving.

Temperature

Most homes maintain a year-round temperature between 60°F and 75°F, to which the average houseplant is perfectly suited. However, keeping temperatures cooler at night than during the day helps plants do best. If you can, lower the temperature in your home at least 5°F at night. A 10°F drop triggers blooms in orchids, flowering maples, and other plants.

Even though indoor temperatures are stable compared to outdoor ones, they do vary somewhat, not only from season to season, but also from room to room and even within a single

LOCATING TEMPERATURE VARIANTS

When finding places for your plants, it helps to know just where in your home you have a cool spot or a warm one, and where the temperature most radically changes during a 24-hour period. For that, you'll need a minimum/maximum thermometer. Leave in it the same spot for 24 hours: It will record the minimum and maximum temperatures during that period. Then reset it and start again in a different place. Keep a chart of your results and when you bring home new plants, place them according to temperature needs.

room. Although most houseplants do well in average indoor temperatures, there are always a few exceptions, and these are the plants that can profit from any special temperature levels within your home.

For example, if you have plants that require cool temperatures, such as cyclamens, azaleas, and some orchids, a sunny, unheated porch or place close to a window in winter provides a cool microclimate.

Since cool air sinks, the air near the floor is cooler than the rest of the room. This is a great place to put plants that don't tolerate natural summer heat or home heating in winter. If you close the shades to keep the house cool in summer, you may need to supply bright-light plants with some additional lighting.

Since hot air rises, the top shelf of a bookcase or the top of a kitchen cabinet provides an extra bit of warmth for a plant that doesn't tolerate cold. These out-of-the-way locations ensure that the plant won't suffer from too much air movement. Because they are out of the way, however, you'll need to be extra careful not to neglect them.

In your home's hottest areas, such as around fireplaces, heat vents, incandescent lights, and windows in the summer, use plants that thrive on heat, such as cacti and euphorbias. In areas that are both hot and humid—such as near a dishwasher, clothes dryer, or humidifier—try tropical flora, such as prayer plants and bougainvilleas.

Great variations within a single room can be used to your advantage once you are aware of them. They can also spell disaster if you're not. For example, cold drafts near windows and entrances in winter can make plants cold and cause their leaves to droop. When the temperature drops below 50°F, chilling drafts can injure plants. The injury shows up on the leaves, which appear water-soaked or blackened. In these places, use plants, such as Norfolk Island pine, that enjoy the chilly microclimate.

Air circulation

A certain amount of air movement is vital to good plant growth. Air movement removes moisture from the leaves and therefore prevents disease. It also benefits plants in other ways. Regular movement of the leaves produces sturdier, denser plants. In addition, good air movement may keep some insect populations in check.

You can increase air movement by opening a window in warm weather (do this only when it's not raining). A ceiling fan also keeps the air moving, as do small fans placed near plants.

PLANTS HARMFUL TO PEOPLE AND PETS

Although most houseplants are perfectly harmless, the following are toxic if ingested or if the sap gets on the skin:

African milkbush
Amaryllis
Anthurium
Caladium
Chenille plant
Chinese evergreen
Clivia
Crinum lily
Croton
Crown-of-thorns
Dumb cane
English ivy
Euphorbia
  (except poinsettia)
Fern palm

Ficus
Heliotrope
Jerusalem cherry
Lantana
Mandevilla
Natal plum
Oleander
Ornamental pepper
Peace lily
Philodendron
Pothos
Pregnant onion
Sago palm
Swiss-cheese plant

Plants grouped together create a higher humidity level than plants spaced apart. Air circulation removes some of the humidity.

Temperature, Air Circulation, and Humidity
(continued)

A room humidifier adds moisture during the winter, when home heating dries out the air.

Humidity

Humidity level describes the degree of moisture in the atmosphere—that is, the percentage of water in the air. It tends to be highest in summer, although air-conditioning lowers indoor humidity dramatically. Humidity tends to be lowest (often desert-dry) in winter, when home heating systems dry out the air. Generally the colder the air outside, the drier the air indoors.

The humidity in the native habitat of tropical and subtropical plants runs about 80 percent; most houses average between 35 and 65 percent humidity and sometimes fall below 20 percent in winter. Although many plants have adapted to lower humidity levels, most do better when the air humidity is at least 50 percent.

When humidity is too low, plants exhibit a variety of symptoms, the most common being brown leaf tips and edges. Low-humidity problems are intensified if soil is allowed to dry out, if the plant's location is drafty, or if it is in full sun.

High humidity is seldom a problem except in rooms devoted to indoor pools and hot tubs.

Increasing humidity

The most efficient way to increase humidity is to install a humidifier on your furnace. Even with such a system, though, humidity levels may vary from room to room. If you don't have access to a central humidifier, a room humidifier provides localized moisture control in the air.

Grouping plants helps raise humidity, as each plant gives off a considerable amount of moisture through transpiration. Put the plants with the highest humidity needs in the center of the grouping and the more adaptable plants on the outer edges.

One effective way to raise the humidity immediately surrounding a plant is to set its pot on a humidity tray, a tray of pebbles sitting in water. The water in the tray simply evaporates into the air. When adding more water to the humidity tray, make sure the top pebbles remain partially exposed so the plant isn't sitting directly in water.

Mulching a plant also increases the humidity in the air around the plant, as does double-potting (see page 39). You can keep plants that need very high humidity in a terrarium (an extremely humid microclimate) during the winter when air is particularly dry. See "Terrariums and Bonsai" on pages 74–75 for more information.

Misting plants by hand is no longer considered efficient in raising humidity, as its results are so temporary. Any moisture applied evaporates quickly, so you would have to mist every few hours for this technique to be effective. Also, wetting the leaves of many plants invites disease.

Home microclimates

WINDOWS: South windows give a room extra warmth in winter and are a good place to put tropical plants, especially since light is brightest there. In summer, a south window can become too hot for most plants. Unless the room is air-conditioned, use southern exposures only for plants that can take heat, such as cacti and succulents.

A north-facing room stays quite cool in winter, making it the perfect spot for plants that need a cool, dormant period. The same north room in summer provides a cool spot for plants that don't tolerate high heat, but supplemental light may be necessary.

Be careful not to set cool-sensitive plants too near cold windows in winter. On the other hand, those that require a cool, dormant period during the winter are perfectly suited to a cold windowsill.

VENTS: Areas around heat registers and air-conditioning vents often cause special problems. They produce high air turnover and, as a result, dry things out. Plants native to arid climates tolerate dry air blowing over them, but many tropical plants cannot. If your plants need good air circulation to prevent fungal problems, you will be better off using a fan to move air than to set plants near vents and registers.

FIREPLACES: The space above a fireplace withstands

fluctuating dry, hot periods. Beware of putting a plant directly on a mantel, regardless of how good it looks. You may have a beautifully draped English ivy gracing your fireplace only to find it sizzled and crisp if you forget to move it before the first fire of the winter season.

BATHROOMS AND KITCHENS: Rooms with running water naturally have more humidity than the rest of the house. You can take advantage of these locations with plants that are used to and need the almost constant humidity of the rain forest.

Keep in mind, however, that plants in the kitchen will, over time, accumulate greasy dirt on their leaves. Allow extra time in your plant maintenance schedule to wash them regularly, spraying or sponging the leaves with a soapy solution (a teaspoon or two of mild dish detergent per gallon of water).

To maintain correct temperature, air circulation, and humidity, watch your plants carefully. Raise the humidity if plants show signs of drying out, and increase the air circulation if you see insect or fungal problems. If you pay attention to your plants, they will show you what suits them best.

A ceiling fan circulates the air, helping to inhibit some plant infestations and diseases.

PLANTS TO MATCH MICROCLIMATES

STEAMY BATHROOM (WITH GOOD LIGHT)
Flamingo flower
Cape primrose
Coleus
Croton
Ferns
Hibiscus

COOL FOYER
Cactus
Citrus
Japanese fatsia
Spider plant
Umbrella plant

DARK CORNER IN COOL LIVING ROOM
Cast-iron plant
Chinese evergreen
Dracaena (some)
Snake plant
Philodendron
Pothos

COOL SUNROOM (IN WINTER)
Asparagus fern
Cactus
Christmas cactus
Clivia
English ivy
Artillery plant
Swedish ivy

WARM SUNROOM (IN SUMMER)
Bromeliads
Cactus
Crown-of-thorns
Grape ivy
Wax plant
Jade plant
Panda plant
Nerve plant
Ponytail palm
Ficus

Growing Media

You can create your own potting mix by combining ingredients such as bark chips, perlite, and sphagnum moss.

Ahouseplant needs an "anchor" to hold it in place and provide nutrients. Some plant roots can thrive in water only, in hydroculture systems (see pages 48–49), but most plants are grown using soil or a similar potting mix.

Plant roots require air and water for health, so the mixture in which their roots reside must provide plenty of both. It must also retain moisture and nutrients for the plant's use.

Growing mix

Garden soils are generally too heavy for use in containers and bring with them problems of disease and insects. Many potting mixes for indoor plants are actually soilless. You can customize them according to individual plant needs if you want, but commercial mixes available at your local garden store are adequate for most plants.

Most commercial soilless mixes are composed of peat moss or decomposed bark and vermiculite or perlite in various proportions. They are free of pests, diseases, and weed seeds. They are also inexpensive, simple to use, and widely available.

If you find you need a potting mix with other ingredients, you can mix your own or purchase a ready-made specialty mix. Commercial potting blends for flowering plants contain more organic materials that retain moisture, such as shredded bark or compost, because flower buds are sensitive to water loss. Cacti and other succulents need a mix that has sand or calcined clay for extremely good drainage. Bromeliads and orchids need a coarse mix of bark chips, which provide plenty of air for the roots.

When choosing a growing mix, look for one that is of medium weight. Those that are too light, such as straight peat moss, can't adequately anchor a plant. Too heavy a mix, such as sterilized topsoil, causes drainage problems. If you are potting a very large plant that will not be repotted often or has the potential to become top-heavy, mix one part commercial sterilized topsoil to three parts standard potting mix.

Measuring acidity and alkalinity

An important factor in the composition of any growing medium is its acidity or alkalinity, measured in terms of pH. The pH scale ranges from 0 to 14, with 7 being neutral. A pH reading higher than 7 is alkaline, and one lower than 7 is acid. Highly acid mixes cause yellowing and leaf drop. Alkaline soil causes stunted growth and dull green, yellowish, or purplish leaf color.

Most packaged potting mixes are slightly acid; they have a pH of about 6.5 to 6.8, which is ideal for most plants. Most of the mixes suggested here include dolomitic lime to raise the pH to this level. For acid-loving plants (azaleas, gardenias, citrus, ferns, and others), prepare the mixes without the dolomitic lime. Many cacti and succulents prefer a neutral or slightly alkaline soil, easily provided by adding extra lime.

Soilless potting mixes work well in all types of containers and can be customized according to the pot as well as to the plant.

You can grow a plant in a decorative pot that has no drainage holes by nesting a draining container inside the nondraining pot.

Fill in the space between the growing container and the cachepot with potting mix or sphagnum moss.

Specialty mix ingredients

■ **African violets, flowering plants:** Equal parts sand, peat moss, sterilized topsoil, and leaf mold.

■ **Epiphytes, orchids, bromeliads:** Equal parts sphagnum moss, coarse bark, and coarse perlite. Add 1 tablespoon dolomitic lime and 1 cup horticultural charcoal to 3 quarts mix.

■ **Cacti and succulents:** Two parts sterilized soil, 1 part coarse sand, 1 part calcined clay. Add 2 tablespoons dolomitic lime and ⅓ cup charcoal to 4 quarts mix.

■ **Ferns:** Three parts peat moss-based potting mix, 2 parts perlite, 3 parts leaf mold. Add 1 cup charcoal to 2 quarts mix.

■ **Soil-based mix:** One part sterilized soil, 1 part peat moss, bark, or leaf mold, 1 part coarse sand or perlite.

Individual ingredients

■ **Peat moss:** Partially decayed plant materials mined from the middle and bottom of peat bogs. It has acid pH and is highly moisture retentive, but adds no nutritive value.

■ **Sphagnum moss:** Plant matter harvested from the top of peat bogs, fibers longer than those of peat moss, decomposes slowly. Used mainly to line baskets and in orchid mixes; rarely used in regular potting mixes.

■ **Perlite:** Expanded volcanic rock that is moisture and nutrient retentive, lightweight, and improves drainage and aeration.

■ **Vermiculite:** Mica expanded by heating to become moisture-retentive.

■ **Sand:** Adds drainage and weight. Lime-free, coarse river sand is best. Beach sand may contain harmful salts.

■ **Shredded bark:** Finely shredded or ground hardwood or pine bark. Equivalent in use to peat moss. No nutritive value.

■ **Charcoal:** Absorbs salts and byproducts of plant decay, keeps the soil sweet, removes acidity. Use only horticultural grade.

■ **Leaf mold:** Decayed leaves of all types. Excellent organic additive for moisture retention, some nutrition.

■ **Calcined clay:** Clay pulverized by heating, most commonly available as unscented cat litter, adds weight, drainage, and aeration.

Add extra potting mix around the base of the plant to disguise the lip of the inner pot.

Water thoroughly to settle the potting mix and add more mix if needed.

Growing Media
(continued)

A tiled surface, impervious to water, is a perfect spot to let freshly watered plants drain.

Containers

The only two essential considerations to keep in mind when choosing a pot are how it drains and what the shape and size are in relation to the size of the plant and its root system. Beyond that, selection is a matter of personal preference.

DRAINAGE: Good drainage is imperative. No matter what type of plant you are growing, the pot must have holes for drainage. If you want to use a decorative pot that doesn't have drainage holes, use it as a cachepot (see pages 45 and 47–48) or drill one or more drainage holes in its bottom.

A common myth says that if you put a layer of stones or sand in the bottom of a nondraining pot, it will give the water somewhere to drain. In actuality, the roots still soak in water that tends to stagnate in the gravel and causes rot.

There is no substitute for a pot that drains well.

SIZE: Make sure your pot is large enough to contain plenty of growing mix to accommodate the root system and maintain an inch of room above the soil, called head space, for watering. A good design principle to keep in mind is that the pot should be no taller than one-third of the plant/container combination. Thus a 9-inch pot supports an 18-inch plant.

Standard pots—those in which the depth is equal to the diameter of the pot—were once the usual format for both clay and plastic pots. Azalea pots—those in which the depth is equal to three-quarters the diameter—now are the preferred format for plastic pots since the mix tends to stay more evenly moist in a squatter pot.

Pots come in a wide variety of materials, with plastic and terra-cotta the most commonly available. Both are fairly inexpensive, and an outstanding selection of decorative types is available.

PLASTIC: Plastic pots are easy to handle, relatively unbreakable, and easy to clean and store. They keep the potting mix moist longer than terra-cotta but are sometimes too lightweight for top-heavy plants. They are the

Always use a tray or saucer underneath a pot—even a pot without drainage holes—to catch moisture that eventually seeps out.

best choice for moisture-loving plants.

CLAY: Unglazed terra-cotta and clay pots are porous and allow air and moisture through the sides of the pot. Thus, soil dries more quickly in clay than in plastic. This is an advantage for cacti and succulents but may keep you on your toes with moisture-loving plants. Clay is breakable and harder to store but provides weight for stability. Soak new clay pots in a basin of water for several hours before planting. Otherwise, the dry clay absorbs water from the potting soil, robbing the new plantings of moisture.

SELF-WATERING: These pots, which allow you to water less frequently, are discussed on page 39.

SAUCERS AND TRAYS: You must place all pots with drainage holes on a saucer or tray of some sort. In fact, even cachepots (pots without drainage holes) are best placed on saucers, especially if they are made of unglazed clay because sooner or later water may seep through or condense on the pot's side and drip down. To do a good job, the saucer must be at least as wide as the pot's upper diameter and also deep enough to hold any excess water that may flow through the pot during watering.

Clear plastic saucers are widely available and inexpensive. You also can recycle old plates or shop for saucers that complement your pot. Beware of unglazed clay saucers, as they are porous and can stain the surface they sit on. Some terra-cotta saucers have an unglazed outer surface but are glazed inside so water won't flow through. You also can paint the inside of an unglazed saucer with waterproof varnish or enamel, or place it on a round of cork.

CACHEPOTS: The most practical way to grow houseplants is in "grow pots" or "culture pots," which are classic plastic or clay pots. They come in all sizes, so it is easy to move plants up one size at a time as they grow. They aren't always attractive in a decorating sense, however. That's where growing in cachepots helps.

Any ornamental container that can hide a grow pot is essentially a cachepot. It may be ceramic, plastic, metal, wood, or any other material, and it needn't have drainage holes, although it can have them as long as you place a waterproof saucer either inside or underneath. It needn't even be a dedicated plant container: Old watering cans, washbasins, teakettles, and other items are often used as cachepots. You also can find cachepots sold for this purpose from gardening products retailers.

A shallow tray garden shows off the cachepots as well as the artful arrangement of plants.

Growing Media

(continued)

Fill a windowsill box with plants that have similar light needs. The attractive box hides the plants' plain plastic growing pots. Line the box with a protective tray.

Ideally the cachepot should be about 2 inches wider than the grow pot so you can insert and remove the latter readily and easily see if the there is any standing water in the bottom. You can rapidly convert a cachepot into a double pot (see page 39) by filling the space around and under the grow pot with peat moss, sphagnum moss, Spanish moss, or perlite, or by covering the potting mix and pot edge with decorative mulch. If the grow pot is too low for the cachepot, raise it on an inverted pot or saucer placed in the bottom of the cachepot.

■ **Be careful watering cachepots.** Excess water may sit in the bottom or in the saucer inside, leaving the plant to soak. Half an hour after you water, check the pot and drain if necessary.

WOVEN BASKETS: These attractive containers make wonderful homes for plants but must be used as cachepots due to their tendency to rot when they contact moisture. Either carefully line them with plastic before inserting the grow pot or put a saucer in the bottom. In case water accidentally seeps through,

place baskets on plastic mats or cork pads. As with other cachepots, you can use Spanish moss or some other mulch to hide the grow pot.

WINDOW BOXES AND WOOD PLANTERS: Planters made of rot-resistant redwood or cypress fill a decorative niche. Because their construction may not be as watertight as that of plastic, clay, or ceramic containers, they are probably best used as cachepots. Line them with plastic and conceal the grow pots and drainage trays inside. You also can opt for waterproof plastic and metal window boxes.

HANGING POTS: To add an interesting dimension to a room, use hanging planters. They highlight fine architectural details and disguise unattractive ones. They also make efficient use of space and avoid monotonous concentration of plants at one level. A trailing plant with its vines cascading over the edges of a planter hung high in the air provides a graceful effect. Choose hangers that have built-in swivels so you can rotate each side of the planter toward the sun. Watering hanging pots is difficult since they may dry out rapidly; see page 38 for ideas on how to keep them moist.

Hydroculture

Hydroculture takes the self-watering pot (see page 39) one step further, and does it without soil or organic material of any kind as a support. The plants grow entirely in stones or, more frequently, clay pebbles. Hydroculture reduces the danger of soil pests and diseases while supplying the plant with exactly the amount of water it needs. Since the plants in this system require watering only once every two to three weeks, it is the ideal technique for people who don't have time to baby their plants. In addition, many of those who are allergic to plants (in fact, they more often are allergic to soil-borne organisms) find that a soilless solution allows them to enjoy houseplants as a hobby. Virtually any houseplant—even cacti and succulents—will adapt to hydroculture.

■ **Hydroculture simply means "growing in water."** It is a simplified or passive version of another technique called hydroponics. In hydroponic systems, water is recirculated on a regular basis using pumps or other mechanical means. Hydroculture systems consist of an outer pot that serves as a reservoir for a liquid nutrient solution and a grow pot filled with stones or clay pebbles. A screen sits between the two pots. In hydroculture systems, water simply moves from one clay pebble to the next via capillary action, much as water moves into the growing mix in a self-watering pot.

The texture of the pebbles allows plentiful air circulation, which is necessary for healthy root growth, while giving the roots all the moisture they require. There are no circulating pumps or bothersome tubes to fuss with in hydroculture.

Before transferring plants to a hydroculture pot, rinse them thoroughly to remove soil particles, and trim off any dead or dying roots; otherwise rot can result. To make the transition easier for the plants, place them inside a clear plastic bag for the first 10 days after transplanting. In many cases, it is easier to start with new cuttings rooted in the hydroculture pot using special rooting stones (smaller versions of the regular clay pebbles) than it is to transplant soil-grown plants. Transfer the cuttings to their final hydroculture pot once they have rooted. Some merchants stock plants already raised in hydroculture units.

■ **Maintenance of a hydroculture system is simple.** You need to add water only when there is none left in the outer pot. In most cases, this means waiting until the indicator reads empty, then delaying two more days. To check that the container is empty, tip it and note whether the indicator moves. Then add enough water to bring the indicator up to the halfway mark. If you fill the pots to the top each time, the roots may rot. Use the maximum capacity of the container only when you will be away for several weeks. Leach the plants every two to three months using tepid water.

Since there is no soil to buffer pH levels and mineral concentrations in the water, it is important to use a fertilizer formulated for hydroculture. Some liquid and soluble hydroculture fertilizers must be added each time the container is filled with water. Others are slow-release fertilizers, usually in the form of crystals or disks. They should be applied according to instructions, usually once every six months.

Supplies and pots for hydroculture are readily available from hydroponics stores and some nurseries.

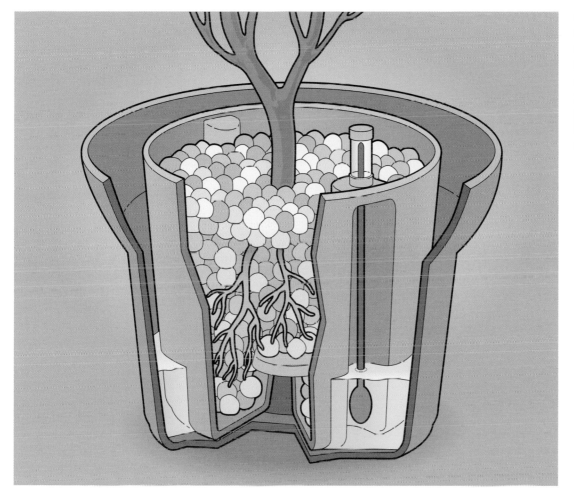

A hydroculture container employs an outer pot as a nutrient reservoir and an inner grow pot filled with clay pebbles or stones. No soil or potting mix is used.

Potting and Repotting

Young plants need to be repotted as soon as they have filled their pots with roots—that might be twice a year or more. Surprisingly, though, many mature houseplants seldom need repotting. Some plants even perform better or bloom better if they are pot-bound. Other plants need repotting if they outgrow their pots, if the soil has become depleted, or if the plant is infested with soil-dwelling pests. A plant needs repotting when you can't seem to water it enough. This is a sign that it has used up all of the soil's water storage capacity.

You can repot anytime, but the prime time occurs right before active growth starts in spring. Avoid repotting plants during a plant's dormant or resting period.

Is it time?

To determine whether a plant needs repotting, tap the plant out of its pot and look at the root system. If the roots are spread out with few (or none) growing through the drainage holes, repotting may not be necessary. However, if the root ball is such a mass of roots that virtually no soil is left, the time has come.

If a plant has outgrown its pot, you have the option of putting it into a bigger pot or pruning the root ball and putting the plant back into its original pot. If you want the plant to grow bigger, give it a larger pot—but only 1 or 2 inches larger in diameter. If you pot a plant in a container that is too large, the pot will hold more soil and, in addition, more water than the plant can use, a situation that could lead to rot.

If you want to maintain the plant's size, tap it out of its pot and slice off about an inch all around the root ball, including underneath, with a sharp knife. When you disturb the root system this way, you will need to prune some of the top growth at the same time. Otherwise the plant will drop some of its foliage in response to losing its roots.

When a plant looks like it needs feeding but doesn't respond to fertilizer, it's probably time to replace all or part of the soil. For partial replacement, remove the plant from its pot and knock off some of the old soil; tease out the roots a bit to encourage them to grow into the new soil and repot the plant. Another option is to top-dress the plant, or scrape off the top inch or so of soil and add new soil. Topdressing is the easiest way to replace soil for plants that should not have their roots disturbed, such as amaryllis.

If the soil is completely depleted or infested by insects, remove as much of the soil around the roots as possible. Tap off loose soil, then wash the roots with warm water. Examine the roots for any problems, prune out diseased or damaged areas, and repot.

It is never necessary to add a "drainage layer" of gravel or pot shards when repotting. Studies have shown that such layers actually hinder proper drainage and waste valuable root space. If you're worried that the potting mix will run out of the drainage hole or holes, place a piece of newspaper or plastic screen across the bottom of the pot.

Steps for potting or repotting

■ Thoroughly water the plant several hours before repotting.

REPOTTING

A. To prepare for repotting, loosen the plant from its old pot and slip it out gently, taking care not to injure it.

B. Gently tease apart any tight or circling roots. Loosen old soil gently from the roots with your fingers.

C. Clip any damaged or diseased roots. If returning the plant to the same pot, remove some healthy roots too.

■ Gather needed supplies such as a pot, screen to cover drainage holes, newspaper to cover your work surface, and potting mix.

■ Moisten potting mix by adding warm water and mixing it in with a spoon to make it easier to handle. Potting soil is hard to wet once it's in the pot.

■ Loosen the plant by running a knife around the inside edge of the pot or tapping the pot on a table. Slip out the plant. Hold the top of a small plant between your fingers, supporting the root ball in your palm. Remove a larger plant by laying the pot on its side and sliding out the plant.

■ Unwind circling roots and cut off any that look rotted. If the plant is pot-bound, make shallow cuts from the top to the bottom of the root ball with a sharp knife. Cut off an inch or so of the root ball if you intend to put the plant back into the same pot.

■ Pour some potting mix into the new pot and center the plant at the same depth as it was planted before. Then fill in more mix around the roots.

■ Tamp the soil lightly with your fingers as you work;

1. To divide a plant, remove it from its pot, separate the leaves, and pull or cut apart the root ball.

2. Place a section of the plant with healthy roots and leaves into a new pot proportional to the size of the division.

pressing too hard will compact the growing mix. Water the plant well.

■ If the roots were pruned substantially, cut back the top of the plant accordingly.

Dividing

While you're repotting, you also can divide overgrown plants that have multiple stems or crowns. Doing so rejuvenates plants that have overgrown their pots and provides you with new plants.

Remove the plant from its pot and slice through the root ball with a sharp knife or spade. You may need to saw

some plants apart, but others gently break apart by hand. Make sure each division includes some of the main root and stem system. Plant the divisions immediately in permanent containers with potting soil, and water thoroughly. Keep them in bright light but out of direct sun, watering frequently until they root. You also can put the potted divisions inside clear plastic bags to reduce moisture loss. When they appear upright and healthy, place them in a permanent location and care for them as you would mature plants.

3. Center each section in a new pot, fill in with soil, and water well.

D. Center the plant in its new container, making sure the crown is at the same depth as in the old pot.

E. Fill in soil around the root ball, tamping and firming it gently with your fingers.

F. Water the newly potted plant thoroughly, allowing it to drain well into a saucer or decorative container.

Propagation

Starting new plants from old ones is fun and rewarding. It's neither difficult nor time-consuming in most cases. Propagation is a great way to develop healthy new plants from an aging specimen and allows you to have beautiful gift plants to share with friends and relatives.

Propagation is best done when plants are in active growth but can be carried out any time of the year.

Cuttings

Growing houseplants from cuttings is the most popular method of vegetative propagation. It is an easy way to duplicate the attractive features of the original plant— the new plant is a clone of the original.

Depending on the plant, you can take cuttings from stems, leaves, or roots. Cuttings will root in a variety of media: in a commercial rooting medium, in water, in an artificial soil mix, or in vermiculite. Prepare the rooting medium before you take the cutting from the parent plant.

Although some gardeners routinely dip all cuttings in powdered rooting hormone before planting them, this step is not usually necessary and may actually inhibit fast-rooting plants, such as coleus (*Solenostemon*) and Swedish ivy (*Plectranthus*). Plants with

STEM CUTTINGS

1. Select a healthy stem and take a 3- to 5-inch cutting with several nodes (the point where the leaf attaches to the stem).

2. Pinch or cut off all but the top two or three sets of leaves. If leaves are very large, as on rubber trees or dieffenbachias, cut the leaves in half widthwise to prevent excess transpiration.

3. For slow-rooting plants, dip the end of the cutting into rooting hormone and tap off the excess.

4. Make a hole in the potting mix with a pencil or your finger, then insert the cutting in the hole and firm the soil around the stem.

5. Water gently and cover the cutting with a plastic bag to retain moisture. Check to see if the cutting has rooted after a few weeks by tugging lightly (a rooted cutting resists). Do not water or cover cuttings of cacti and succulents. They root best in dry mix with ample air circulation. Begin watering them only when roots have formed.

LEAF CUTTINGS

1. Remove an African violet leaf with its petiole (leaf stem) attached by clipping close to the crown of the plant.

2. Make a hole in the potting mix. Rooting hormone is not necessary. Simply insert the cutting in the hole, burying three-quarters of the petiole.

3. Firm the soil, then water thoroughly. Cover the pot with a plastic bag. Check every few days for new plants forming at the base of the leaf.

slightly woody stems, such as fuchsia and miniature rose, are more likely to benefit from use of a rooting hormone. You can buy extra-strong rooting hormones for especially difficult-to-root woody cuttings, and bottom heat from heating cables may be useful for some cuttings.

STEM CUTTINGS: This is the most common type of cutting,

good for most plants that have stems.

LEAF CUTTINGS: Only a few plants reproduce from leaf cuttings, including African violets, some begonias and peperomias, florist's gloxinias, sedums, kalanchoes, echeverias, and crassulas.

Certain plants, such as snake plant, also produce a new plant from just a section of leaf. Cape primrose and

some begonias also root from leaf segments.

ROOT CUTTINGS: A few plants propagate from latent buds in their roots, such as the ti plant *(Cordyline terminalis)*. To propagate from a root cutting, simply set 2-inch sections of thick root horizontally in rooting medium. When a plantlet forms, transplant it as you would other cuttings that have rooted.

LEAF CUTTINGS

1. Cut a snake plant leaf into 3-inch sections, making sure to keep them oriented upright. Making a notch in the top of each piece helps.

2. Stick the leaf cuttings into the potting mix, notched side up. Then firm the soil and water the cuttings. Cover each pot with a plastic bag.

Propagation

(continued)

Layering

Layering is a technique similar to rooting cuttings, except that the part of the plant (usually a branch) to be rooted remains attached to the parent plant. The great advantage of layering is that the parent plant supplies the cutting with water and nutrients while the cutting's roots form. Daily maintenance is therefore unnecessary. There is one disadvantage: New plants develop more slowly from layering than from cuttings.

A suitable plant for layering has a branch that's low enough for you to bend into contact with the growing mix. Creeping and trailing plants are ideal subjects for the technique. Note that many plants self-layer wherever they touch the soil. In this case, simply detach the rooted branch and transplant it into a new pot.

AIR LAYERING: Air layering—rooting from a notch in a stem—works well for some genera, such as dumb cane (*Dieffenbachia maculata*), dracaena, and rubber trees, that lack branches conveniently close to the ground. It is especially useful for salvaging leggy plants or mature specimens that have lost their lower leaves.

AIR LAYERING

1. Make a notch in the stem, removing a tiny sliver of growth.

2. Dust the notch with rooting hormone, then loosely wrap plastic around the stem, holding it at the base with tape or a twist tie.

3. Fill the plastic with dampened sphagnum moss.

4. Close the top of the plastic with electrical tape or twist ties. Check weekly for moistness, opening slightly to add water if needed.

5. After roots develop, cut the stem of the plant below the plastic. Remove the plastic and the moss.

6. Plant in fresh potting soil. New stems will probably sprout below the cut on the parent plant.

1. Move the parent plant to a stable location and place a pot with fresh potting mix next to it. Pin a trailing stem to the potting mix, but leave the growing tip free.

2. When roots develop at the node (this can take months), cut the new plant free of the parent plant.

OFFSETS

Plantlets

Several common houseplants reproduce by sending out miniature new plants on runners or shoots. These include the spider plant (*Chlorophytum*), flame-violet (*Episcia*), and many varieties of Boston fern (*Nephrolepis exaltata*). Some even produce plantlets on leaves, such piggyback plant (*Tolmeia menziesii*) and several kalanchoes. The plantlets can be cut away from the parent plant and repotted.

Offsets

Small new plants that form at the base of an old plant and remain attached to it are known as offsets. You can break them off and plant them just as you would for divisions. Detach offsets only when they are mature enough to survive on their own— usually when they have taken on the look of the mature plant. You can propagate the screwpine (*Pandanus veitchii*) and many bromeliads using this method.

1. Gently separate an offset from the parent, using a knife if necessary. It may be necessary to remove the parent plant from its pot for easier access.

2. Plant the offset in growing mix at the same depth it grew in the original pot. Tamp the soil lightly, then water. Give the offset the same care as the parent plant.

You may need to tease apart the roots in order to remove the offsets of some plants.

Offsets will propagate easily if they are well developed and have healthy roots.

Propagation
(continued)

Seeds

Most houseplants may be grown from seed, but usually they are easier to propagate vegetatively. A number of excellent houseplants, however, can be propagated only from seed. Single-trunk palms, cyclamen, and many annuals used in hanging baskets fall into this category. As an experiment, try starting citrus plants from seeds that you've washed and allowed to dry. Lemon, lime, orange, and citron all make lovely houseplants, although they will not produce fruit.

Houseplant seeds are available from garden centers and mail-order nurseries. Sow them the same way you would sow seed for outdoor plants, in warm temperatures (70°F to 75°F). Bottom heat from heating cables expedites germination.

For containers, you can use flats or small pots. Soak large seeds that have hard coats and slow-germinating seeds in tepid water (use a thermos) until the coat softens, then sow.

Scatter tiny seeds on top of moist growing mix and leave them uncovered. Sow medium-size seeds on the growing mix, then cover them with a thin layer of milled sphagnum moss (passed dry through a kitchen flour sifter). Not only does the fine moss hold the seeds in place when it is watered, it also helps prevent damping off, a common fungal problem with germinating seeds. Cover large seeds to a depth twice their diameter, firming the growing mix around each seed by pressing gently.

Water lightly and slip the seed tray into a plastic bag or cover it with paper or glass. Check the seed packet for any special needs: Many require light for germination; others must be kept in darkness. Check seeds regularly, watering when necessary. If you are growing tropical houseplants, be prepared to wait, as some are slow to germinate.

When seedlings emerge, remove the tray covering and move them into brighter light. Wait for true leaves (they look like mature leaves, only smaller) to appear before potting the seedlings individually. After two or

1. Fill a pot or tray with moistened, well-drained potting mix or seed-starting mix and press gently. Sprinkle seeds on the surface of the mix, then cover with milled sphagnum moss.

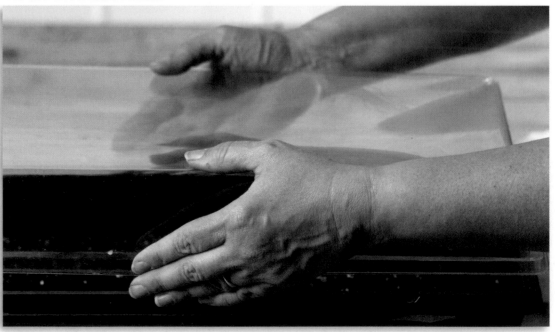

2. Water gently with a mister, then cover the container with plastic and move it to a warm spot.

three days, move them into the same light you would give the mature plant. When the seedlings are three to four weeks old, fertilize them every two weeks with a diluted solution of liquid fertilizer (one-quarter to one-third the regular strength).

3. When two to four true leaves develop, separate the seedlings to pot individually.

4. Transplant seedlings to small containers and, after a few days, move them to the same light conditions required by mature plants.

HOUSEPLANTS TO GROW FROM SEED

BOTANICAL NAME	COMMON NAME
Abutilon spp.	Flowering maple
Asparagus densiflorus	Asparagus fern
Begonia spp.	Begonia
Various	Bromeliads
Browallia speciosa	Browallia
Various	Cacti
Calceolaria herbeohybrida group	Calceolaria
Capsicum annuum	Ornamental pepper
Clivia miniata	Clivia
Coffea arabica	Coffee plant
Crossandra infundibuliformis	Firecracker flower
Cyclamen persicum	Florist's cyclamen
Cyperus alternifolius	Umbrella plant, dwarf papyrus
Exacum affine	Persian violet
Various	Ferns
Fuchsia ×*hybrida*	Fuchsia
Heliotropium arborescens	Heliotrope
Hypoestes phyllostachya	Polka-dot plant
Impatiens walleriana	Impatiens
Iresine herbstii	Bloodleaf
Mimosa pudica	Sensitive plant
Various	Palms
Pelargonium spp.	Geranium
Pentas spp.	Star flower
Persea americana	Avocado
Primula spp.	Primrose
Punica granatum nana	Dwarf pomegranate
Saintpaulia ionantha	African violet
Senecio ×*hybridus*	Florist's cineraria
Sinningia spp.	Sinningia, gloxinia
Solanum pseudocapsicum	Jerusalem cherry
Solenostemon scutellarioides	Coleus
Streptocarpus hybridus	Cape primrose

Propagation
(continued)

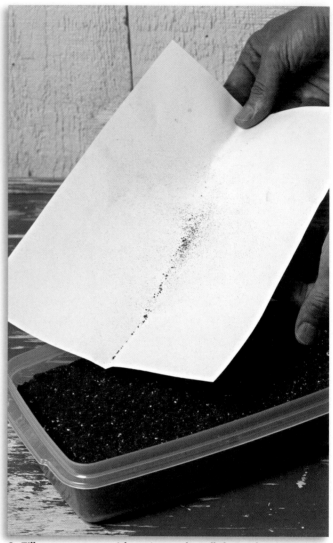

1. When tiny round bumps (spore cases) on the back of a fern frond have turned dark, lay the frond on a piece of white paper in a protected area. Spores will deposit on the paper when they are ripe.

2. Fill a pot or tray with moistened, well-drained potting mix or seed-starting mix and firm gently. Sprinkle spores on top of the mix, then mist.

Fern spores

Unlike most other plants, ferns produce spores, not seeds. The spores are tiny, very slow to germinate and grow, and need to be protected continually from dry air, so mist them frequently. If you want to propagate ferns, you will need plenty of patience. The technique is similar to sowing seeds but is more delicate and slow.

Dividing bulbs, corms, and tubers

Many bulbous plants, such as amaryllis *(Hippeastrum)*, are divided by cutting them into sections as you would slice an onion, each with at least a section of the flattened basal plate at the bottom of the bulb. Even if the bulb is left unplanted on a shelf, the sections produce tiny bulblets that you can pot. Most home gardeners prefer not to lose the mother bulb by chopping it into pieces. They'd rather wait until it produces offsets, which can be separated and potted on their own.

Tubers and rhizomes offer other possibilities. Over time, tubers often develop two or more separate growing points. At planting time, just before potting them, you can cut carefully between two points to produce two separate tubers. Leave the cut to heal for a week, then pot the sections as you would adult tubers.

3. Cover with a piece of glass or a clear plastic bag and place in a warm spot. Check periodically to see if spores are germinating and to make sure the starting mix is moist. Be patient. New plants take a long time to develop.

4. Ferns go through an intermediate phase when they look something like algae before they begin to look familiar. Keep misting the starting mix if it feels dry. When fronds develop, transplant them into small pots.

By nature, rhizomes creep and crawl, dividing at their tips, so pots usually offer plenty of material for division. Simply cut the rhizome so each piece has its own growing point. You can break apart scaly rhizomes, such as those produced by achimenes, into individual scales. They're tiny, but treat them like seeds (see pages 56–57) and they'll quickly sprout, producing full-size blooming plants the same year.

To divide tubers, cut carefully between two growing points. Pot the sections after they have had time to heal.

Fertilizer

Many people believe that fertilizer feeds plants because we call it "plant food." Actually fertilizer feeds the soil they're planted in. Photosynthesis provides plants with the sugar and other carbohydrates they need for energy. Fertilizers amend the soil with minerals that plants need to sustain healthy growth. Because houseplant potting mixes are highly fertile with plenty of organic matter, houseplants can survive for months without additional fertilizer.

Over time, however, watering leaches nutrients from potting mixes. Plants that lack nutrients grow slowly and may exhibit pale or dropped leaves, weak stems, and small or nonexistent flowers. Under most circumstances, you'll need to add some fertilizer on a regular basis, but forgetting or skipping a fertilizer application does not have the same disastrous results as forgetting to water.

Follow label directions carefully. Too much fertilizer damages plants.

Read the label

Fertilizers come in many different formulations to suit various types of plants. Their labels list three numbers that represent the percentages of nitrogen, phosphorus, and potassium in the fertilizer. These three elements are the nutrients plants need most. A fertilizer labeled 12-6-6 is 12 percent nitrogen, 6 percent phosphate (phosporus), and 6 percent potash (potassium).

Nitrogen primarily enriches the greenness of the foliage and promotes stem growth. Phosphorus encourages flowering and root growth. Potassium contributes to stem strength and disease resistance. Fertilizers formulated for flowering plants usually contain less nitrogen and more phosphorus and potassium. Those designed for foliage plants tend to have higher nitrogen content and less phosphorus and potassium. You also can find specialized fertilizers for some plant groups, such as orchids. If you grow many different types of plants, it's simpler to apply a good all-purpose fertilizer or to alternate between a flowering plant fertilizer and one for foliage.

In addition to the three major nutrients, plants need three secondary nutrients—sulfur, calcium, and magnesium—and minute quantities of iron, zinc, manganese, copper, chlorine, boron, and molybdenum. The latter are called micronutrients, or trace elements. A lack of trace elements causes hard-to-diagnose symptoms, such as stunted growth and yellowing or reddening of leaves. If you suspect such a problem in your plants, apply a fertilizer rich in trace elements.

Fertilizer types

Fertilizers are available in many forms: water-soluble pellets, time-release pellets, powders, liquids, dry tablets, and sticks that you insert in the soil. Their value and strength vary widely; if you have questions, consult a houseplant specialist.

When applying fertilizers, always read the label first and follow the directions carefully. Remember that more is not better: Excess fertilizer can burn roots and leaves.

SOLUBLE AND LIQUID FERTILIZERS: Most fertilizers on the market are soluble or liquid concentrates designed to be diluted in water. (Ready-to-use liquid fertilizers contain mostly water.) These fertilizers usually have been formulated for use once a month. If that's how you prefer to use them, simply follow the instructions

Soluble fertilizers usually are formulated for once-a-month application. If you prefer, dilute them for use each time you water.

Time-release fertilizer pellets are sprinkled directly onto the potting mix.

on the label, remembering that it's okay to use less fertilizer but not more.

Many gardeners find it easier to add small doses of fertilizer each time they water. That way, it becomes part of their regular watering routine and they are less likely to forget. If that's your choice, reduce the suggested dose of fertilizer to one-quarter of the monthly amount, if you water weekly, or one-eighth of the amount if you water on demand, and apply with each watering.

Apply soluble and liquid fertilizers whenever plants are in active growth, usually spring through summer. Reduce or dilute applications in fall and stop entirely during the winter. Plants maintained in constant growth under artificial lights require fertilizer throughout the year.

SLOW-RELEASE FERTILIZERS: These fertilizers are generally designed for a single yearly application and last for six to nine months under normal growing conditions. Many indoor gardeners find them practical. Apply time-release fertilizers according to instructions on the label. Some are tablets or sticks you insert into the soil.

FOLIAR FERTILIZER: You can also nourish plants by spraying or misting diluted fertilizer onto their leaves. Use only fertilizers recommended for foliar application and follow the label directions. Foliar fertilizing acts quickly but lasts a relatively short time. It is best used as a supplement to fertilizers applied directly to the potting mix.

If you overfertilize

Before deciding that a plant needs extra fertilizer, review its other care requirements to determine whether they are being met. The worst time to fertilize is when a plant is ailing or lacking in light.

Sickly plants decline even more rapidly if heavily fertilized and may die.

Overfertilization is a common mistake that people make, particularly with plants growing in low light. Such plants do best with little or no fertilizer. Dormant plants also do not require fertilizer. Too much fertilizer causes leaf burn, poorly shaped leaves, and a white crust on the pots and the surface of the growing medium.

LEACHING: If you accidentally overfertilize a plant, leach it thoroughly several times with tepid water and discard the drainage water. In mild weather, you can do this outdoors using a garden hose.

Leaching also helps wash out accumulated mineral salts, which can build up and harm the plant. Salt buildup shows up as a whitish deposit on pot surfaces or as salt burn on the edges of leaves. You may have to leach weekly for several weeks to alleviate it.

Another way to control salt buildup is to gently wash the old soil from the roots, then repot the plant in fresh growing mix.

Pruning

Pruning is one of the most rewarding aspects of plant care. Not all plants benefit from it, but many need pinching and cutting back to stay shrubby and full. Pruning acts like a spring tonic. It encourages and directs growth, and it corrects structural problems so a plant becomes a prime specimen. In some cases, pruning is essential to remove diseased or damaged wood or to limit a plant's growth.

Tools

Before pruning, arm yourself with sharp, high-quality, bypass pruning shears. They will pay for themselves many times over by giving you clean cuts and allowing you to carefully control your pruning. Anvil-type pruners tend to crush the stem rather than slice it off, so opt for the bypass type. You also can use scissors, but make sure they are very sharp. A plant stem crushed or torn by dull tools takes a long time to recover.

Goals

Keep in mind the overall form of a plant. The main reason for pruning is to make the plant look better, and careful work leaves it looking almost as if it were never pruned. There are some exceptions to this rule, such as when you need to cut back a plant drastically to reduce its size or cut off nonflowering wood. Always think carefully before making any cuts. A major stem that is cut off accidentally will take a long time to be replaced, leaving your plant with "bad haircut" syndrome.

You'll also prune to remove diseased parts or to rejuvenate a plant. To remove diseased tissue, prune back into healthy tissue, always keeping in mind the overall shape of the plant. Dispose of the prunings immediately (don't leave them near the plant) and sterilize your pruners with rubbing alcohol between cuts to avoid spreading disease.

If you are pruning to rejuvenate an aging or leggy plant, the plant's shape and growth pattern should dictate how you prune. Some plants do well with drastic pruning while others do not. Know your plant before you start cutting. The "Gallery of Houseplants" beginning on page 100 can help.

Some plants, such as African violet and peperomia, send up leaves from a flat crown in a basically round, symmetrical shape called a rosette. Plants of this form need pruning only to maintain an even shape. Remove older leaves from the underside of the rosette, pinching off the leaf and petiole as close to the base as you can. Also

Before: A weeping fig tree needs periodic pruning to keep it healthy and attractive.

After: Wayward stems are pruned out or headed back, and dead stems and crossing interior branches are completely removed to direct growth toward a more pleasing shape.

To keep plants bushy, regularly pinch off the stems just above a leaf. Also pinch off the flower spikes of plants grown only for their foliage.

remove any leaves that detract from the overall balance, such as misshapen or large ones.

Trailing plants, such as Swedish ivy and pothos, need regular pruning to keep them in the peak of health. They produce new leaves on the ends of long stems, and regular snipping will keep the plant bushy and full by forcing new leaves to grow along the stem. Pruning them is a matter of cutting a stem just above a leaf joint or node. Try to clip the stems at different lengths to keep the plant looking natural.

Other plants, such as ming aralia and fishtail palm, have naturally irregular shapes so you need only remove an occasional unhealthy leaf. Stemmy plants, such as fibrous begonia and Swedish ivy, benefit from an occasional severe pruning to force healthy new growth.

Crown-of-thorns, citrus, dracaena, and other woody houseplants may need occasional pruning of an entire branch or part of a branch to look pristine. These plants have woody stems that take much longer to grow back than herbaceous stems, so choose your cuts carefully.

Weeping figs develop a distinct umbrella shape as they age; pruning them while they're young encourages this shape and helps achieve it sooner. Prune out all branches that point straight up and trim back side branches to give the plant a symmetrical shape.

Pinching

Pinching, one type of pruning, is often done with the fingernails rather than pruners. Pinch out the tip of a stem and its topmost few leaves to promote growth of the side buds. Pinching is a great way to keep shrubby plants full at the center and robustly dense. In some plants, such as coleus, pinching out flower spikes encourages development of the more attractive foliage.

Root pruning

A specialized type of pruning, root pruning, is occasionally used to hold back a plant's growth. A plant naturally grows new roots at a root cut or break, so deliberately pruned roots and the breaks that naturally occur during repotting stimulate new growth. Severe root pruning is done to keep a plant in a small pot, although there are limits to how much of the root system you can remove without hurting the plant. A reduction in the number of roots means less nutrient uptake, so when you root prune a plant, remove some foliage at the same time to keep things in balance.

Grooming

Dust on leaves blocks light. Gently wipe off dust with a soft, dry cloth while supporting the leaves from underneath.

Remove faded leaves at their base using sharp scissors or pruners. If many leaves have faded, use this opportunity to check the plant for signs of pest and disease problems, and treat accordingly.

Houseplants need regular grooming to look their best. It doesn't take much time and makes the difference between plants that look healthy and attractive and ones that look neglected. More important, regular grooming keeps you literally in touch with your plants, providing an opportunity to catch and eradicate disease and insect problems early, when they can be easily controlled.

The amount of time you spend grooming will vary according to the type of plant. Some plants naturally shed and require more time than others to have their leaves removed and dead stems pruned out. A little grooming performed each time you water, however, reduces the need to do major work often.

Leaves

The first step in grooming is to remove old, dead leaves. If a leaf turns yellow-brown and withers, it won't green up again. Pull off the leaf. Some plants don't give up their leaves easily, so keep a pair of scissors handy to prevent tearing the stem. (Leaves on nutrient-deficient plants turn pale green and yellowish. In this case, fertilize.)

Remove the entire leaf instead of trimming off brown parts. Trimming may make the plant look better temporarily, but the leaf will end up browning at the cut edge again, starting an endless cycle in which the final step is to remove what's left of the leaf. Grit your teeth and remove it when it begins to brown. Chances are, you won't miss it.

While you are removing dead or yellow leaves, determine whether they are being lost due to normal leaf shedding or if there might be a disease, infestation, or environmental problem. This is a good time to reassess the plant's cultural situation. Examine the plant thoroughly and make adjustments as necessary. Rotate the pot a quarter turn. This lets all parts of the plant have access to the light and keeps it from growing lopsided.

Flowers

Unless the plant develops attractive fruits, such as citrus, Jerusalem cherry, or ornamental pepper, simply cut or pinch off faded flowers. They add nothing to the plant's appearance, and seed formation drains the plant's energy. Make flower removal part of your regular plant-grooming routine.

After a plant has finished blooming, you probably will want to remove it from your living room or other prominent spot. Simply toss temporary plants, such as chrysanthemums, florist's cinerarias, and calceolarias, into the compost. Move houseplants that rebloom, such as African violets, clivias, and amaryllis, to a light garden, a bedroom, a workshop, or some other spot where they can recuperate, then bring them out again when they flower anew.

Dusting and washing

Just as dust on a table masks the wood's beauty, dust on a plant hides its natural sheen and makes it look neglected. Moreover, dust clogs the leaves' stomata, preventing air exchange. If the dust gets thick enough, it can even block light. Spray small-leaved plants with water or gently shake off the dust. To dust large-leaved plants, carefully wipe with a soft cloth while you hold and support each leaf in your other hand.

Use a dry cloth for dust that wipes off easily. Dampen the cloth only if the dust is greasy, such as on a houseplant located in the kitchen. In that case, you will probably need to use a mild detergent solution to clean the leaf. If your water tends to leave white mineral deposits on foliage, you may need a damp cloth to remove them.

Once you clear away the dust, a leaf's natural shine will come through. There are plenty of "shine" products commercially available, but most contain a sticky wax that clogs leaf pores and makes a dust problem worse.

Plants sometimes benefit from a quick, yearly shower, although you may choose to shower them several times a year or not at all. Small-leaved plants that are hard to clean with a duster respond well to a quick rinse in the tub with tepid water. In good weather, you can do this outdoors in a protected area. Don't use too strong a spray from the hose. Warm the water by letting the hose lie in the sun before you spray the plant. Extremely cold water will shock even the toughest plant.

Mulch

Mulch is an easy plant enhancer. Potting mix looks great when the plant is first potted but eventually begins to show fertilizer deposits and to collect dead leaves and stems around the base of the plant. Adding mulch not only makes a plant look better but also reduces evaporation from the soil.

You can use almost anything as mulch. Generally something natural works best, such as small stones, shredded bark, or sphagnum moss, but if you want to use colored aquarium stones to accent your decor, go ahead. Use your imagination!

Groundcover plants make superb mulches. Not only do they perform many of the same duties as other mulches, but they also add another texture to the planting. Choose a groundcover plant that shares the same cultural requirements as the larger plant. For example, you can add coleus or English ivy around the base of your weeping fig.

Add moss, stones, or a groundcover on top of the soil to enhance a plant's beauty and help retain moisture.

Staking and Training

Tying a plant to a post or stick is often necessary and functional when helping a wobbly plant to stand up or when training a plant to grow in a particular direction. But staking and training go far beyond putting a stick in the soil and tying a plant to it.

Stakes offer endless opportunity for artistic expression. With them, you can train a vine to a topiary form or natural arch, shape plants into a living wall or curtain, or create a sculpture that combines a plant with an imaginative trellis.

SOLVING PROBLEMS: A stake used to hold up a plant that has been poorly grown doesn't accent the plant but rather accentuates the fact that the plant is lopsided or uneven. In these cases, it's probably better to start over by drastically pruning the plant or tossing it altogether.

Sometimes a stake is necessary only to temporarily correct a problem; once the plant starts growing well, the stake can be removed. In other cases, the stake is an integral part of the plant/pot combination, a permanent addition to the overall look of the plant.

Staking and training usually work best if you start with young plants. Older plants have stems that don't bend as easily, while young plants are not only pliable but also can be pruned as they grow to cover their support. Training plants onto a form may require a couple of years.

WHAT KIND OF STAKE? Choose a stake or support system that is at least as thick as the stem you are supporting. Stakes made of natural materials or painted natural colors, such as green or brown, tend to disappear when engulfed with foliage. Black is the least visible color. Green or tan bamboo stakes are readily available and inexpensive. They are amazingly strong and long-lasting.

In addition to stick-type stakes, ready-made forms and trellises also are available. A popular trend uses twigs and stems to create arches

TRAINING A STANDARD

A standard is a plant trained to a single stem—usually in a lollipop form. Indoor plants that lend themselves well to this type of training are those with strong or woody stems, such as coleus, flowering maple, fuchsia, geranium, lemon, calamondin orange, ming aralia, and herbs such as rosemary.

1. Choose a well-rooted cutting or seedling with a single sturdy stem. Pot the plant in a heavy pot in well-drained, heavy potting mix. Tie the stem loosely at several intervals to a firmly seated stake, taking care not to bind the stem.

2. Pinch off side shoots, letting leaves remain along the main stem to sustain the plant. When the plant has reached the desired height, pinch out the growing tip to force side shoots for the main head. As side shoots develop, prune them to achieve the shape you want.

3. As the plant gains size and becomes more top-heavy, repot into a larger heavy pot. It may be possible at some point to remove the stake if the plant stem can stand on its own.

Some plants must be staked, so use your creativity to make the stakes disappear in the foliage or at least add to the decorative nature of the plant.

You will find all types of stakes and supports available commercially, although some of the most attractive support systems can be made from twigs and branches from your garden. Whatever you use, make sure it is sturdy and doesn't detract from the plant.

Use natural materials to tie plants to stakes. Make a snug loop around the stake and then a loose loop around the plant, creating a figure eight. This allows the plant stem some movement. Tie the plant in several places instead of one. With just one tie, the stem becomes vulnerable to breakage.

and trellises. Plant-training devices also come in wire and wooden forms of all shapes. **WHAT ABOUT TIES?** For tying the plant to a stake, again choose green or brown materials, such as twine, raffia, or even green twist ties or plastic tape. Remember that the wider or softer a tie, the less chance it will injure the plant stem. Tape or pieces of nylon stocking make good choices if the tie won't be seen. Because they stretch, there is less chance they will girdle a stem if they are forgotten. If the ties will be visible, choose raffia or another natural fiber that will look as if it's part of the design. You can even use grapevine tendrils to loosely tie a plant.

When tying a plant to a stake, make the shape of a figure eight, with one loop around the stake and one loop around the plant. This allows the plant a little movement, which may prevent breakage. Tie the plant in several places, and tie loosely so expanding stems have plenty of room.

Once you have a plant staked, it is crucial to check the ties regularly. Plants grow quickly, so you must make sure the ties are not girdling stems, that there is not a problem with disease under a plastic tie, and that the plant still needs its stake.

SEASONAL CHORES

In order to efficiently groom and care for your plants, keep this list handy for reminders of monthly chores.

JANUARY
Give plants a shower; adjust for short days.

FEBRUARY
Check for new insect outbreaks.

MARCH
Prune for spring growth. Check carefully for pest outbreaks and control as needed. Fertilize.

APRIL
Repot if necessary. Fertilize.

MAY
Fertilize.

JUNE
Fertilize; move plants outdoors if desired.

JULY
Fertilize.

AUGUST
Inspect plants for insects. Prune where needed. Fertilize lightly.

SEPTEMBER
Bring in plants; take cuttings of annuals for

growing on the windowsill. Fertilize lightly.

OCTOBER
Check carefully for pest outbreaks and control as needed.

NOVEMBER
Check humidity levels after you turn on the furnace.

DECEMBER
Relocate plants as necessary to compensate for shorter day lengths.

Move your houseplants outside in containers for the summer. It's healthy for them and brightens your outdoor living space.

Special Care Concerns

Now that you've learned how to choose plants and provide them with basic care, you know enough to keep typical houseplants in great shape for years to come. That means it's time to dig into the special care needs of unique plants and special growing environments.

For example, did you know that a summer spent outdoors can quickly recharge a plant's growing energy? Many houseplants go from weak and spindly to vigorous and luxuriant when moved into the brighter light and better air circulation of a patio or balcony. You can keep them in their indoor pots or combine them in colorful container gardens that will brighten up your outdoor living space. In fact, some plants are grown especially for use as container plants, decorating your deck or garden in summer and overwintering indoors.

Container gardening is not just a seasonal outdoor pastime. Instead of growing all your plants in individual pots, you can group them together in dish gardens or terrariums to create an unusual indoor garden feature. Plants that barely survive other indoor environments often thrive in a terrarium.

Some plants lend themselves well to bonsai, the art of growing and training dwarfed plants. Such miniaturized trees are grown under unusually stressful conditions, including severe underpotting and harsh pruning, but the results are worth the extra effort.

What indoor gardener doesn't dream of owning a greenhouse one day? With the increasing availability of window greenhouses and add-on sunrooms, it's easier to create a conservatory environment at home for a reasonable cost. In these pages you'll learn the role of greenhouses in houseplant culture and what type might be right for your home.

Spectacular flowering bulbs, such as amaryllises, tulips, daffodils, and hyacinths, are easy to grow indoors, even in winter. You also can raise herbs in your kitchen window to use all year round. Their care is different from that of typical houseplants but the rewards are great.

There are three categories of houseplants so unlike the others they need special discussion: bromeliads, with their central tanks and water-absorbing leaves; orchids, with their unique potting needs and special root systems; and cacti and succulents, which need bright light and careful watering. The plants in these groups aren't difficult to grow but their care needs are different from more common houseplants. After reading this chapter you'll be ready to include some of these unique plants in your own home.

Moving Plants Indoors and Out

Use houseplants outdoors in places where they are protected from harsh weather.

After a long, dark winter, many houseplants enjoy a dose of fresh air, filtered sunlight, and rainwater. This treatment rejuvenates them and adds a bright touch of greenery to porch, patio, or yard.

Outside for the summer

Take only the toughest plants —those that can withstand unexpected wind and cold— outdoors. Wait until all threat of frost has passed and temperatures remain above 45°F at night. Make the transition gradually, keeping the plants for at least a week in a protected, well-shaded spot. After a week or so, you can settle most plants in a spot where they'll get a few hours of filtered sunlight each day and protection from the wind. Some houseplants, such as many cacti, tolerate full sun outdoors once they are acclimated to their new environment.

Keep a close watch for evidence of excessive dryness, pest infestation, or shock. Houseplants growing outdoors for the summer are subject to more wind movement and evaporation than indoor plants and may dry out more quickly. You might even want to install a drip irrigation system to make sure they never lack moisture.

Display houseplants outdoors in their pots, insert the pots into flower boxes, or plant the pots directly in the garden, sinking them just below ground level (provided the site has good drainage). Dig a bed 3 or 4 inches deeper than the pots and wide enough to accommodate the foliage spread without overlapping. Layer the bottom of the bed with 3 inches of gravel and 1 inch of peat moss. Set the pots in the bed and fill the bed with soil up to the pot rims. The gravel should prevent the roots from spreading out of the drainage holes, but twist the pots every now and then to make sure the plants don't root into the ground.

Indoors for the winter

Bring plants back indoors before temperatures begin to dip in autumn. That way the plants need only adapt to a drop in light when they move inside; the temperature and humidity remain essentially the same. A plant left outdoors during cool evenings will begin to slow down for winter and may react badly to the drier air of a heated interior. There are exceptions: You can keep plants that prefer cool weather, such as azaleas, Japanese aralia, and holiday cacti, outside late into fall, until frost threatens, even when evenings are chilly.

Set each plant on a bench or table outdoors where you can examine it carefully, and clip off every yellowed leaf, spent flower, and seedpod. If the plant has grown too large for its pot, reshape it with some careful pruning or repot it into a larger container. Clean both the plant and the outside of the pot with warm water. Examine the foliage carefully for pests and disease, and treat pest-infested plants with the appropriate control (see pages 89–92), following label directions. Even if you don't see any pests, you may want to spray or wipe the whole plant with insecticidal soap. To get rid of insects hiding in the soil, soak the root ball in a vat of soapy water for 20 minutes or so, then drain.

Bringing the outdoors in

You can also bring outdoor plants inside. Many garden annuals, such as impatiens, wax begonias, and pelargoniums, already have a long history of use as houseplants, but have you considered petunias, calibrachoas, or diascias? These (and many others) are tropical or subtropical perennials grown as annuals in cooler climates. Take cuttings in the fall or dig up specimens from the garden and cut them back severely before you bring them indoors. Doing so rejuvenates them and the new foliage produced under indoor conditions better adapts to its new environment.

You must acclimatize any plants brought indoors (see page 19) just as you would with new houseplants.

Tuck potted plants into perennial beds for added color and texture. Check them often for excessive dryness and signs of pests or disease.

Bring warmth-loving plants indoors before cool autumn nights trigger dormancy.

Container Gardening

Container gardening is one of the hottest trends in horticulture. On patios, balconies, and terraces across the continent, people are displaying boxes and pots and even bags full of flowers and foliage. Container gardening offers outdoor gardeners the ultimate in flexibility because everything about it is movable. You can "clear the deck" when you have a party and afterward re-create mini-landscapes—a shady corner for reading, a flower-filled dining area, a tropical spot for lazing in the sun—simply by rearranging the furniture and pots.

Lack of space presents no problem: A container garden fits along a staircase or on a window ledge, or you can even hang pots from fences and walls or an overhanging roof. Containers may be small enough to hold one plant apiece or large enough to display a jungle of foliage and flowers so heavy they have to be moved on casters. Container gardening provides the ultimate means for

You can arrange houseplants moved outdoors for the summer to mimic a natural landscape setting even on a deck or patio.

showcasing your plants: Move flowering plants to the front when they are in bloom, then push them to the back when they rest.

Container gardens can be entirely composed of houseplants spending the summer outdoors or may be used to rejuvenate tropical plants that must be overwintered indoors. Some tropicals, such as canna and ginger lily, conveniently go dormant in the fall; you can store them dry in a basement. You can force others, such as New Zealand flax and oleander, into semidormancy by keeping them in a cold but frost-free garage. The rest do well in the brightest possible light you have available indoors. Keep them a bit cooler in the winter (below 65°F at night, if possible) and water only moderately until new growth begins to appear in March. Then resume full watering and fertilizing as temperatures warm up, so the plants easily acclimatize to the

outdoor garden again in late spring. See "Outside for the Summer" on page 70 for information on moving plants outdoors for the summer.

Caring for outdoor containers

Container plants need care similar to the care of houseplants, except when it comes to watering. Because they are exposed to both sun and wind, evaporation from container plants is significant. In sunny spots, it may be necessary to inspect the containers daily, watering those that have dried out overnight. For convenience, use large containers: Their greater soil mass holds more moisture so you can water less often. Also, look for growing mixes specifically designed for container use. They are lightweight yet hold ample quantities of water, while letting excess moisture drain. Many contain water-absorbing polymer crystals

EXOTIC PLANTS FOR CONTAINER GARDENS

Agave	Grass palm
Allamanda	Hibiscus
Angel's trumpet	Licorice plant
Banana	Mandevilla
Bird of paradise	New Zealand flax
Blue trumpet vine	Oleander
Bougainvillea	Palms
Caladium	Passionflower
Canna	Persian shield
Castor bean	Plumbago
Citrus	Red fountain grass
Flowering maple	Star flower
Ginger lily	Sweet potato vine

1. Create a small dish garden by planting three to five cactus specimens together in one container. You'll need potting mix, gravel, and newspaper.

2. Start with the largest plants first, adding cactus potting mix as you include the smaller plants. Use folded newspaper to handle cacti with spines.

3. When you're satisfied with the arrangement, fill in around the plants with potting mix, then top off the mix with sand or decorative gravel.

that capture water during times of excess and release it slowly to plants as the mix dries out. A drip irrigation system is even more efficient. Put the system on a timer and your containers will be amply watered even when you're out of town.

Containers indoors

Creating a garden in a pot need not be limited to the outdoors. It's possible to create beautiful container gardens indoors as well.

In a large pot or basket, for example, you can place several smaller potted plants, raising them on inverted pots or saucers if necessary to bring them up to the right level. It's best not to unpot them: By keeping the plants in individual pots, you can quickly remove any overly exuberant or tired plants and replace them with something more appropriate.

Consider using a majority of smaller foliage plants for a pleasing background along

with a single pot of whatever plant is in bloom at the time. Blooms are not mandatory, however. Even miniature gardens entirely composed of a variety of foliage plants are charming.

When you have an arrangement that suits you, fill around and over the pots with a decorative mulch, such as sphagnum moss, or ornamental stones to give it a finished look.

DISH GARDENS: You can also put together a small cactus dish garden to place in a brightly lit spot. Find a tray or other relatively shallow container with a drainage hole, plus a saucer or other tray to catch any surplus water. Add a bit of cactus and succulent mix (see the recipe on page 45) to the bottom of the container, then arrange your plants in a pleasing manner on its surface. When you like the results, unpot the plants, set them in the tray of mix, then fill in around the roots with more growing mix. Use a bit of decorative gravel

or sand as mulch and you can have a very attractive mini-desert in a pot.

Care for your desert dish garden as you would any cactus or succulent. Choose a location with very bright to intense light and let the mix go dry between waterings.

A woven basket makes an attractive container for a dish garden that combines a variety of houseplants.

Terrariums and Bonsai

Terrariums are miniature landscapes created by combining a collection of plants in a glass container. Suitable containers include fish tanks, bubble bowls, brandy snifters, or bottles. Depending on the choice of plants, the location, and the type of container used, you can create the effect of a woodland dell, a rocky coastline, or a tiny jungle.

Plants do best under clear rather than tinted glass. Wide-necked containers are easiest to plant and maintain because you can reach inside them with your hands.

Keep a terrarium in bright but indirect light to prevent heat build up inside the closed container.

Use a funnel made of rolled-up paper to guide potting mix into a bottle terrarium.

Planting a terrarium

Clean and dry the chosen container thoroughly before you start planting. Before you add any plant to a bottle garden or terrarium, inspect it carefully for insects, diseases, and rotted roots. These problems are especially contagious under glass.

Most containers used for terrarium gardening have no drainage holes. To keep the growing mix sweet smelling and healthy, line the bottom of the container with ½ inch of charcoal chips (available where indoor plants are sold). Then add at least 1½ inches of ordinary commercial soilless mix with a little extra vermiculite or perlite added to improve air circulation to the roots.

Small-necked bottles require delicate, long-handled tools for planting. Use a rolled-up piece of newspaper to funnel the growing medium into such a bottle. To shape the terrain, use a chopstick or bamboo skewer with a small measuring spoon taped to the end. When you are ready to "bottle" the plants, gently remove most of the potting mix from the roots, drop each plant through the neck of the bottle, coax it into the right position with your miniature "spade," and cover the roots with growing media.

Once the plants are in place, a final mulch or ground carpet of moss completes the

POPULAR TERRARIUM PLANTS

Miniature plants that tolerate moderate light and high humidity are best for terrariums. Plants that need dry conditions, such as cacti and succulents, rot rapidly under such circumstances.

Baby's tears	Miniature	Pilea
Earth star	sinningias	Rex begonia
Euonymus	Moss fern	Strawberry
Ferns	Norfolk Island	begonia
Miniature African	pine*	
violets	Parlor palm*	*Young plants
	Pellionia	only.

scene. Mist with clear water to settle the roots and to remove soil particles from the leaves and the sides of the bottle.

Maintaining a terrarium

The most common misconception people hold about terrarium plantings is that they require no care and will thrive just about anywhere indoors. In fact, they need occasional watering and regular grooming to remove spent growth and to contain fast-growing plants. A terrarium stuffed with plants soon becomes overgrown.

Terrariums do best in bright but indirect light. Sunlight shining directly through the glass for more than a few minutes is likely to cook the plants. Terrariums do well under fluorescent tubes lit for 12 to 14 hours a day.

Watering can be tricky, especially in bottle gardens. When the soil appears dry or there are no moisture droplets on the container, add a tablespoon of water. If the soil is still dry, add another spoonful the next day. If you accidentally add too much water, remove the surplus with a paper towel or a turkey baster.

Grooming is easy if the container has an opening big enough to insert your hand. To remove yellowing leaves, spent flowers, or excess growth from a narrow-necked bottle garden, tape a single-edge razor blade to a thin stick and use it as a cutting tool. You can remove the clippings with slender pieces of wood or a pair of chopsticks. Remove dying leaves and flowers before they rot: A tiny amount of rot

quickly infects healthy leaves and shoots.

Bonsai

Bonsai is the Japanese art of growing plants in containers. Over thousands of years, the term has come to mean miniaturized trees and landscapes in a small pot or tray. Although some bonsai specimens are several centuries old, it is quite possible to create an acceptable young bonsai in only a few years. You can buy preformed or partially formed bonsai, or start your own from small plants or cuttings.

Bonsai are not necessarily indoor plants; in fact, most true bonsai are hardy plants kept outdoors year-round. However, some very interesting tropical and subtropical shrubs make excellent bonsai subjects and can be maintained indoors year-round.

If possible, choose plants with naturally small leaves, flowers, and fruits; also look for those that respond well to pruning and produce rough, aged-looking bark from the time they are young. An already formed bonsai is readily maintained by annual root pruning in the spring and regular pinching. You also can form your own bonsai plant in one of many different styles: formal upright, slanting, cascade, or forest. You'll

Houseplants with naturally small leaves and flowers respond well to pruning as bonsai subjects.

find a variety of bonsai pots on the market, each adapted to a specific style of bonsai.

Caring for a bonsai partly depends on the plant grown. Some need intense light, but others adapt to bright or even moderate light. Since they have little root space, watering must be done with utmost care. When the mix begins to feel slightly dry, set the pot in tepid water and let it soak up what it needs. The frequency of watering depends on many factors, including the light level and the season. Fertilize only moderately with all-purpose fertilizer.

English ivy can be trained in the root-over-rock bonsai style.

POPULAR PLANTS FOR INDOOR BONSAI

Azalea
Bougainvillea
Buddhist pine
Dwarf
    pomegranate
Elfin herb
English ivy
Fig (dwarf
    varieties)
Jasmine
Natal plum
Serissa

Greenhouses and Solariums

A greenhouse window attached to your house is an affordable way to increase light and humidity.

The term greenhouse refers to any structure that traps and stores energy by means of transparent panels. In common parlance, however, a greenhouse is a structure specifically designed to have as much transparent surface as possible oriented toward the sun. A sunporch, a sunroom, or even a sunny window provides some of the benefits of a greenhouse.

Greenhouses

Greenhouses come in a vast range of sizes and materials, but all are especially designed for growing plants and thus let abundant light in through a transparent roof and walls. Their structure may be either lean-to or freestanding and covered with glass, acrylic, or fiberglass. The smaller greenhouses that are becoming increasingly available are more appropriate for home gardeners. They allow you to extend the outdoor growing season by intensifying the warmth and humidity of a section of backyard or balcony without going to the trouble of installing a foundation, plumbing, and lights.

More permanent greenhouses, though, need water and electricity, so you must plan where to place the hookups. Locating the greenhouse close to these connections makes it easier and less costly to install the utility lines.

Consider the walking distance between the house and the greenhouse. If you have to contend with freezing weather or blinding snow, a greenhouse should be close—or better yet, attached—to the house.

Solariums

Solariums, or sunrooms, have become a common architectural element in modern homes. Builders and remodelers install them because of their unique appeal as an indoor/outdoor living space and because of the benefits of adding sun-provided warmth and light to a home. Although these additions often are not primarily designed for indoor gardeners, they are as effective as greenhouses for plants that need plenty of direct light.

Greenhouse windows

If the idea of a greenhouse interests you, a full-size structure is not the only option. A greenhouse window falls well within most budgets, and just about everyone has at least one window that's suited to such a project. Greenhouse windows do not require expensive plumbing, electricity, or heating systems, and kits that you can assemble in as little as one afternoon are available. Down the road, if the greenhouse window becomes too small for your needs, you can always add another one or a full-size greenhouse.

The best greenhouse windows come with temperature-controlled vents that open automatically to let out hot air. However, it's wise to install a small circulating fan near the window to blow warm air into the structure in winter and vent hot air in the summer. Due to their small size, window greenhouses tend to heat up quickly during the day and cool off rapidly at night.

Greenhouse uses

Besides growing a range of ornamentals, you can use your greenhouse for vegetable gardening and solar heating as well as a setting to display your plant collection as part of your home decor.

FOOD PRODUCTION: The environment of a greenhouse is in many ways well-suited to food production. Though growing food in a greenhouse is not cost-effective at the outset, doing so provides many benefits: absolute freshness, freedom from contaminants, and the possibility of growing exotic varieties. Vegetables, fruits, and herbs all can be successfully grown in a greenhouse. Off-season vegetable crops are becoming a particularly popular choice.

HOME DECORATION: In a greenhouse, you can grow plants to a degree of perfection that's difficult to achieve in the house itself. It is natural to want to show off your perfect plants by bringing them inside, but keep their stays in the house to a few days or so, or they will lose their greenhouse luster and perfection.

PLANT COLLECTIONS: A greenhouse is the perfect place to bring similar kinds of plants together in a collection, whether they are plants in the same family or genus, plants with the same cultural requirements, or plants that have the same aesthetic impact. The most common greenhouse groupings are alpines, begonias, bromeliads, gesneriads, orchids, and succulents. Most need a well-heated greenhouse; only alpines fare well with little heating in most climates.

SOLAR HEATING: A greenhouse attached to the home is a natural source of passive solar heating. To make the best use of this heat, install a fan or other type of air circulator to force it from the greenhouse into the house.

Growing plants in a greenhouse

The needs of greenhouse houseplants are much the same as those kept in the home. Use the same growing media and fertilizer used for other indoor plants. Watering requirements are also much the same. Although plants grow faster under glass and therefore need more frequent watering, greater air humidity inside the greenhouse helps compensate for water loss from the soil. Remember to water according to the needs of the plants rather than by the calendar.

Proper temperature is vital, and most greenhouses and solariums require a controlled means of ventilating excess

heat in summer and providing warmth in winter. See your local greenhouse supplier for heating and cooling ideas to fit your particular situation.

Overall the increased light, greater humidity, and easier temperature control in the greenhouse allow you to grow a wider range of plants than a typical home interior can sustain.

A sunroom can be as effective as a greenhouse in providing the bright light many houseplants need.

Some ornamentals require the bright light and humidity of a greenhouse in order to flower and fruit.

Forcing Bulbs

Those beautiful pots of flowering bulbs that you see in retail stores in the spring have been "forced," that is, pushed into flowering well before they normally would. You can buy forced bulbs already in bloom, or you can force bulbs at home.

The technique itself is simple, duplicating but shortening the stages bulbs go through outdoors, so rather than blooming in April or May as they would naturally, they bloom as early as December. You can force tulips, crocuses, narcissi, Dutch irises, grape hyacinths (*Muscari*), squills, and ornithogalums. Perhaps the all-time favorites, with their exquisite perfume, are hyacinths.

Plant tulip bulbs with their flat sides toward the outside of the pot so the leaves will grow facing outward.

Pot Dutch irises in autumn for midwinter blooms indoors. Forcing takes at least 12 weeks.

Choose pots in proportion to the size and number of bulbs you want to force.

How to force bulbs

Buy the largest bulbs you can find. Select only those varieties recommended for forcing. In general, early flowering plants with short stems give the best results.

Forcing bulbs normally takes at least 12 weeks. Therefore, if you want blooming flowers during the December holidays, plant in September. Only the very earliest bulbs bloom that soon. Pot them later, in October or November, for flowers from February through May. Use a growing medium that drains well, such as ordinary commercial soilless potting mix.

Pot size depends on the type and quantity of bulbs you are forcing. One large daffodil or tulip bulb or three small crocuses will fill a 4- to 5-inch pot. Six tulips, daffodils, or hyacinths require an 8- to 10-inch pot. When planting several tulips in one pot, place the bulbs with the flat sides facing toward the outside of the pot so the leaves emerge facing outward.

Nearly fill each pot with premoistened potting mix. Place the bulbs in the pot so their tops are just below the rim and cover them with mix. Avoid pressing the bulbs; the mix should remain loose, allowing roots to grow through it easily. Water thoroughly to settle the mix, letting the excess water drain. Label each pot as you plant it with the name of the flower and the planting date.

Hardy bulbs need a period of cold temperatures after potting in order to form a vigorous root system that can support lush foliage and blooms. Without a potful of roots, bulbs will not bloom prolifically. Some nurseries precool the bulbs so buyers can plant or force them immediately. More often, you'll need to place most bulbs in a cool, frost-free place, such as an unheated garage or basement, in the refrigerator, or any location where the temperatures stay between 35°F and 50°F (cold but above freezing). Keep the soil evenly moist while bulbs root; check the pots weekly to see if they need water.

When the pots have filled up with roots (lift them to check the state of the roots through the drainage hole) and their tips are well-developed, move the pots out of the cool environment into warmth and light. The change triggers bloom in about two weeks. For a succession of blooms over a long period, force only a few pots each week. Place the bulbs in a sunny, mild (55°F to 70°F) spot. The cooler the area, the longer the flowers last. You can force bulbs into bloom at warmer temperatures, but they'll grow taller and may need staking. Keep the soil moist and the bulbs away from direct heat; flowers fail to open if the soil dries out.

After the flowers fade, continue to provide moisture and sunlight. As soon as any danger of hard frost passes, move the bulbs to an out-of-the-way place outdoors where the foliage can continue to mature. Bulbs will not stand forcing for a second year, so plant them in the garden when their leaves fade. Forcing is hard on bulbs, and and a few years may pass before they resume flowering.

Forcing tender narcissi

Hardy daffodils require a lengthy period of cold temperatures to bloom, but there are also precooled tender varieties of narcissus, such as 'Paper White' and 'Grand Soleil d'Or', which you can force relatively quickly even in a somewhat sunny location. Simply pot and set in a cool (50°F to 65°F), dark place until the roots form. After the bulbs have grown a good root system (usually in

two to four weeks), bring them into a warm room with bright sunlight. They will quickly send up stems topped with clusters of fragrant white or gold blossoms.

Discard tender narcissi after forcing if you live in an area where winter temperatures dip below 20°F. In warmer regions, you can plant them in the garden outdoors.

Forcing bulbs in water

Hyacinths, tender narcissi, and crocuses are often grown in specially designed glass bulb vases that hold the bulbs above a well of water into which the roots grow. Growing these bulbs is especially fun for children, who can watch the roots and flowers develop.

Fill the container so the base of the bulb is just above the water, and add water as needed to maintain this level. Place the container in a dark,

cool area until roots have formed, then move it into the light to force blooming.

TIPS

■ Flower buds of forced bulbs will blast (fail to open) if the potting mix is allowed to dry out after they've begun to grow.
■ Bulbs forced under regular indoor temperatures tend to stretch and may need staking. Cooler temperatures result in shorter, more solid stems.

Hyacinths forced indoors can be planted outdoors but they may take several years to recuperate and bloom again.

Daffodils chilled under mulch outdoors can be forced indoors once green growth begins.

Growing Herbs Indoors

An indoor herb garden is both practical and decorative. Even an apartment-dweller who is without outdoor garden space can produce an herb crop. And all cooks appreciate the convenience of having fresh herbs at their fingertips.

With the right growing conditions, you can successfully grow a surprising variety of herb plants indoors. Most cooking herbs grow well in small- to medium-size pots. Clay or terra-cotta pots contrast well with foliage, but you can also grow herbs in glazed or plastic pots, a window box, or even a hanging basket with the proper care.

Most herbs are accustomed to full sun in an outdoor garden, and many are hardy plants that require a cold winter period. Therefore, one secret to the success of growing herbs indoors is to put them outside in the summer. Doing so allows them to store up energy for the winter months, when they will be subjected to the lower light levels of most homes. Leave herbs that are winter-hardy outdoors until late fall, exposing them to frost once or twice. This way, they are sure to get the winter break they need. When brought indoors, they'll immediately burst into growth under the springlike conditions of an indoor environment.

Herbs grown indoors require bright light, high humidity, and consistent temperatures. Pinch them back to keep them compact and bushy, and rotate them each time you water so all sides get equal access to light.

Most herbs require a growing mix with good drainage; herbs with moisture-soaked roots won't flourish (mint is an exception). Keep herbs away from gas fumes and areas subject to abrupt temperature changes, such as by a gas stove. Good humidity is vital, so consider running a humidifier if your indoor air is usually dry.

Make sure the plants receive plenty of light. Full sun in winter is barely enough for many herbs, although there are a few, such as mint, that do well in only medium light. If the plants stretch for the light, pinch them back to encourage bushier foliage and rotate the containers occasionally to ensure even growth. This is especially important if you are growing herbs in a hanging basket.

You also can grow herbs under artificial lights. If you use fluorescent bulbs, keep the plants as close as possible to the tubes without letting them touch. A four-tube installation provides better lighting for these sun-lovers than the typical two-tube fluorescent fixture.

You can start herbs from seeds or cuttings, or take divisions from the garden. Many supermarkets also offer potted herb plants. If you find that your potted herbs dry out too quickly after each watering, repot them into a larger container.

Watch for plant pests. Indoor herbs are not as pest-resistant as outdoor plants, and spider mites, aphids, and whiteflies are common visitors. Because you'll use the herbs in food, avoid resorting to chemical pest control products. A few treatments of insecticidal soap should take care of pests. Wait at least a week before eating herbs that have been washed with insecticidal soap.

Good herbs for indoors

The best herbs for indoor gardens are those grown for their foliage. Those grown for their seed are better left outdoors. Here are a few herbs you might like to try.

BASIL (*Ocimum* spp.): Fairly easy to grow indoors. Plants tend to decline after a few months, so start new plants from seed.

BAY (*Laurus nobilis*): Actually a tree or shrub, bay is probably the most readily adapted herb to indoor use and lives for decades with only minimal care. See page 164 for more details.

CHIVES (*Allium schoenoprasum*): Needs a rest period in cold temperatures. Expose to frost outdoors, then bring in for the winter. Bring in divisions from the garden or grow from seed.

DILL (*Anethum graveolens*): Grows quickly from seed. Start new plants two or three times a year since mature plants decline rapidly.

LEMON VERBENA (*Aloysia triphylla*, syn. *Lippia citriodora*): A tropical shrub that needs considerable pinching indoors to remain compact. It may lose its leaves for a short period in winter but soon produces new ones.

MARJORAM (*Origanum* spp.): Sweet marjoram (*O. majorana*) is the most popular type to grow indoors. Grow new plants from seed when mature plants falter.

MINT (*Mentha* spp.): Does well in less light and moister soil than other herbs. Start new plants from cuttings at any time. Many different varieties are available.

PARSLEY (*Petroselinum crispum*): Grow new plants from seed rather then bringing summer plants in, as mature plants tend to turn bitter once they're indoors.

ROSEMARY (*Rosmarinus officinalis*): Since this herb is not hardy in many regions, it must overwinter indoors. Requires intense light to do at all well. Water carefully: It tolerates neither soggy soil nor drought.

SAGE (*Salvia officinalis*): Needs intense light. Start new plants from cuttings yearly, as older plants decline.

SCENTED-LEAF GERANIUMS (*Pelargonium* spp.): Many choices are available. Particularly easy to grow indoors: lemon-, rose-, mint-, orange-, and apple-scented. Some varieties need a lot of pinching to stay compact.

TARRAGON (*Artemesia dracunculus*): Use only French tarragon, grown from cuttings rather than seed. It prefers slightly dry soil, so water moderately indoors.

THYME (*Thymus* spp.): Many different varieties are available and easily started from cuttings. Thyme tolerates indoor conditions well.

Parsley and basil grown from seed in a sunny window are attractive and tasty too.

Growing Bromeliads

HINT

Bromeliads usually bloom when they reach their full mature size (this can take several years), but if yours don't, place them in a plastic bag with a ripe apple for a few days. The ethylene gas from the apple initiates flower buds.

More than 2,700 bromeliad species and a wide variety of bromeliad hybrids exist. Increasingly popular for indoor use, most are easy to grow and attractive for long periods of time. Some are grown for their flowers and others for their foliage, but most are attractive both in and out of bloom.

Some bromeliads grow a stalk of colorful bracts that emerges from the center at flowering time, creating a spectacular display. The bracts are modified leaves and of sturdier texture than the short-lived flowers that peep out timidly from among them. Bromeliads that have no stalk feature flowers borne in the center of their rosettes. Their central leaves generally turn brilliant colors at blooming time to attract pollinators to the insignificant blooms. Still other bromeliad species completely change color at flowering time.

Bromeliads bloom only once, then slowly die over as many as three years. After flowering, however, offsets (called "pups") form and you can cut them free and pot them on their own, thereby ensuring your plants' longevity.

For the most part, bromeliads originated in the New World Tropics, where the majority grow as epiphytes—that is, they live on tree branches and trunks rather than in the ground. Many, however, will tolerate a more terrestrial habitat if conditions are appropriate (many grow on rock faces, for example). From their aerial perches, they gather moisture from rainfall and dew, and nutrients from particles in the air and falling debris. They collect their nourishment in a cup-shaped rosette of leaves called a "tank," which is also their most distinctive feature. In nature, the tank catches and stores rain, ensuring the plants of water though they often are exposed to drying sun and winds. Insects, spiders, and even frogs are known to set up house in these small "ponds," living in or laying their eggs in the tank. This curious way of growing, on treetops yet with their growing point underwater, has led one expert to describe them as "the only aquatic plants that grow on trees."

Not all bromeliads have tanks, nor are they all epiphytic. In fact, they divide into three different groups.

Some bromeliads have central "tanks" that collect and store food and water.

Terrestrial bromeliads

Although some tank-type bromeliads are terrestrial, having returned to the ground after evolving as epiphytes, for the purpose of this book this category includes those species of bromeliads that grow strictly on the ground and have no particular adaptations to an epiphytic habit. Most botanists consider them to be more primitive species, relicts of an era millions of years ago when all bromeliads were still terrestrial.

Terrestrial bromeliads, such as pineapples and earth stars (*Cryptanthus* spp.), have a normal root system and are not particularly efficient at absorbing water and nutrients by way of their leaves. To water them, moisten their soil as you would any other houseplant. They do well planted in ordinary potting mixes, although desert dwellers, such as dyckia, prefer a cactus and succulent mix (see page 45).

Tank bromeliads

Mostly epiphytic, this is the largest group of bromeliads. You can grow them on bark slabs, much like orchids (see page 85), but most also do well in pots, even in regular potting mix, although a specially well-aerated mix for epiphytes (see page 45) is preferable. On bark slabs, they develop only a limited number of roots that absorb little water and serve mainly as anchors that attach the plant to its support. Those grown in pots develop a more extensive root system that does absorb water.

Grow tank bromeliads in humid air, watering them mainly through their tanks. Keep these topped with water at all times. Water the pots of those grown in soil whenever they start to dry out. Avoid hard water or water that's rich in fertilizer; distilled water or rainwater is best. Hard mineralized water causes irremediably stained leaves.

Air plants

Epiphytic bromeliads (also called mesic or xerophytic) come from less humid climates where evaporation is intense and water is more scarce. Under such circumstances, a tank is useless. Instead these plants have evolved thick grayish scales (scurf) that cover their leaves. When misted with water, these scales rapidly absorb moisture. As a result, air plants can grow in dry locations, even deserts, as long as there is dew or an occasional mist. They usually produce only a few anchoring roots that are incapable of absorbing water or nutrients. Some even grow along telephone wires in their native lands!

In nurseries, air plants are often sold glued to ceramic figures or to pieces of driftwood. They also are sold loose. You can affix them to your favorite support using plumber's glue. You can even create a "bromeliad tree" by gluing or attaching them to a large branch solidly anchored in a pot. Air plants generally do not grow well in soil or potting mix.

To water these extreme epiphytes, mist them regularly or plunge them into tepid water for about 20 minutes once or twice a week.

Air plants rapidly absorb water through the scales on their leaves. They thrive with periodic misting.

Growing Orchids

No other group of plants offers as wide a choice as orchids: Some 600 genera, 25,000 species, and 100,000 hybrids are known. Orchids grow over such a wide range of conditions that there's bound to be at least one suited to your home.

Center a monopodial orchid in the the pot with the lowest leaf at the bark surface.

Position a sympodial orchid with the oldest pseudobulbs against the rim and the newest growth toward the center of the pot.

Growth habits

Orchids are found all over the world, but most are of tropical or subtropical origin. Most of those grown as houseplants are epiphytes that grow naturally on tree branches and have thick aerial roots. They typically have smooth, untoothed leaves and bear flowers with three sepals and three petals, one of which—the labellum—is highly modified and showier than the others. Orchid flowers are generally long-lived: The blooms of the most common orchids last for at least one month. Many orchids bloom seasonally, but with so many varieties, you can have plentiful flowers all year long. Some hybrid moth orchids are almost never without flowers.

The two main growth habits in the orchid family are monopodial and sympodial.

MONOPODIAL ORCHIDS: These orchids, which include moth orchids and vandas, produce a usually upright stem that continues to grow for years, producing new leaves at the top and losing lower ones at the bottom. They may eventually produce offsets at their bases, along their stems, or even on flower stems. These offsets are called keikis (keiki means "child" in Hawaiian). You can remove and pot them when they have a few aerial roots of their own. You also can cut off and root the top of an ungainly stem to force the older section to produce numerous keikis.

To repot monopodial orchids, remove the old mix, cut off any dead or damaged roots and the bottom of the stem if necessary, then set the plant lower in its new pot, up to the base of the lowest leaves. Fill the pot with orchid mix (see page 45 for a recipe) and tamp lightly. If you pruned off many roots, wait a few days before watering and temporarily put the plants in a shady spot until they adjust to the change.

SYMPODIAL ORCHIDS: This group includes the popular cattleyas, slipper orchids, and oncidiums. Sympodial orchids have a sideways, rather than upright, growing pattern. They develop a rhizome that usually grows over the surface of its growing mix, producing individual stems that each blooms only once, then slowly dies. Most common are orchids with pseudobulbs— fat, bulblike, and often wrinkled stems that bear only a few leaves—but others bear thickened canes, and yet others only clusters of foliage.

Sympodial orchids typically are divided when they need repotting. Divide them into clumps of at least three stems, preferably four or five. You can cut out yellowing, leafless pseudobulbs, but leave the healthy ones (even those that have already bloomed) intact. Nearly fill the pot with orchid mix. Repot a bit off center, with the older pseudobulbs near the edge of the pot, so new growth will be directed toward the middle of the pot. Add more mix to fill in around the roots and press lightly. You may need to stake the plant in place for the first few months. Put newly repotted sympodial orchids in a shady spot at first, and don't water for a week or so until the cut surfaces have healed.

Cultural needs

Orchids have a wide range of cultural needs, from full sun to shade and from constant warmth to seasonal cold, so it is advisable to consult the the "Gallery of Houseplants" (pages 172–175) for more information on specific genera. In general, though, orchids prefer high humidity at all times, fairly average indoor temperatures much of the year (a short, cool period in the fall can sometimes help stimulate bloom), some ventilation, regular but light fertilizing, and careful watering.

Watering is a special concern because orchids are not usually grown in standard moisture-retentive potting mixes. Instead they grow in light aerated mixes designed for epiphytic plants. Touching the mix helps you decide if the plant needs water: If it feels dry, it's time to water; if not, wait. When you do water, add water slowly and let the excess drain out of the pot. A few orchids without canes or pseudobulbs, such as paphiopedilums, prefer to remain slightly moist at all times.

Growing on slabs

One very interesting thing about orchids is that they don't have to be grown in pots. Like many epiphytic plants, they can attach to slabs of wood, cork, or tree fern. To grow an orchid on a slab, start by making a small, slim pad of sphagnum moss. Staple or loosely tie the pad to a slab and put the plant on top of it, arranging the roots so they extend outward. Fasten the roots to the slab, putting

small rolled-up pieces of moss between them and the staples or wire. Keep the plants lightly shaded and water them infrequently until they become established—this usually takes six to eight weeks. Afterward, whenever the slab feels dry to the touch, spray thoroughly or soak the plant and its slab in water for half an hour, as explained on page 38.

Another option is to grow orchids in slatted wooden or plastic pots, which offer the roots the aeration they need.

Like other epiphytes, orchids don't have to be grown in pots. Try a wood-slatted orchid basket filled with sphagnum moss. Anchor the orchids with wire.

Growing Cacti and Succulents

One reason cacti and succulents are popular houseplants is because they are so easy to grow. Many people find that these plants withstand considerable neglect— a definite plus if you're very busy. Benign neglect is actually the secret to their successful culture!

Cacti and succulents exhibit a wide variety of colors, shapes, textures, and sizes. These are the camels of the plant kingdom: Their well-developed water conservation techniques can carry them through periods of drought.

Most cacti and succulents need to dry out between waterings. Water well, then wait until the growing mix is completely dry to the touch before watering again. Clay and other porous containers make it easier to control the moisture level because they allow excess water to evaporate. You also can use plastic pots for these plants if you water less frequently.

The right clay pot is one just large enough to accommodate the plant without overcrowding its roots. If a small plant is placed in too large a pot, its roots may rot in unabsorbed water. Clay pots have an advantage over plastic because clay is heavier, a definite plus for taller cactus specimens as they tend to become top-heavy over time. Bonsai containers are splendid for displaying succulents: They really make them stand out, and the larger-than-usual drainage holes are the right size for allowing unabsorbed water to drain freely. Put a screen over the drainage hole to keep soil from pouring out.

Although cacti and succulents will grow in regular commercial potting mixes, it's better to provide a mix that drains more quickly. You'll find a recipe for such a mix on page 45.

During their growing season, cacti and succulents need water whenever the soil begins to dry out. During dormancy, however, water sparingly (just enough to keep the roots alive). Never let them get dehydrated; water before the foliage and stems go limp and shrivel. In springtime, when plants show signs of fresh growth, begin thorough watering again. Set the pots in a pan of water and allow them to "drink" until the soil is just moist on top.

Fertilize succulents dilutely, at half or one-quarter of the recommended strength for the fertilizer, and only during the growing period. If you prefer a constant feed method, dilute to one-eighth of the regular rate. When plants cease their seasonal growth, stop fertilizing.

Place cacti and succulents where they will get as much light as possible; full sun is not too much for these stalwart plants. Many will adapt to bright or even medium light, although their growth may slow drastically. Thin, elongated, or pale growth indicates a serious lack of light.

Cacti and succulents are predictably heat-resistant and not much bothered by the burning heat of a south

CACTUS FLOWERS?

Those brightly colored balls growing on top of a triangular green stem are not flowers. They're albino cacti. Without green chlorophyll, these cacti show pigmentations that would otherwise be hidden: pinks, yellows, oranges, and, in the case of the most popular one, *Gymnocalycium mihanovichii* 'Hibotan', bright red. Since they lack chlorophyll, albino cacti cannot carry on photosynthesis and normally would die. However, you can graft them onto a green cactus (usually *Hylocereus),* which provides the energy they need to survive. *Hylocereus* stem sections are not long-lived, however, nor very tolerant of cold. If you want an albino cactus to thrive for years, regraft it onto a slower-growing but longer-lived cactus, such as *Trichocereus.*

Cacti can live happily in the same pot for years, but when the time comes to repot them, it helps to know how to do it without getting your fingers full of needles. One solution is to use a jar lifter (rubber-coated tongs) to hold and lift the plant, but you have to be very careful because it is easy to squeeze too hard and damage the cactus. Another solution involves a section of newspaper folded into a 3-inch-wide strip. Wrap the newspaper around the plant and hold the two ends together with one hand. You can readily lift even a moderately heavy cactus this way with no harm to either the cactus or yourself.

window. But they do prefer cooler evenings. During the fall and winter, cacti generally need cool to cold night temperatures, or they may not bloom. Most other succulents don't depend on cool winters for flowering.

Both cacti and succulents are usually propagated by stem cuttings. Unlike other plants, though, pot their cuttings in dry mix, not moist, and don't cover with a plastic bag as you normally would. Watering before the cut ends have healed over may lead to rot. Begin to water only when you see new growth or when the plant resists when you tug on it (a sign that it is rooted).

For specific details on growing cacti and succulents, see individual plant listings on pages 121–125 and 206–209 in the "Gallery of Houseplants."

Check for signs of infection or infestation every time you water your plants. Most problems are easy to remedy if you catch them early and take prompt action.

Troubleshooting

In a perfect world you could bring new plants home, find a spot where the environmental conditions are exactly right, and maintain them with basic care. But sometimes environmental conditions aren't perfect, and people forget to water and fertilize. When plants seem healthy it's easy to forget about them, but stressed or neglected plants are susceptible to insect infestations and diseases that can cause serious damage

Since you can correct a problem much more easily when you catch it early, make it a habit to examine and touch your plants every time you water them. Check for signs of insects or disease, and if you any, move the plant away from others while you take steps to control the problem. Check nearby plants to make sure any infection or infestation has not already spread. Then use the information in this chapter to diagnose and fix the problem.

With just a little know-how, you can easily keep your houseplants in top shape.

Insects

APHIDS

PROBLEM: New leaves are curled, discolored, and smaller than normal. A shiny or sticky substance may coat them. Tiny (⅛-inch), wingless, soft-bodied green insects cluster on buds, young stems, and leaves. Aphids in small numbers do little damage, but they are extremely prolific and populations rapidly build up to damaging numbers. Damage results when aphids suck sap from the leaves and stems. Aphids are unable to digest all the sugar in the plant sap and excrete the excess in a fluid called honeydew, which often drops onto leaves or surfaces below.

SOLUTION: Wipe off small infestations with cotton swabs dipped in rubbing alcohol or rinse the foliage under the faucet two or three days in a row. If the weather permits, take infested plants outdoors and knock off the aphids with a strong stream of water. If necessary, spray with insecticidal soap, neem oil or an insecticide labeled for aphids, repeating weekly until the aphids have disappeared.

Aphids excrete honeydew, which leads to a fungus called sooty mold—both telltale signs of infestation.

CYCLAMEN MITES

PROBLEM: The stem tips or the newest growth in the plant center becomes severely stunted. Leaves become stunted, brittle, stay very small, and may be cupped or curved. Color may change to bronze, gray, or tan. Flower buds fail to develop properly and do not open. Cyclamen mite (*Steneotarsonemus pallidus*) is an extremely small mite that's related to spiders. These mites attack many types of houseplants and can be particularly damaging to cyclamens. They infest the new growth most heavily but will crawl to other parts of the plant and to other plants as well. Cyclamen mites reproduce rapidly. Their cousins, broad mites (*Polyphagotarsonemus latus*), cause similar problems.

SOLUTION: Spray infested plants several times with insecticidal soap or a miticide. Make sure your plant is listed on the product label and follow label directions carefully Isolate mildly infested plants. Discard severely infested plants. Scour the pots and wash the area where the pots were sitting with a solution of 1 part household bleach to 9 parts water. Observe nearby plants closely so you can spray if symptoms appear. Avoid touching leaves of infested plants before touching leaves of healthy plants.

Cyclamen mites attack all kinds of houseplants. Isolate infected plants while you treat the problem.

Insects
(continued)

Fungus gnats are small flies that do little damage but can be a nuisance.

FUNGUS GNATS

PROBLEM: Small (up to ⅛-inch), slender, dark insects fly around when plants are disturbed. They frequently run across the foliage and soil and may also be found on windows. Plant roots may be damaged and seedlings may die. Fungus gnats and their close relatives, shore flies, are small flies that do little damage, but they are unpleasant in large numbers. They lay their eggs in soil that contains organic material. After a week, the eggs hatch and the larvae crawl through the upper layer of the soil. The larvae are white, ¼ inch long, and have black heads. They feed on fungi that grow on organic matter. The larvae usually do not damage plants, but when present in large numbers, they may feed on the roots of some plants, killing seedlings. The larvae feed for about two weeks before maturing into adults. Many generations may be born in a year.
SOLUTION: Hang sticky traps among infested plants to catch adults. Let potting mix dry out slightly between waterings: Larvae cannot survive in dry soil. Apply a labeled insecticide or *Bacillus thuringiensis israelensis* according to label directions.

Leaf miner damage is unsightly but easily controlled.

LEAF MINERS

PROBLEM: Irregular, winding white to brown tunnels or patches appear on upper leaf surfaces. Small, dark-headed white grubs sometimes are seen in the tunnels. Leaf miners are minuscule flies that lay white eggs in clusters on the undersides of leaves. The larvae bore inside the leaves of susceptible species, such as chrysanthemums and cinerarias (*Senecio* ×*hybridus*). Leaf miners spread through contact with other plants and may also come indoors through open windows.

SOLUTION: Damage from leaf miners is unattractive but not fatal to a mature plant. Removing infested leaves is usually sufficient, as this pest rarely can reproduce in the average home environment. Nevertheless keep infested plants isolated from other susceptible species. Surface sprays are generally ineffective against the larvae, but a systemic insecticide solution may be helpful. The roots take the insecticide up to the leaves where larvae feed. A neem solution applied weekly to the potting mix may also be helpful.

Mealybugs feed on all parts of the plant, especially tender new shoots.

MEALYBUGS

PROBLEM: White cottony or waxy insects up to ¼ inch long cluster on the undersides of leaves, on stems, and in the axils where leaves are attached. Egg masses also may be present. Some species live below ground on roots. Honeydew, a sticky substance, may cover the leaves or drop onto surfaces below the plant. Leaves may be spotted or deformed. Infested plants are unsightly, do not grow well, and may die.
SOLUTION: Control is difficult. If only a few mealybugs are present, wipe them off with a damp cloth or use cotton swabs dipped in rubbing alcohol. Wipe off any egg sacs under the rims or on the bottoms of pots. For larger infestations, thoroughly spray stems and both sides of leaves with a labeled insecticide, neem oil, or insecticidal soap. For soil mealybugs, drench the potting mix with the insecticide, insecticidal soap, or neem solution. Make sure your plant is listed on the product label and follow the label directions carefully. Discard severely infested plants, and do not take cuttings from them for new plants.

NARCISSUS FLIES

PROBLEM: Amaryllis bulbs fail to produce new leaves after their dormant period. When squeezed, they appear soft. Upon inspection, frass (brownish insect excrement) may be found at a hole at the bulb's base. When cut open, you find a single (rarely more) large brown larva inside and often substantial rotting material. You may see a bumblebee-like insect (the adult fly) with black and yellow stripes hover around the plants.

SOLUTION: Unpot the bulb and remove the soil to reveal the insect's entry point. Carefully extract the larvae with a piece of wire. If the center of the bulb is intact, dust the opening with powdered sulfur to help stop the rot. (Repot after the wound has healed, and drench the bulb and potting mix with a labeled insecticide.) If the bulb is gutted, cut it open and remove rotted material. Lay the bulb in vermiculite in a cool spot. New bulblets may appear from intact bulb scales but may be years away from flowering. Avoid putting amaryllis plants outdoors where narcissus fly infestation occurs.

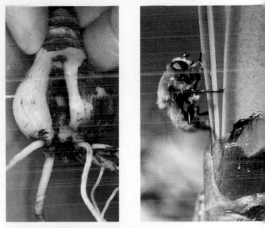

Narcissus flies cause bulbs to rot.

SCALE INSECTS

PROBLEM: Nodes, stems, and leaves or fronds are covered with cottony white masses, brown crusty bumps, or clusters of flattened reddish-gray or brown scaly bumps that scrape off easily. Leaves or fronds turn yellow and may drop. A sticky excretion called honeydew may cover the stems and leaves or fronds, and drip on surfaces below. Scale insects of several different types attack houseplants. The young, called crawlers, are small (about $\frac{1}{10}$ inch) and soft-bodied. They insert their mouth parts into the plant and feed on the sap. Eventually their legs disappear, but the scales remain in place. Some develop a soft covering, while others are hard.

SOLUTION: Pick off by hand or brush all plant surfaces with a soft toothbrush dipped in soapy water. Young can hide under adult shells, so make sure scales are removed as soon as possible. Insecticidal soap or an indoor horticultural oil is most effective on crawlers. Make sure your plant is listed on the product label and follow label directions carefully. Repeated applications may be necessary.

Scales suck plant sap, weakening and damaging the plant.

SPIDER MITES

PROBLEM: Leaves are stippled, yellow, and dirty; they may dry out and drop. There may be webbing over flower buds, between leaves, or on the lower surfaces of the leaves. To determine whether a plant is infested with mites, hold a sheet of white paper beneath an affected area and tap the leaf or stem sharply. Minute green, red, or yellow specks the size of pepper grains will drop to the paper and begin to crawl around. Spider mites, related to spiders, are a common problem for many houseplants. They cause damage by sucking sap from the undersides of the leaves. Under warm, dry conditions, these insects multiply rapidly.

SOLUTION: Thoroughly rinse infected plants in the shower or with a hose to remove the majority of the insects. Then spray infested plants with insecticide or an insecticidal soap. Make sure your plant is listed on the product label and follow label directions carefully. Plants need several weekly sprayings to kill the mites as they hatch. Inspect new plants thoroughly before bringing them into your home. Increase humidity to discourage reproduction and prevent future infestations.

Spider mites thrive in the dry, heated air of a home in winter.

Insects
(continued)

SPRINGTAILS

PROBLEM: Small white to black insects up to ⅕ inch long jump when plants are watered. Lower leaves and young seedlings may be nibbled. Springtails are common insects in indoor conditions and seem to prefer potting mixtures rich in peat moss. They do little damage to mature plants but are harmful to seedlings.

Springtails thrive in moist organic potting mixtures.

SOLUTION: Springtails thrive only in damp conditions, so allow the potting mixture to dry out slightly between waterings. Use pasteurized mixtures when sowing seed, and cover seed containers with plastic film to prevent the pests from reaching young seedlings. In severe cases, take the plants outside and treat the soil with an insecticide containing malathion. Or soak the plants in water to bring springtails to the surface, then spray them with an insecticide containing pyrethrins.

Remove damaged leaves and flowers to reduce thrips infestation.

THRIPS

PROBLEM: Flowers and leaves are abnormally mottled or streaked with silver. Young leaves and flowers may be distorted. Pollen sacs on African violets *(Saintpaulia)* spill open, leaving yellow powder on flowers. Dusty black droppings collect on leaves or flowers. Tiny (¹⁄₁₆ inch long or less) insects scuttle away when the plant is breathed on. Both adult and immature thrips damage plant surfaces with their rasping mouth apparatus, used to suck plant sap. Nymphs are pale in color and wingless. Adults are dark and, although they bear feathery wings, tend to hop rather than fly. They hide in crevices between stems and flowers and lay their eggs inside plant tissues or in the potting mix. Therefore they are relatively immune to most spray pesticides.

SOLUTION: Thrips reproduce many times each year, so remove heavily damaged leaves and flowers to reduce infestation. Apply an insecticide or insecticidal soap to affected plants and potting mix weekly until no further symptoms are apparent. Make sure your plant is listed on the product label and follow the label directions carefully.

Whiteflies excrete honeydew, which encourages sooty mold fungus.

WHITEFLIES

PROBLEM: When you touch the plant, tiny, winged white insects flutter around it. Translucent scalelike larvae are present under leaves. Leaves may be mottled and yellow. Whiteflies feed mainly on the undersides of the leaves. They cannot digest all the sugar in the sap and excrete the excess in a sticky honeydew, which coats the leaves and may drop from the plant.

SOLUTION: Isolate heavily infested plants as soon as you spot the problem. Use yellow sticky traps to catch adults. If only a few leaves are infested, wipe off larvae with a damp cloth or cotton swab soaked in alcohol, or shake the plant and vacuum up the cloud of flies. Spray severe infestations with insecticidal soap, neem or insecticide labeled for control of whiteflies. Check labels to determine which product can be used on your particular plant. Spray weekly as long you continue to see any whiteflies.

Diseases

BACTERIAL STEM BLIGHT

PROBLEM: Soft, sunken areas with water-soaked margins appear on the stems. Cracks sometimes appear in the affected areas. Lower leaves may turn yellow and become severely wilted. They tend to hang on the stem even when collapsed. If the condition is severe, the stem may rot through so the top of the plant breaks off. Inner stem tissue is discolored brown. Cuttings from infected stems may produce infected plants, or they simply may not root. Bacterial stem blight is caused by the bacterium *Erwinia chrysanthemi*.

SOLUTION: No cure exists for this disease. Discard severely infected plants. If some stems are still healthy, cut them off above the diseased area and reroot them. Do not reroot any stems that have brown streaks.

To prevent bacterial stem blight, use a potting mix that drains well and avoid splashing leaves when you water. If possible, water from the bottom of the plant and discard excess water after 20 minutes. Make sure air circulation is sufficient around the plant.

Bacterial stem blight cannot be cured.

BOTRYTIS

PROBLEM: Light brown patches appear on leaves, stems, or flowers, gradually darkening and turning soft and moist. A grayish mold covers the affected surfaces. Infected plant parts curl up and fall off. Botrytis, or gray mold, is a common airborne fungal disease that affects a wide range of plants and spreads quickly. When the plant stem is affected, the entire plant may rot away. This disease is especially common during periods of intense humidity and inside closed containers, such as terrariums.

SOLUTION: Remove infected plant parts. Treat the rest of the plant with a fungicide or a fungicidal soap. Make sure your plant is listed on the product label and follow label directions carefully. To prevent this disease, avoid overly humid air and improve air circulation around the plants to keep humidity low. Do not mist susceptible plants.

Fungal spores emerge on the leaves of a plant infected with botrytis.

CROWN, STEM, AND ROOT ROT

PROBLEM: Plants fail to grow. Leaves appear dull, then turn black. Lower ones may turn yellow and drop. Leaves in the center of the plant turn dark green, then black. Roots are dead and rotted. When the condition is severe, all the roots are rotted and the plant may wilt and die. Rot is caused by soil-dwelling fungi (*Pythium* spp.), or water molds, that attack the roots, and usually indicates that the plant has been watered too frequently or that the soil mix does not drain well. The fungi are common in garden soils

and can be introduced on a plant or dirty pot, or transferred on dirty fingers or tools. Rot spreads quickly through a root system if the soil remains wet. Plants weakened by other factors are most susceptible.

SOLUTION: If the plant is only mildly affected, let the soil dry between waterings. If the soil mix is heavy or the container does not drain well, transplant into fast-draining soil mix in a container that drains freely. Discard severely infected plants and soil. Soak pots in a mixture of 1 part household bleach to 9 parts water

for 30 minutes. Rinse with water, and dry thoroughly before reuse. After handling infected plants, wash your hands thoroughly before touching healthy plants.

Slow growth and discolored leaves are the first symptoms of rot.

Diseases
(continued)

Remove infected leaves to prevent fungal spread.

LEAF SPOT

PROBLEM: Circular reddish brown spots appear on the leaves. The spots are surrounded by a yellow margin. Several spots may join to form blotches. Badly spotted leaves may turn yellow and die. Septoria leaf spot is caused by a fungus (*Septoria* spp.). In most cases, spotting is unsightly but not harmful, but on susceptible plants, the leaves may weaken and die.

SOLUTION: Clip off badly spotted leaves. Water carefully to avoid leaf splash and keep the foliage dry to prevent the spread of the fungus. If spotting continues, spray the plant with a fungicide or a fungicidal soap. Make sure your plant is listed on the product label and follow label directions carefully.

Stressed plants are most susceptible to infection from powdery mildew.

POWDERY MILDEW

PROBLEM: White or gray powdery patches appear on the leaves, stems, and flowers. Leaves and flowers may be covered with the powdery growth. The mildew usually appears first on the upper surfaces of older leaves. Tissue under the powdery growth may turn yellow or brown. Affected leaves may drop. Powdery mildew is caused by several genera of fungi. The powdery patches are fungus strands and spores. The wind-borne spores are capable of infecting leaves, stems, and flowers on the same plant or on nearby plants.

The disease favors dim light and warm days with cool nights. Older leaves are more susceptible than new ones. Plants in dry soil are more susceptible than those in moist soil.

SOLUTION: Remove infected leaves and spray plants with a fungicide or fungicidal soap until the disease is gone. Make sure your plant is listed on the product label and follow label directions carefully. Move plants to locations with more light and keep them out of cool drafts; locate them in rooms that have consistent temperatures and adequate air circulation.

Plant viruses cannot be cured.

VIRUS

PROBLEM: Plants grow slowly and without vigor. Leaves are lightly mottled or streaked with yellow; they also may show ringed yellow spots. Leaves can be distorted. Virus diseases often are subtle, with the main symptoms being stunted growth and a generally lackluster performance. They are carried from plant to plant by insects or on infected tools.

SOLUTION: No cure exists for infected plants. Destroy them. To prevent viruses, keep insects at bay through preventive treatment. When pruning, dip tools into a disinfectant (bleach or rubbing alcohol) between each cut.

Cultural Problems

BUD BLAST

PROBLEM: Flower buds form but fail to open. They may turn brown shortly after forming or attain nearly full size before brown patches appear. Sometimes they simply drop off with no other symptom. Dry air is the most common cause. Other causes are air pollution, excessive heat or cold, too much fertilizer, too little or too much water, and fungal disease. Bud blast is normal in certain circumstances, such as when a plant has produced more buds than it has energy to feed. Young plants, for example, will often lose many of their flower buds at their first flowering.

SOLUTION: As flowering approaches, place plants on a humidity tray or in a room with a humidifier to increase humidity. You might also move plants out of direct sunlight (air loses humidity as it heats up) and away from air-conditioning vents. Check for other symptoms that may explain the cause of the buds blasting (for example, wilting from too much or too little water or a sudden temperature change) and treat the problem accordingly.

Bud blast may be caused by too much direct sun or too little humidity.

EDEMA

PROBLEM: Brown, corky patches form on stems or leaves. When scratched away, underlying, healthy cells are revealed. Too much water, especially during humid weather, is usually the cause. Cells swell up with moisture and burst, then scab tissues form as the plant heals, leading to a corky appearance. Sucking insects, such as spider mites, may also cause edema on some plants, notably succulents. Many plants tend to develop edema on their lower stems as they age.

SOLUTION: Once edema appears, cutting away the affected tissues can cure it. It can, however, be prevented by less frequent watering, especially when the air is humid and light levels are low. Also check for symptoms of spider mites and treat accordingly.

Edema is usually caused by overwatering but may also be a symptom of a sucking insect infestation, such as spider mites.

GUTTATION

PROBLEM: Drops of water or sap form at leaf tips or on the underside of the leaf. They may blacken or form translucent crystals as they dry. Too much soil moisture is the most common cause. The plant absorbs more water than it can use, causing it to secrete the excess through its leaves. In plants such as grape ivy *(Cissus)*, West Indian holly *(Leea)*, chestnut vine *(Tetrastigma voinieranum)*, and dieffenbachia *(Dieffenbachia)*, a certain amount of guttation is normal.

SOLUTION: Reduce watering so the plant does not absorb excessive amounts of liquid. Improved light helps the plant to use the water rather than secrete it through its leaves. Increase air circulation and lower humidity so any liquids that are exuded evaporate rapidly rather than accumulate.

Overwatering is the most common cause of guttation.

Cultural Problems
(continued)

HIGH TEMPERATURE

PROBLEM: Outer leaves turn yellow. Leaves may die and turn brown. Stems become soft. Plants stop flowering. High temperatures cause problems for cool-weather plants, which tolerate warm days as long as they have cool nights (below 55°F). Cool temperatures initiate flower buds. Constant high temperatures inhibit flower buds. High temperatures also keep plants from growing well, causing leaves to lose their green color and die.

SOLUTION: Grow cool-weather plants in a cool room with as much light as possible. If a cool room is not available, put them near a window at night. If temperatures are not below freezing, put the plants outside at night. Under alternating temperatures, they will flower for long periods. Keep plants adequately watered and fertilized.

When temperatures are too warm, leaves turn yellow, then brown and plants stop forming flower buds.

INSUFFICIENT WATER

PROBLEM: Leaves are small; the plant fails to grow well and may be stunted. Plant parts or whole plants wilt. Margins of broad leaves or tips of narrow leaves may dry and become brittle but still retain a dull green color. Bleached areas may occur between the veins. Leaf tissues may die and remain bleached or turn tan or brown. Plants may die.

SOLUTION: Water plants immediately and thoroughly. If the soil is completely dry, soak the entire pot in water for a couple of hours.

Too little water stresses plant leaves.

IRON DEFICIENCY

PROBLEM: The newest leaves turn yellow at the margins. The yellowing progresses inward; in the advanced stages, the last tissues to lose their green color are the veins. In severe cases, the entire leaf is yellow and small. The plant may be stunted.

Iron deficiency is a common problem for acid-loving plants, which grow best in soil with a pH between 5.5 and 6.5. Although soil is seldom deficient in iron, when the pH is 7.5 or higher (alkaline), iron is chemically unavailable to some plants.

SOLUTION: To correct iron deficiency, make a solution containing chelated iron according to label directions, spray the foliage with it, and apply it to the soil in the pot. Or apply a fertilizer containing chelated iron the same way. Use acid-based fertilizers for the plant's regular fertilizing. When planting or transplanting acid-loving plants, use an acidic growing medium that contains at least 50 percent peat moss. Do not add lime or dolomite to the growing mix.

Iron deficiency causes leaves to yellow.

LACK OF BLOOM

PROBLEM: The plant fails to flower during its blooming season. It seems in perfect health otherwise and no signs of insect or disease are visible.

SOLUTION: There are many reasons plants don't bloom, including the plant being too immature to flower (some houseplants bloom the first year, while others take several years to reach blooming size). The three most common culprits are a lack of light, insufficient humidity, and improper temperature. Move the plant to a somewhat brighter spot, place it on a humidity tray, and check its entry in the "Gallery of Houseplants" to learn its temperature requirements. A lack of minerals or an excess of nitrogen could be the cause. Give the plant a flowering plant fertilizer, one with a high middle number in the fertilizer analysis. Check for insect populations; an infestation could be sapping the plant's strength.

Low light, low humidity, and incorrect temperatures can cause lack of bloom.

LACK OF LIGHT

PROBLEM: Plants fail to grow well. Leaves may be lighter green and smaller than normal. Lobes and splits normal in mature leaves may not develop. Lower leaves may yellow and drop. Stems and leaf stalks may elongate and grow spindly and weak. Plants bend toward a light source. Flowering plants fail to produce flowers, and plants with colorful foliage become pale. Variegated plants may lose their variegation and become green. Although foliage plants generally need less light than plants grown for their flowers or fruit, plants with colorful foliage have a relatively high need for light.

SOLUTION: Gradually move the plant to a brighter location. To avoid burning sensitive plants, close lightweight curtains when the sun shines directly on the plant. If the available light is not bright enough, provide supplemental lighting as described on pages 30–33.

Variegated plants lose their colorful markings in low light.

LOW HUMIDITY

PROBLEM: Growth is slow and leaves tend to curl downward. Plants wilt rapidly and need frequent watering. Flower buds and new leaves wither or fail to develop properly. Leaf edges and tips may turn brown and dry up. Low humidity causes plants to lose water to the air more quickly than they can replace it. It is a major problem, especially during the heating season when indoor air is naturally drier.

SOLUTION: Place plants on a humidity tray or keep them in a room with a humidifier. Water as soon as the potting mix is dry just below the top inch. Group plants together so the transpiration given off by each increases the air humidity around them all. Regular misting also helps, as does moving the plants to a cooler, less sunny spot. Grow plants that require very high humidity in terrariums.

Dry air causes leaf tips to turn brown.

Cultural Problems
(continued)

NITROGEN DEFICIENCY

PROBLEM: The oldest leaves, usually the lower ones, turn yellow and may drop. Yellowing starts at the leaf margins and progresses inward without producing a distinct pattern. The yellowing may progress upward until only the newest leaves remain green. Growth is slow, new leaves are small, and the whole plant may be stunted. Nitrogen is easily leached from soil during regular watering. Of all the plant nutrients, it is the one that the soil is most likely to lack.

SOLUTION: For a quick but temporary response, spray leaves with a foliar fertilizer. Then fertilize plants with a soluble plant fertilizer rich in the first label number, such as 23-19-17. Add the fertilizer at regular intervals as recommended on the label. Add pasteurized organic material to the pots of plants that can tolerate the weight. Otherwise amend or replace potting soil when plants begin to show symptoms of nitrogen deficiency.

Foliage plants need more nitrogen than flowering plants.

SALT DAMAGE

PROBLEM: The leaf margins of plants with broad leaves or the leaf tips of plants with long, narrow leaves turn brown and brittle. This browning occurs on the older leaves first; when the condition is severe, new leaves also are affected. On some plants the older leaves may yellow and die. Salt damage is a common problem found on container-grown plants. Salts can accumulate from water or from the use of fertilizers, or they may be present in the potting soil. Salts also accumulate faster if plants are not watered thoroughly.

SOLUTION: Leach excess salts from the soil by flushing with water as described on page 61. Never let a plant stand in the drainage water. If the plant is too large to lift, empty the saucer with a turkey baster. Do not overfertilize. Trim off dead stem tips with sharp scissors.

Accumulated salts in the potting mix cause leaves to turn brown and brittle.

SUDDEN LEAF DROP

A sudden change in conditions can cause leaves to drop off.

PROBLEM: After you move the plant to a new location, leaves first turn yellow, then drop off. Most of the leaves may fall off if nothing is done, and soon the only green leaves left are a few of the youngest ones.

SOLUTION: All plants react to changes in their environment and some more so than others. The weeping fig and the croton are two plants famous for sudden leaf drop. Try to purchase plants that have been pre-acclimated to local conditions rather than shipped directly from a field to the store. Put plants in the brightest light possible and increase humidity. Cover newly arrived plants with clear plastic bags to temporarily increase humidity while they adjust to lower light, as described on page 19. Once susceptible plants have adapted to a particular spot, do not move them to another one without good reason. Sudden leaf drop may also occur if a plant is suddenly exposed to a cold draft.

SUNBURN OR LEAF SCORCH

PROBLEM: Tan or brown dead patches develop on leaves exposed to direct sunlight. Leaf tissues may lighten or turn gray. In some cases the plant remains green but growth is stunted. Damage is most severe when the plant is allowed to dry out. Sunburn or leaf scorch occurs when a plant is exposed to more intense sunlight than it can tolerate. Plants that are grown in low light burn easily if they are suddenly moved to a sunny location.

SOLUTION: Move plants to a shaded spot or close curtains when the plant is exposed to direct sunlight. Prune off badly damaged leaves, or trim away damaged leaf areas to improve the appearance of the plant. Keep plants properly watered.

Leaf scorch is easily cured by moving the plant.

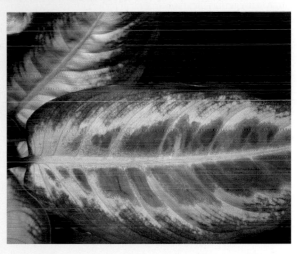

TOO MUCH WATER OR POOR DRAINAGE

Poor drainage causes roots to take up too much water, then leaves wilt.

PROBLEM: Plants fail to grow and may wilt. Leaves lose their glossiness and may become light green or yellow. An examination of the root ball reveals mushy brown roots without white tips. The soil in the bottom of the pot may be soggy and have a foul odor. Plants may die.
SOLUTION: Discard severely wilted plants and those without white root tips. For plants that are less severely affected, do not water again until the soil is almost dry (barely moist). Prevent the problem by using a light soil with good drainage.

WATER SPOTS

PROBLEM: White to light yellow blotches in various patterns occur on older leaves. Small islands of green may be left between the discolored areas. Brown spots sometimes appear within the discolored areas. Water spots are a common problem for African violets (*Saintpaulia*) and other fuzzy-leaved plants. They occur most commonly when cold water is splashed on the leaves while the plant is being watered.

SOLUTION: Avoid getting cold water on leaves when watering. Use tepid water, which will not cause spotting if it touches the leaves. Spotted leaves will not recover. Pick them off if they are unsightly.

Fuzzy-leaved plants are sensitive to cold water splashes. Water them from the bottom with tepid water.

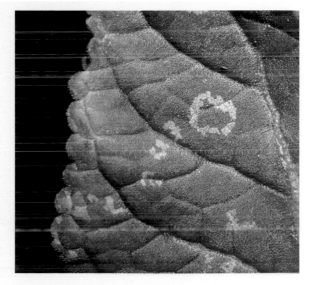

Gallery of Houseplants

IN THIS CHAPTER

Plant Gallery **102**

Flowering plants, foliage plants, easy-to-grow plants, tough-to-please plants—you'll find them all in this chapter.

The more than 200 plants featured here have been placed in alphabetical order according to their botanical names. Some plants, such as cacti, orchids, and succulents, have been gathered together and described in alphabetical order within their group. If you know the Latin name of the plant you're seeking, such as *Ficus*, you can go straight to it. Look up common names, such as English ivy, in the index at the back of this book. If you're not sure of a plant's name, flip through the gallery and look at the photos to help you find it.

Each plant entry includes general appearance and special characteristics as well as light, water, humidity, and temperature needs. You can also read advice on watering, fertilizing, and repotting, as well as learn how big the plant will grow and how to propagate it. You'll find a few tips on each plant's idiosyncrasies too. The definitions that follow will help you understand the requirements listed.

With such a great variety of plants to choose from, you'll find some that are just right for your home.

LIGHT: All plants need light, but some need more than others. A plant grown in proper lighting has a better chance of being healthy.

■ **Low light** usually refers to an eastern or northern exposure that receives little or no direct sun. At this lighting level, there's enough light available to read a newspaper easily.

■ **Medium light** is the equivalent of an eastern or western exposure, where the plants receive indirect light all day but only a few hours of early-morning or late-afternoon sun. It also could be a location well back from a south window. A space directly under a two-tube fluorescent fixture also offers medium light.

■ **Bright light** corresponds to a southern or western exposure that receives at least two hours of full sun per day but only indirect sun during the hottest part of the day. It also could be a spot several feet back from a south-facing window. A space directly under a four-tube fluorescent fixture offers bright light.

■ **Intense light** refers to a southern exposure that receives full sun for much of the day or a greenhouse or sunroom that receives diffused but bright light from the east, south, and west.

HUMIDITY: Dry air plays havoc with many plants, so it is important to know which ones require special effort to ensure proper humidity.

■ **Average** refers to the humidity that prevails in most homes much of the year. Plants in such environments fare better with added humidity when the heating system or air-conditioner is running, as both cause humidity to drop.

■ **High** means the plant needs extra humidity throughout the year. A humidifier or a humidity tray almost certainly is necessary during the winter, when air is particularly dry.

■ **Very high** refers to a level of air moisture rarely obtained in the home. You'll need to grow such plants in a terrarium or greenhouse.

TEMPERATURE: Most plants do well in average home temperatures but may prefer cooler conditions during the winter or at night. You can pick the right plants for your home by knowing the temperatures they prefer.

■ **Cold:** below 50°F but above freezing.

■ **Cool:** between 50°F and 65°F.

■ **Average:** between 65°F and 80°F.

■ **High:** above 80°F.

101

FLOWERING MAPLE

Abutilon
a-BEW-ti-lon

Flowering maples bloom year-round if given adequate light. Prune regularly to maintain a short, dense shape.

Old-fashioned types are tall with an open habit and hanging flowers, such as *A. pictum*, with salmon-orange blooms. Modern flowering maples (generally *A. ×hybridum*) are shorter, denser plants with outward-facing cup-shaped flowers in white, pink, yellow, orange, and red. Blooming occurs all year long when light is good but is often most intense in spring and summer. The slightly fuzzy leaves range from deeply cut and maple-like to nearly rounded and can be green or splotched with white or yellow. *A. pictum* 'Thompsonii' (syn. *A. striatum* 'Thompsonii'), for example, has salmon-orange flowers and green leaves with abundant yellow spots. Other cultivars, such as 'Souvenir de Bonn', have white marbled leaves.

A. megapoticum, with yellow flowers and reddish calyxes, and golden 'Victoria,' are trailers.

LIGHT: Medium to bright.
WATER: Keep evenly moist, slightly drier in winter.
HUMIDITY: Average to high.
TEMPERATURE: Average; cooler in winter if possible.
FERTILIZER: Rich in phosphorous.
DIMENSIONS: 1 foot to 8 feet tall and 1 foot to 4 feet wide, depending on type.
REPOTTING: Annually.
PROPAGATION: Stem cuttings, seed.
PROBLEMS: Low light causes spindly growth and poor bloom. Excess mineral salts cause leaf-tip burn and stem dieback, so repot or leach frequently. Susceptible to whiteflies, mealybugs, and scale insects.
TIPS: Prune occasionally to prevent legginess, either throughout the year or cut back severely in mid-winter. Grow cultivars with white variegation as foliage plants; they rarely bloom.

CHENILLE PLANT

Acalypha
a-ka-LEE-fa

Jacob's coat (A. wilkesiana) is grown for its dramatic foliage. Pinch out the flower spikes to keep the plant dense.

The chenille plant, or red-hot cat's tail, is a stunning indoor shrub with shiny, oval, lightly toothed green leaves and spectacular spikes of downy, pendant red flowers. Prune to keep it under 3 feet tall and wide. It flowers in spring and summer, sometimes all year.

The flying foxtail (*A. repens*) is similar but has much smaller leaves, stems that spread out and downward, and shorter red chenille-like flower spikes. It is generally used in hanging baskets.

A. wilkesiana (copperleaf, Jacob's coat) has insignificant flower spikes but brightly colored foliage, often copper red or splotched pink, orange, white, and other shades. Numerous cultivars exist in various combinations and leaf shapes, ranging from oval to deeply cut and fringed.

LIGHT: Medium to bright.
WATER: Keep evenly moist.
HUMIDITY: Average to high.
TEMPERATURE: Average. Keep away from cold drafts.
FERTILIZER: All-purpose during growing period.
DIMENSIONS: 3 to 10 feet tall and 3 to 6 feet wide.
REPOTTING: As needed.
PROPAGATION: Softwood cuttings at any season.
PROBLEMS: Low light, cold drafts, dry air, and soil kept either too dry or too wet cause leaf drop. Spider mites, whiteflies, mealybugs, and fungal diseases are possible.
TIPS: Acalypha dislikes sudden changes; small plants adapt better to new environments. Regular pinching and pruning keep plants dense. Sap may irritate sensitive skin and is also slightly poisonous if ingested. Wear gloves when pruning and keep the plant away from children and pets.

ACHIMENES, ORCHID PANSY

Achimenes
a-kim-EE-neez

This relative of the African violet is a seasonal houseplant, grown from rhizomes in spring for summer-long bloom, then allowed to go dormant. It produces abundant trumpet-shaped flowers in white, pink, red, purple, mauve, blue, orange, and yellow, often with spotted or netted throats. The growth habit of *Achimenes* ranges from naturally bushy to open and arching. The latter varieties look best in hanging baskets. Leaves are shiny and smooth to slightly hairy and can be green or bronze.

×*Achimenantha* is a cross between *Achimenes* and *Smithiantha*. The resulting plants look much like *Achimenes* but with more numerous flowers.

LIGHT: Medium to bright.
WATER: Keep evenly moist; do not water when dormant.

HUMIDITY: Average to high.
TEMPERATURE: Average; cooler during dormancy.
FERTILIZER: Rich in phosphorous.
DIMENSIONS: 10 to 24 inches tall and wide.
REPOTTING: Pot three to seven per pot in early spring, barely covering rhizomes with growing mix.
PROPAGATION: Numerous new rhizomes provide ample material for propagation. Or break rhizomes into individual scales: Each produces a new plant. Achimenes may produce supplementary rhizomes from leaf axils. You can also take tip cuttings.
PROBLEMS: Dry soil leads to premature dormancy. Low light prevents blooming. Avoid hard water. Whiteflies, mealybugs, and aphids are possible pests. Spraying may cause leaf spots.
TIPS: Needs active care in summer and neglect in winter. Keep rhizomes dry at cool to average temperatures in winter; either leave them in the pot or store in peat moss. Repot each spring. Pinch for fullness.

Orchid pansies, such as A. *admirabilis* 'Affinity', require winter dormancy in order to produce blooms in summer.

LIPSTICK PLANT

Aeschynanthus lobbianus
(A. radicans)
eye-skee-NAN-thus lo-bee-AN-us

The lipstick plant gets its common name from its flowers: Dark purple tubular cups appear at the tips of the branches, each one encircling a tiny unopened bright scarlet flower bud. The bud opens into a curved, hooded corolla. Lipstick plant produces branches that arch outward, then downward (perfect for hanging baskets) and waxy looking dark green leaves, often with a reddish margin. It tends to bloom most heavily in fall and sometimes sporadically throughout the year.

A. pulcher is similar but has green calyxes and yellow-throated red flowers. *A. longicaulis* (syn. *A. marmoratus)* is a semitrailer more popular for its purple-mottled leaves, reddish below, than the unobtrusive green and brown flowers; its hybrid 'Black Pagoda' has similar but darker leaves and brighter red-orange flowers. Bushier, more upright *A. hildebrandii*, only 8 by 10 inches, produces a constant show of tubular orange flowers.

LIGHT: Medium to bright.
WATER: Allow to dry slightly between waterings.
HUMIDITY: Average to high.
TEMPERATURE: Average.
FERTILIZER: Rich in phosphorous.
DIMENSIONS: 10 to 24 inches tall and 24 to 36 inches wide.
REPOTTING: Infrequently, in any season.
PROPAGATION: Grows best from softwood cuttings.
PROBLEMS: May need some full sun or supplementary light to bloom. Mineral salt buildup burns leaves. Mealybugs, scale insects, aphids, and thrips are possible pests.
TIPS: Prune after flowering if necessary. Take cuttings of *A. hildebrandii* while the plant is still young, as mature specimens may bloom themselves to death. Plants placed outside in summer attract hummingbirds.

The scarlet flowers of a lipstick plant unfurl like lipsticks rolled out of their tubes. Bright light aids blooming.

Aglaonema commutatum
a-glah-o-NEE-ma ka-mew-TAH-tum

Chinese evergreen is a slow-growing but dependable choice for use indoors in average household light.

CHINESE EVERGREEN

A foliage plant appreciated for its slow, regular growth even under low-light conditions, Chinese evergreen is essentially an upright plant with thick, nonbranching stems and long, leathery, often silver-mottled dark green leaves. Three or more plants are usually grown per pot for a bushier appearance. Older plants may lose their lower leaves over time, exposing bare stems.

Chinese evergreens occasionally bloom indoors, but the blooms are insignificant. Long-lasting, bright red berries follow. You can sow the seeds from the ripe berries.

Its many species and cultivars come in various sizes.

LIGHT: Low to medium.
WATER: Keep evenly moist. Avoid overwatering Chinese evergreen under low-light conditions.
HUMIDITY: Average to high.
TEMPERATURE: Average to high. Avoid cold drafts.
FERTILIZER: All-purpose during growing period. Not a heavy feeder.
DIMENSIONS: 10 to 60 inches tall and 12 to 30 inches wide.
REPOTTING: Infrequent, in any season. Keep the root ball intact.
PROPAGATION: Stem cuttings, air layering, or root division; or from seed when available.
PROBLEMS: Leaf edges turn brown in cold or dry air or if mineral salts build up. Mealybugs, scale insects, and aphids are possible. Waterlogged soil causes rot.
TIPS: Keep the leaves dry to avoid leaf spots. Buy plants of the size you want because *Aglaonema* grows very slowly. It tolerates low light but eventually declines. To hide bare stems, cut off the bottom of the root ball, then repot, covering the base of the stems. New roots will form on the buried parts. Chinese evergreen sap contains oxalic acid, which causes irritation if ingested.

Alocasia
ah-lo-KAH-see-a

A. ×amazonica is popular because of its striking dark green foliage and prominent silver veins.

ALOCASIA

The striking foliage of alocasia, also known as elephant's ear (see also *Caladium*), is its claim to fame, as it rarely blooms indoors and when it does, its Jack-in-the-pulpit-type flowers are not particularly striking. The leaves, however, are outstanding. Usually arrow- or heart-shaped in basic outline, sometimes with lobed or wavy margins, they are often a shiny dark green very close to black, with contrasting silvery veins. In fact, you may find visitors touching them, convinced they are plastic.

About 70 different species of alocasia and dozens of hybrids exist, most either rhizomatous or tuberous in nature, but only a few are offered as houseplants. Perhaps the most available is *A.* ×*amazonica*, simply because it combines beautiful leaves with a relatively sturdy constitution. It very much resembles *A. sanderiana*, one of its parents, which is less well-adapted to indoor growing due to its need for constant high humidity. Both are large plants that can eventually reach up to 6 feet tall, although they are usually under 2 feet tall when sold. They have the typical dark green arrow-shaped leaves with silvery veins. Similar plants include *A. lowii* and *A. korthalsii* and an ever-increasing list of hybrids.

Quite different is giant taro (*A. macrorrhiza*), with entirely green leaf blades up to 4 feet in length, although usually much less. The arrow-shaped leaves point upward instead of downward like other alocasias. It is also unique because it is frequently sold as a large dormant rhizome (other alocasias are sold as potted plants). The rhizome is edible when cooked and a staple food in some countries. Golden and variegated forms of this plant are

ALOCASIA *(continued)*

available, as are other giant alocasias that are similar in appearance, such as *A. odora*.

LIGHT: Medium. Tolerates low light for short periods.
WATER: Let dry slightly between waterings, then water thoroughly.
HUMIDITY: High.
TEMPERATURE: Warm to hot. Avoid cold drafts.
FERTILIZER: All-purpose during growing period.
DIMENSIONS: Depending on variety, 1 foot to 6 feet tall and wide.
REPOTTING: Infrequently, in any season.
PROPAGATION: Divide in spring.
PROBLEMS: Too much moisture causes crown rot. Dry air causes leaf dieback. Spider mites, mealybugs, and scale insects are possible pests.
TIPS: Can be difficult to maintain unless you keep the air humid and let the growing mix dry out a bit between waterings. Overwatered plants usually rot. Leave the top of the rhizome/tuber exposed when repotting to help prevent rot. Can theoretically go dormant, but it's best to keep most types in active growth during the winter months. Keep those that do lose their leaves only slightly moist; begin watering when new sprouts appear.

Giant taro's huge leaves grow up to 4 feet long. Use this dramatic plant outdoors in summer in a container garden. It thrives in humidity as long as it does not receive too much water.

Aphelandra squarrosa
ay-fel AN-dra skwah-RO-sa

ZEBRA PLANT

This plant is usually sold in full bloom during the fall or winter. At that time, its broad dark green leaves striped with ivory veins (spectacular on their own) play second fiddle to the conical inflorescence that tops the plant. The bright golden bracts last for months and bear shorter-lived tubular flowers in a similar shade. After blooming, the zebra plant goes back to being a spectacular foliage specimen until the following fall, when it blooms again.

Modern cultivars are compact plants that rarely exceed 15 inches tall. The most commonly available are 'Dania', with compact growth and nearly black leaves highlighted by bright ivory veins, and 'Apollo', so covered with creamy white veins that there is little green visible.
LIGHT: Medium to bright.

WATER: Keep evenly moist.
HUMIDITY: High.
TEMPERATURE: Average; keep cool in winter.
FERTILIZER: Rich in phosphorous.
DIMENSIONS: 10 to 24 inches tall and 30 inches wide.
REPOTTING: In late winter or early spring.
PROPAGATION: Stem cuttings.
PROBLEMS: Dry air and cold drafts cause leaf scorch. Soil kept too wet or too dry and mineral salt buildup causes leaf drop. It is difficult to encourage to rebloom. Aphids, thrips, whiteflies, mealybugs, and scale insects are possible pests.
TIPS: Best considered a one-season wonder, to be bought and enjoyed in bloom, then composted. Simple enough to keep in good shape once it is in bloom but not as easy to get it to rebloom without high humidity and very careful watering. Easier to grow in a greenhouse than at home.

Zebra plant's flowers are as dramatic as its foliage, but it is difficult to make it rebloom except in a greenhouse.

Anthurium
an-THEWR-ee-um

Anthurium blooms are long-lasting, and many species are repeat bloomers when grown in bright light.

Few plants offer such a wide variety of possibilities as the genus *Anthurium*. Among the up to 900 species are both flowering plants and foliage plants, as well as

ANTHURIUM

terrestrial plants, epiphytes, and climbing plants, all in a huge range of shapes and forms. Most adapt readily to the low light and less-than-perfect humidity of the average home.

One unusual characteristic of many epiphytic anthuriums (by far the largest group) is the production of thick aerial roots, much like those of orchids. They are used in the same way as well, to capture and absorb water and nutrients and to affix themselves to their support. Since anthuriums, unlike most orchids, adapt readily to regular potting mixes, these aerial roots can be seen simply as curious appendages of little practical use in pots.

The best-known anthuriums are those grown as flowering plants. They produce a spike of tiny, insignificant flowers, sometimes scented, called a spadix, but the main attraction is provided by a large leaflike bract, often leathery in appearance, called the spathe. Each single inflorescence often lasts a month or more, and since many

anthuriums are repeat bloomers, they can be attractive for months on end. Many of the species anthurium have bright red blooms, but hybrids are now more common than the species and come in a wider range of colors.

LIGHT: Medium to bright for flowering types; foliage anthuriums adapt to low light.

WATER: Water thoroughly, then let the medium dry slightly.

HUMIDITY: Average to high. Very high for some varieties.

TEMPERATURE: Average to high. Avoid cold drafts.

FERTILIZER: All-purpose during growing period. Not a heavy feeder.

DIMENSIONS: Depending on the species, from less than 8 inches by 8 inches to over 6 feet by 6 feet.

REPOTTING: Every two years or so, in any season.

PROPAGATION: From offsets or softwood cuttings from plants with visible stems.

PROBLEMS: Excess mineral salts cause leaf-tip burn and stem dieback. Overwatering causes crown rot. Low light or dry air causes poor

Pig-tail anthurium is a good choice for growing indoors because it tolerates drier air than some of the other species.

Flamingo flower is easily identified by its large leaf-shaped spathe. The actual flowers on are the yellow spadix.

Anthurium 'Pink Frost' is a popular stem in cut flower arrangements.

blooms. Mealybugs, thrips, and scale insects are possible. Avoid spraying leaves to prevent leaf spots.

TIPS: Thin-leaved anthuriums need high humidity; leathery-leaved anthuriums can cope with drier air. Pot into well-aerated growing mixes, using half orchid mix and half regular potting mix, leaving the upper roots exposed; cover those with sphagnum moss to replicate the treetop growing conditions of most species. As plants age and produce abundant aerial roots, repot into deeper containers, again covering the upper roots with moss. Or cut off the top and reroot. New offsets will form at the base.

■ **Flowering Anthuriums:** All anthuriums flower under the right conditions, but the following are specifically grown for their attractive flowers.

The huge heart-shaped bracts of flamingo flower *(A. andraeanum)*—up to 8 inches wide in some hybrids, but 4 inches is more common—is probably the most striking of the flowering anthuriums. The bract is so shiny that it appears to be made of patent leather, and it is set off by a contrasting yellowish spadix. The

original species had bright red bracts, but you'll also find pinks, whites, and even greens. The flamingo flower is popular for cut arrangements. The foliage is just as attractive as the flowers: shiny, heart-shaped dark green leaves. This species needs very high humidity, however, and rarely makes a long-lasting houseplant.

Pig-tail anthurium *(A. scherzerianum)* is much easier to grow and an altogether smaller plant with thicker, less shiny lance-shaped leaves and twisting spadices, usually the same orange-red color as the bracts. Its greater tolerance of dry air makes it a long-lasting, yet slow-growing, flowering plant. Several cultivars exist, some with white-speckled bracts.

■ **Hybrid Anthuriums:**
Many hybrid flowering anthuriums are available, often close to *A. andreanum* in general appearance but with smaller flowers in a wider range of colors. Developed specifically for use in the average home, they bloom abundantly all year long (even under low light) and are not at all difficult to maintain. Popular cultivars include the 'Lady' series in shades of red, pink, and white, and 'Southern Blush' with lavender blooms, along with new releases every year.

■ **Foliage Anthuriums:** You'll find a wide range of foliage anthuriums. Their flowers, while interesting, tend to bloom in shades of green and dull purple. Hence, the plants are grown for their attractive foliage.

Crystal anthurium *(A. crystallinum)* is one of the most striking foliage anthuriums, with long-stemmed, heart-shaped, emerald green leaves up to 12 inches across and 20 inches long and beautifully overlaid with silver veins.

Bird's nest anthurium *(A. hookeri)* is so called because its stemless, leathery, paddle-shaped dark green

A. *crystallinum* is grown for its striking veined foliage. The leaves can grow up to 20 inches long.

leaves form a dense rosette vaguely resembling a bird's nest. In the wild, the leaves capture fallen tree leaves, then the plant sends aerial roots up into the resulting compost, thus creating its own aerial potting mix. With time, bird's nest anthuriums become huge plants up to 6 feet across and tall, but they are usually sold as modest 1-foot foliage plants. A. 'Fuch's Ruffle' is similar to A. *hookeri*, but with wavy leaf margins.

Hybrid anthuriums are smaller and easy to grow at home, even in low light. They bloom in a variety of colors.

Araucaria heterophylla
ah-row-KAH-ree-a heh-teh-RO-fil-la

NORFOLK ISLAND PINE

Not a true pine *(Pinus)* but a conifer that originated on Norfolk Island, off Australia. It produces one new whorl of symmetrical branches each year, each wider at the base than the previous one, giving it the appearance of an upside-down spruce or fir. Its formal appearance makes it a hit indoors, where it can serve as a replacement for the family Christmas tree, decorations and all. The shiny dark green needles are short, cylindrical, and borne all around the branches. For a fuller look, growers usually plant several seedlings to a pot, although over time one or two of the plants will gradually dominate the planting.
LIGHT: Medium. Tolerates low light for short periods.
WATER: Keep evenly moist.

A Norfolk Island pine looks like an upside-down fir tree. Humidity helps it retain its lower branches.

HUMIDITY: Average.
TEMPERATURE: Average; keep cool in winter.
FERTILIZER: All-purpose during growing period. Not a heavy feeder.
DIMENSIONS: From 1 to 8 feet tall and 1 to 4 feet wide indoors. Will grow much taller outdoors or where ceilings are high.
REPOTTING: Infrequently, in any season.
PROPAGATION: Not feasible indoors.
PROBLEMS: Dry soil, overwatering, excess mineral salts, insufficient light, and hot, dry air all cause lower branches to drop off. Spider mites, mealybugs, and scale insects are possible. Reacts badly to pruning.
TIPS: Under poor conditions or when watered erratically, Norfolk Island pine loses lower branches and looks bare; hide its "bare legs" behind other houseplants. It grows slowly, so buy one large enough for your immediate needs.

Argyranthemum
ar-gi-RANTH-e-mum

ARGYRANTHEMUM, OX-EYE DAISY, PARIS DAISY

Also called marguerite, the ox-eye daisy is basically a shrubby daisy, producing deeply cut leaves and typical flowers on branching, woody stems. You can train it into a treelike shape through careful pruning, but it's probably best pruned back each spring or simply pinched regularly to keep it dense and full. Flowers typically appear from spring through fall, but blooms are prolific in mid- to late summer.

   A. frutescens (Chrysanthemum frutescens) is the original species. It tends to be faster-growing than hybrid varieties, with leaves that have a silvery tinge. Flowers are simple white daisies with a yellow center. It is still readily seen in homes, but mostly as a pass-along plant. Nurseries tend to stock only the more colorful, more compact modern hybrids, available with single or double flowers in white, pink, and yellow.

LIGHT: Bright to intense.
WATER: Water thoroughly, then let dry slightly between waterings.
HUMIDITY: Average.
TEMPERATURE: Average, cool to cold in winter.
FERTILIZER: All-purpose during growing period.
DIMENSIONS: 1 foot to 8 feet tall and 1 foot to 3 feet wide.
REPOTTING: Occasionally, in any season.
PROPAGATION: Tip cuttings.
PROBLEMS: Low light causes spindly growth and lack of bloom. The chrysanthemum leaf miner is a possible pest.
TIPS: Pinch regularly; ox-eye daisy is most attractive when kept under 3 feet in height. It makes an excellent outdoor plant for the summer patio or balcony. With heavy mulching, you can even grow it outdoors as a perennial shrub in USDA Zones 9 and 10.

Marguerite 'Vera' is a shrubby daisy that flowers from spring through fall. Regular pinching keeps it blooming.

Asparagus densiflorus
uh-SPEH-rah-gus den-si-FLO-rus

Not ferns at all, but rather subtropical relatives of the asparagus, these plants get their name from their fernlike appearance: light and airy with plentiful medium green "needles" (actually modified stems called cladodes). The only true leaves are the prickly scales hidden along the stems. Asparagus grows from thick, carrot-like roots, sending shoots upward and outward, which creates an attractive appearance in hanging baskets.

LIGHT: Medium to bright. Tolerates low light for short periods.

WATER: Water thoroughly, then let dry slightly.

HUMIDITY: Average.

TEMPERATURE: Average. Tolerates cool winters.

FERTILIZER: All-purpose during growing period.

DIMENSIONS: 1½ to 10 feet tall and 2 to 4 feet wide.

REPOTTING: Annually.

PROPAGATION: Divide crowns of established plants with a saw. Can be grown from seed.

PROBLEMS: Needles turn yellow and drop if the plant is kept too wet or too dry or moved suddenly to low light. Spider mites are possible.

TIPS: Massive root systems quickly crush growing mixes and fill up all available space, so watering from above is ineffective (water runs around the root ball without moistening the soil). Either repot into increasingly larger pots or soak the pot in a sinkful of tepid water at each watering. Pruning long, ungainly growth stimulates shorter stems. Asparagus is an excellent basket plant for outdoors.

Of the more than 300 species of Asparagus, two are commonly grown indoors: *A. densiflorus* and *A. setaceus.*

Emerald feather, or emerald fern (*A. densiflorus*), provides two popular cultivars, both with small

ASPARAGUS FERN

white flowers, half-hidden among the needles, that turn into bright red berries. Since flowers are generally sporadic and produced only here and there among the foliage, neither the flowers nor the berries are of great ornamental value.

A. d. 'Sprengeri' is the most widely available of the asparagus ferns. It bears 18- to 36-inch arching stems lightly clothed in flat, dark green, l-inch needles. This gives the plant an open, frothy appearance that is much appreciated. Give the plant a regular quarter turn to keep the branches from all growing to the same side. The foxtail fern (*A. d.* 'Myers') has a more upright habit, with densely needled bright green 2-foot stems that resemble foxtails. Unlike other asparagus plants grown in hanging baskets, it looks best as a tabletop plant.

Asparagus fern (*A. setaceus*, also sold as *A. plumosa*) is quite different. Its stems bend at right angles at the tip and, covered with very tiny needles, look very much like fern fronds. When young, it is a bushy plant only a foot or so high and looks best in a hanging basket. When it reaches its adult form,

though, it becomes a climber, with clambering stems up to 10 feet long bearing "fronds" here and there along its entire length. You can either train it up a trellis or other support or cut back the long stems, promoting shorter, denser growth. Its tiny white flowers give way to shiny black berries.

The cascading shoots of asparagus plants look good in hanging baskets.

Foxtail fern (A. densiflorus 'Myers') has an upright growing habit.

Although not a true fern, A. setaceus has a distinctly fernlike shape.

Aspidistra elatior
a-spi-DI-stra ay-LAH-tee-or

Cast-iron plant is an excellent choice for a low-light location. It is slow-growing but tolerates almost any conditions.

CAST-IRON PLANT

Very few houseplants are as easy to grow as cast-iron plant. Its common name refers to its cast-iron constitution: It can tolerate almost any growing condition, from scorching sun to deep shade and from burning heat to near frost. It has traditionally been found in the farthest, darkest corners of barbershops, with its pot used as an ashtray. Cigarette ashes are not, however, a necessary amendment to its health!

Were it not for its tough nature, this plain-looking plant probably never would have become popular. The leathery, dark green, somewhat arching, oblong leaves are borne on 6-inch stalks from an underground rhizome. Insignificant dark purple bell-shaped flowers are borne at the soil surface. Several variegated cultivars are also offered.

LIGHT: Low to bright. Tolerates extremely low light.
WATER: Water thoroughly, then let dry slightly. Keep drier in winter.
HUMIDITY: Low to high.
TEMPERATURE: Cold to high.
FERTILIZER: All-purpose during growing period. Not a heavy feeder. The foliage of variegated cultivars turns all green if overfertilized.
DIMENSIONS: Depending on pot size, 2 feet high and 2 feet wide or more. Its width is almost unlimited in a large pot.
REPOTTING: Infrequently.
PROPAGATION: By division.
PROBLEMS: Susceptible to spider mites; mealybugs and scale insects are possible pests. Rots in soggy soil.
TIPS: Buy a large plant for an instant effect, as it is extremely slow-growing. Remove yellowing leaves. Although tolerant of low light, cast-iron plant grows faster under medium or bright light. It can remain in the same pot for decades.

Aucuba japonica
ow-KEW-ba ja-PON-i-ka

You can grow *Aucuba japonica* as a houseplant, but it will not bloom or produce berries indoors.

GOLD-DUST PLANT, JAPANESE AUCUBA

This broad-leaved evergreen shrub is commonly grown outdoors in many climates (it's hardy to Zone 6 with some protection from winter winds) but also makes an attractive houseplant. The species produces numerous branches covered with shiny, dark, leathery green leaves, usually with a few marginal teeth, but most cultivars are variegated, with small yellow spots over the leaf surface. The small purplish flowers are unobtrusive and, at any rate, rarely produced indoors. Even rarer are the bright red berries produced by female plants: Since there are no insects or wind for pollination indoors, they're normally only seen on outdoor shrubs.

'Variegata' is the classic gold-dust plant and the one most readily available. Its foliage is only lightly sprinkled with yellow spots compared to more modern selections, such as 'Crotonifolia', which has larger, more abundant spots. 'Picturata' has yellow-centered leaves surrounded by yellow spots. All three cultivars are females.

LIGHT: Bright.
WATER: Water thoroughly, then let dry slightly.
HUMIDITY: Average.
TEMPERATURE: Average; cool to cold in winter.
FERTILIZER: All-purpose during growing period. Not a heavy feeder.
DIMENSIONS: Can grow to 10 feet tall and wide but is usually kept under 3 feet tall and wide.
REPOTTING: As needed.
PROPAGATION: Semi-ripe cuttings; use rooting hormone.
PROBLEMS: Too much soil moisture causes root rot. Mineral salt buildup can cause dieback.
TIPS: Place in a cold spot during winter dormancy, or at least avoid night temperatures above 65°F. Prune regularly for dense growth.

BAMBOO

The hollow, woody stems of bamboo sprout new leaves every year. The narrow evergreen leaves are borne on slender branches from knots along the culms. Most indoor bamboos have underground runners; growing plants in pots keeps them under control.

Oriental-style decors seem to cry out for bamboos, but most species grow far too tall for the average home. Also, most need a long, cool winter rest, which is difficult to provide indoors. The species presented here are the best choices for long-term indoor use.

LIGHT: Medium to bright.
WATER: Keep evenly moist.
HUMIDITY: High.
TEMPERATURE: Average; cool to cold in winter.
FERTILIZER: Lightly, if at all, in order to control growth.
DIMENSIONS: Depending on variety, 16 inches to 50 feet tall. Spread is determined by pot width.
REPOTTING: Infrequently, in any season. It does best when grown in a pot that's too small.
PROPAGATION: By division.
PROBLEMS: Low light or high winter temperatures may result in poor growth or leaf loss. It has few insect or disease problems, but naturally drops leaves throughout the year.
TIPS: Remove dead leaves. It may be necessary to break the pot to remove a pot-bound bamboo for division or repotting.

Hedge bamboo (*B. multiplex*, syn. *B. glaucesens*) grows to 50 feet tall outdoors, so needs pruning for use indoors. The thick green to yellow culms provide a distinct bamboo appearance.

Pot-bound Buddha's belly bamboo (*B. ventricosa*) has curiously swollen stems. It can grow over 8 feet tall, so it needs pruning for indoor use.

Pygmy bamboo (*Pleioblastus pygmaeus*, syn. *Arundinaria pygmaea* and *Sasa pygmaea*) is probably the best choice for growing indoors. It is rarely more than 16 inches tall, with thin culms and medium-green leaves.

Variegated pygmy bamboo offers attractive foliage on a plant small enough to be managed indoors.

Beaucarnea recurvata
bo-kar-NEE-a ray-kur-VAH-ta

PONYTAIL PALM, ELEPHANT FOOT TREE

This popular indoor plant gets its first common name from long, narrow, dark green leaves that arch downward like a pony's tail. On some specimens, the leaves stretch down the full length of the trunk. It's also called elephant foot palm, as its thick trunk's greatly swollen base resembles a pachyderm's foot. On large specimens, the base of the trunk can reach 3 feet or more in diameter. *B. recurvata* is not actually a palm but an *Agave* family member. Some plant specialists call ponytail palm *Nolina recurvata*.

Though native to the semi-deserts of Mexico, where it grows in full, blazing sun, this plant has shown itself to be surprisingly adaptable to indoor conditions, thriving in both low and intense light, with or without sun. It is indifferent to dry indoor air, tolerates both cold and heat, rarely needs repotting or fertilizing, has few disease or insect problems, and seems equally adaptable to regular watering and long periods of neglect. In fact, this succulent stores water in its trunk, so it can go without water (and most

other care) for long periods, even months at a time. It rarely blooms indoors, however.

Although it seems to be the ideal houseplant, especially for forgetful indoor gardeners, it does have a flaw: painfully slow growth. It may take years for this plant to grow only a few inches! Because it grows so slowly, always purchase a large enough specimen for your current indoor needs. Should a ponytail palm ever outgrow its welcome you can simply cut it back, as it will resprout (albeit slowly) from lower parts of the trunk.

The Guatemala palm (*B. guatemalensis*, syn. *Nolina guatemalensis*) is very similar and usually sold as *B. recurvata*. It differs in its somewhat reddish foliage and has shorter leaves that don't spiral.

LIGHT: Low to intense.

WATER: Water thoroughly, then let the potting mix dry slightly between waterings. Established plants can tolerate long periods without water.

HUMIDITY: Low but will tolerate high humidity.

TEMPERATURE: Average. Tolerates cool to cold temperatures in winter, but protect from frost.

FERTILIZER: All-purpose during growing period. Not a heavy feeder.

DIMENSIONS: 1 to 8 feet tall and 1 to 4 feet wide.

REPOTTING: In any season.

PROPAGATION: Will grow from seed but very slowly. Well-healed stem tip cuttings might also root. Offsets can be removed and potted.

PROBLEMS: Subject to stem rot when kept too moist. Spider mites, scale insects, and mealybugs are potential problems. Leaf tips may die back and require trimming.

TIP: Remove faded leaves.

Ponytail palm is an ideal houseplant, readily adapting to almost any conditions. It grows slowly, however, so buy a plant large enough for your current needs.

Begonia
bay-GON-ee-a

The begonia's wide range of natural species (more than 1,300) and even greater range of hybrids translates into one widely variable group. Most are readily recognizable by their asymmetric, often colorful leaves and their distinctive flowers, with separate male and female blooms appearing on the same plants (the female is recognized by the triangular ovary at its base). The begonia has many different growth habits, ranging from tall and upright to bushy, creeping, climbing, tuberous, or trailing.

Some are grown essentially for their foliage, others for their flowers, and some for both. Many bloom year round, at least intermittently, but others are distinctly seasonal. Likewise, most remain in growth all year, while others have a dormant or semidormant period.

LIGHT: Medium light for foliage species. Flowering begonias need bright light.

WATER: Water thoroughly, then let dry slightly. Keep drier in winter.

HUMIDITY: Average to high.

TEMPERATURE: Average. Keep plants away from cold drafts.

FERTILIZER: All-purpose during growing period.

DIMENSIONS: Depending on the species or hybrid, from 3 inches to 10 feet tall and wide.

REPOTTING: As needed. May need annual repotting.

PROPAGATION: Stem and rhizome cuttings; sometimes from leaf cuttings or leaf sections. Some produce bulblets. Some can be sown from seed.

PROBLEMS: Overwatering causes crown rot. Low light results in spindly, weak growth. Dry air and cold drafts result in leaf scorch. Examine plants for powdery mildew and mealybugs.

TIP: Pinch or prune occasionally, but don't prune off flower buds.

BEGONIA

Three main groups of begonias exist: rhizomatous begonias, with creeping stems called rhizomes that root as they grow; tuberous and semituberous begonias, with a bulblike structure at their base; and fibrous-rooted begonias, which includes plants that have only ordinary roots, not rhizomes or tubers. These groups subdivide into the following seven categories.

■ **Cane-stemmed begonias** (*Begonia* spp.) are fibrous-rooted, with erect, smooth stems bearing swollen nodes somewhat like those of bamboo. Their leaves are asymmetrical and quite diverse in color, size, and spotting. The plants are not normally self-branching but instead send up new stems from the base. Although grown primarily for their foliage, cane-stemmed begonias bloom intermittently throughout the year if given enough light. Generally they are tough, easy-to-grow plants. Propagate from stem cuttings.

The angel-wing begonias, which have large leaves, silver spotted on top and red underneath, are the best known. The old-fashioned hybrid *B.* 'Lucerna' (or 'Corallina de Lucerna') is the most common angel-wing. It bears coral flowers and can reach over 4 feet at maturity. *B. coccinea* is similar in form but of intermediate height. Some, such as *B.* 'Orange Rubra', are pendulous in habit, making them good choices for hanging baskets. Others, such as *B.* 'Sophie Cecile', are upright in growth and have deeply cut leaves.

■ **Rex begonias** (*B. Rex cultorum* hybrids) are grown primarily for their foliage but will bloom pink or white if given good light. The leaves of most cultivars are large and have asymmetrical blades with diverse, brilliant coloration and textures. Most rex begonias grow horizontally across the soil surface, spreading by rhizomes that root where they touch soil. Some have a more upright habit.

Rex begonias are grown for their colorful foliage. They need consistent warmth and humid air to thrive.

Rex begonias are more fickle than other begonias. Keep them warm and don't overwater. Fertilize lightly. They need humid air at all times. Propagate them from rhizomes or from leaf cuttings or sections. Although there are many cultivars, they are usually sold unlabeled.

Cane-stemmed angel-wing begonias have silver dappled leaves that are red underneath. The blooms are coral.

■ **Rhizomatous begonias** *(Begonia spp.)* are the largest group of begonias. Their jointed rhizomes grow along or under the soil surface and sometimes hang over the edge of the pot. The foliage is often attractively mottled and textured. Although usually considered foliage plants, in ample light most bear tall stalks of white, pink, or greenish white flowers in winter. Propagate these begonias from rhizome or leaf cuttings. Most are fairly to very easy to grow and make excellent, long-lived houseplants. Prune wayward rhizomes to keep the plants under control.

Iron cross begonia *(B. masoniana)* produces large, bumpy, heart-shaped leaves in yellow-green with a dark burgundy Maltese-cross pattern in the center. It needs high humidity. Some old-fashioned hybrids with thick rhizomes and extra-large leaves are still popular, such as beefsteak begonia *(B. erythrophylla)*, which has round, shiny bronze leaves, and lettuceleaf begonia *(B.*

Wax begonias are common in outdoor summer gardens, but also thrive indoors in bright, warm conditions.

Lettuceleaf begonia is an old-fashioned species still popular for its indoor vigor. It may bloom if located in bright light.

×*erythrophylla* 'Bunchii'), which has highly crested leaf edges and the same bronze coloration. More popular these days, though, are the smaller varieties, such as the tiny eyelash begonia *(B. boweri)*, the larger star begonia *(B. heracleifolia)*, and numerous intermediate hybrids, such as *B.* 'Maphil' and *B.* 'Chantilly Lace'.

■ **Semperflorens begonias** *(Begonia ×semperflorens-cultorum)* are best known as wax begonias and are the most popular fibrous-rooted begonias. They are bushy plants with shiny, waxy, somewhat heart-shaped leaves in green or bronze. Given ample light, they bloom profusely in a variety of colors throughout the year. Flowers can be single or double. Wax begonias are best known as outdoor bedding annuals but will flourish indoors with light fertilization, good light, and sufficient warmth. They prefer stronger light than most begonias and are most readily grown from stem cuttings or seed. Popular series include Lotto, Cocktail, Olympia, and Dragon Wing.

■ **Shrublike begonias** *(Begonia spp.)* are fibrous-rooted begonias close to cane-stemmed begonias in general habit and size, but branch abundantly, hiding their stems from view. They are grown exclusively for their foliage, as their bloom is seasonal. They are easy-to-grow, adaptable plants. Those with shiny upper leaves, called hairless begonias, need more light than the hairy types. Propagate them from stem cuttings.

The hairless types have smooth, sometimes metallic-looking leaves. Old-fashioned *B.* ×*thurstonii* has remarkably reflective bronze-green leaves with a red underside. It produces bunches of pink flowers in summer. The trout-leaf begonia, *B.* ×*argenteoguttata*, also falls into the hairless category, although its silver-spotted leaves resemble those of a miniature angel-wing begonia. If given very bright light it produces creamy white flowers from spring to autumn. *B. scharffii* is an example of a hairy-leaf begonia. It has bronze-green leaves dusted with white down. The fern-leaf begonia

BEGONIA *(continued)*

(B. foliosa) has tiny oval leaves on arching stems and produces tiny white flowers.

■ **Tuberous begonias** *(B. ×tuberhybrida)* can be started indoors and their dormant tubers stored indoors over the winter, but they don't make good houseplants. These summer bloomers are best for shady spots in the outdoor garden.

■ **Winter-blooming begonias:** *(B. ×cheimantha* and *B. ×hiemalis)* result mostly from crosses involving semituberous or tuberous begonias. They essentially have fibrous roots, but with swollen, tuber-like bases. Lorraine or Christmas begonias *(B. ×cheimantha)* bloom profusely in winter. They are bushy dwarf plants, most frequently used in hanging baskets because the stems tend to arch outward attractively. In winter, they are covered with pink or white single flowers. After flowering, the plants become

semidormant until late spring. Keep them drier during this period. Lorraine begonias are grown from stem cuttings.

Rieger or Elatior begonias *(B. ×hiemalis)* are low-growing and bushy, with green or bronze foliage. Many are pendulous and used in hanging baskets. The yellow, red,

white, or orange flowers are usually large and often double. Give them cooler temperatures and plenty of light during their winter flowering period. These plants are hard to maintain through the summer, when they are semidormant, and are often best treated as florist plants to be discarded when blooming ceases.

Iron cross begonia has distinctly textured yellow-green leaves with burgundy to dark green Maltese crosses in the centers, which is how it got its common name.

BOUGAINVILLEA

Bougainvillea
boo-gan-VIL-ee-a

Outdoors in warm climates, bougainvilleas are probably the most popular of all climbers, almost always in bloom. Indoors they are not as floriferous but are nonetheless spectacular when they bloom. Although they are normally climbing plants, you can prune their often spiny, woody stems into a shrublike form or allow them to cascade downward from a hanging basket. They produce ovate medium-green leaves and, at the tips of the branches in summer, masses of beautifully colored bracts in shades of pink, purple, red, white, or orange. (They also may bloom in winter under ideal conditions.) The bracts are long-lasting but the tiny tubular white flowers they enclose are ephemeral.

Numerous standard or dwarf cultivars with single or double bracts

exist. Several variegated cultivars also are available. Most are of hybrid origin, but *B. glabra* and *B. spectabilis* also are frequently grown.

LIGHT: Intense.

WATER: Water thoroughly, then let dry slightly. Keep drier in winter.

HUMIDITY: High.

TEMPERATURE: Average in summer, cool in winter.

FERTILIZER: Balanced.

REPOTTING: Infrequently.

DIMENSIONS: Depending on the cultivar, 2 to 10 feet tall and wide.

PROPAGATION: Semi-ripe cuttings. Use rooting hormone.

PROBLEMS: Intense light absolutely needed for bloom. Rots in soggy soil. Spider mites, whiteflies, and mealybugs are possible pests. Some cultivars lose leaves in winter.

TIPS: Prune harshly after blooming, especially older plants, as indoor bougainvilleas tend to become bare at the base.

You can train a bougainvillea to climb a trellis or prune it into a shrubby shape. It needs intense light to bloom.

BROMELIADS

Bromeliads are easy to grow but require special care, as explained in more detail on pages 82–83. If the plants described here interest you, turn to those pages for additional information on their origin and special culture.

Most bromeliads are rosette-forming plants with lance-shaped leaves in a wide variety of colors. Their three-petaled flowers are often very short-lived, but they generally have bracts or leaves that change colors at flowering time, and these may remain colored for months. After flowering, bromeliads usually die but not before producing one or several "pups" (offsets).

You'll find three main types of bromeliads:

■ **Terrestrials** have normal root systems and are treated much like ordinary houseplants.

■ **Tank bromeliads** are generally epiphytes (they grow on trees in the wild) and catch water in their cup-shaped rosettes. Indoors, fill their rosettes with water and moisten the potting mix they grow in. They usually adapt well to pots, especially if an epiphytic growing mix is used

(see page 45), but can be grown on bark slabs.

■ **Air plants** are smaller bromeliads that lack a distinct tank. They are mostly epiphytes and absorb water through their leaves. Spray or mist them, or dunk them entirely in water. Often sold glued to ceramic figures or pieces of driftwood, they do not do well in potting mixes because their roots serve strictly as an anchor and do not absorb water.

LIGHT: Medium for species with spineless green or purple-banded foliage. Bright to intense for those with silvery leaves or sharp spines.

WATER: Water the terrestrial bromeliads' soil thoroughly, allowing it to dry slightly between waterings. Fill the tank bromeliads' rosettes with water and moisten the soil, then let dry slightly between waterings. Spray the leaves of air plants or dunk them in a bucket of water.

HUMIDITY: Low (air plants and terrestrials) to high (tank bromeliads).

TEMPERATURE: Average.

FERTILIZER: All-purpose. Bromeliads are not heavy feeders. In order to prevent staining, avoid applying fertilizers to tanks.

DIMENSIONS: Depending on type, 1 inch to 5 feet tall and 1 inch to 4 feet wide.

REPOTTING: Terrestrial bromeliads have normal root systems, so you can repot as needed. Keep tank bromeliads in small pots with epiphytic mix; repotting is rarely necessary. Mount air plants on wood or bark; never pot.

PROPAGATION: Separate pups, with or without roots, and pot or mount with fishing line or plumber's glue. Some can be grown from seed.

PROBLEMS: Avoid watering or spraying with hard water or water that contains chemical fertilizers, which can stain the leaves permanently. Soggy soil causes root rot. Scale insects and mealybugs are possible.

TIPS: Initiate flower buds by bagging the plant and an apple in plastic. You can use bromeliad tanks as living vases for cut flowers, but avoid those with sharp stems.

■ **Vase plants** (*Aechmea*) are a mostly epiphytic genus of tank bromeliads with spiny leaves. They appreciate bright to intense light. Among the more than 200 species, the most common is *A. fasciata* (living-vase plant, urn plant). Its

'Silver vase' (*Aechmea fasciata*) is a living-vase plant with mottled leaves and long-lasting blue to purple flowers.

Earth star (*Cryptanthus bivittatus*), a small plant well-suited for use in dish gardens, offers colorful foliage.

Domesticated varieties of pineapple (*Ananas*) have been bred without spines and produce small fruit.

broad, thick leaves are mottled with gray and sea-green stripes, and its conical rosette of pink bracts and large dark blue flowers creates a splendid effect. Its flowers last for several months.

An upright rosette of thick silver-banded leaves distinguishes the striking *A. chantinii*. It bears short-lived red-bracted flower stalks and orange-yellow flowers. *A. fulgens discolor*, commonly known as the coralberry plant, has broad leaves that are green on top and purple underneath, highlighted by the purple flower. Its red berries develop after the flower dies.

Pineapple *(Ananas comosus)* is a sun-loving terrestrial bromeliad with gray-green leaves. Normally it is viciously spiny, but most of the domesticated varieties have been cultivated for their spinelessness. To grow a common pineapple plant from a fruit, twist the crown free from the top of a store-bought fruit and plant it in regular potting mix. After several years, it should produce an upright flower stalk with a crown at its top. The red bracts below the crown bear violet flowers that develop into edible fruit.

Most ornamental pineapples are selections of the red pineapple *(A. bracteata)*, similar to the common pineapple but with red flowers and smaller fruit. The spiny leaves of such cultivars as 'Striatus' ('Tricolor') are striped green and white and sometimes pink. The dwarf pineapple *(A. nanus)* resembles a smaller common pineapple with green foliage and much smaller fruit and is more commonly offered in nurseries than *A. comosus*.

Billbergia is a vase plant genus that contains about 60 species of epiphytic tank bromeliads with lightly spined leaves. They look much like a small-scale *Aechmea*, but their upright or arching flower stalks last only weeks, not months.

Guzmania 'Rana' produces showy red bracts in medium indoor light. The true flowers are small and white.

They prefer bright light but tolerate medium light for long periods.

Queen's-tears *(B. nutans)* has grassy gray-green leaves and an arching spray of pink and green flowers. It usually flowers faithfully during the Christmas season in the Northern Hemisphere, producing pups that bloom the following year. It is better adapted to medium light than the others.

B. pyramidalis and *B. pyramidalis striata* sport long green strap-shaped leaves (the latter with longitudinal yellow stripes), bright red bracts tipped with violet, and upright scarlet flowers with yellow stamens. *B.* 'Fantasia' is only one of several cultivars with yellow-spotted leaves. It forms a relatively narrow, upright rosette and an erect flower stalk with bright red bracts and violet flowers.

The pink bracts of *Tillandsia cyanea* are an attractive contrast to the medium-green foliage. Violet-blue flowers also develop in the folds along the bracts.

■ **Earth star** *(Cryptanthus bivittatus)* is a genus of about 20 small terrestrial species and dozens of cultivars with broad, earth-hugging rosettes of wavy, pointed leaves bordered in harmless spines. Unlike most bromeliads, it bears no colorful bracts nor does it change color at flowering, so the small white flowers, borne in the center of the rosette, are of little appeal. The leaves are striped or banded in contrasting colors and constitute the plant's main appeal. Offsets appear on stolons or from the center of the rosette. Medium light best suits these forest dwellers.

C. bivittatus is the most widely available earth star. It has green leaves with creamy white stripes, but many of its cultivars, such as 'Starlite', 'It', and 'Pink Starlite', are boldly striped pink. *C. bromehoides* 'Tricolor' (rainbow-star), which has a more upright habit, displays a colorful array of white and pink stripes down the length of its narrow, wavy leaves. The flattened rosette of *C. zonatus* (zebra plant) resembles zebra skin, banded

in ivory and shades of brown. *C. fosterianus* is similar but larger. The hybrid 'Black Mystic' has similar white-banded leaves, but the background color is a striking deep chocolate brown.

■ **Dyckia** *(Dyckia)* is a slow-growing, medium-size terrestrial bromeliad with dark green to silver spiny foliage. Given intense light during summer, dyckias produce orange flowers on spikes. They are extremely drought-tolerant and should be treated as succulents: Water only when the soil is dry. *D. brevifolia* is a popular species.

■ **Guzmania** *(Guzmania)* has a vase-shaped, spineless rosette that forms a tank and can grow to 20 inches wide, although some cultivars are much smaller. It blooms from late winter to summer, depending on the species, and also can be forced using special techniques. The true flowers are small but surrounded by large, long-lasting, showy bracts. Guzmanias bloom readily indoors: Pups just separated from the mother plant flower within 18 months. This genus does best in medium light.

The intensely colored bracts of *Guzmania* last for several months.

G. lingulata, the most popular species, has brightly colored bracts ranging from red to yellow, and white flowers. Hybrids abound in many shades of red, yellow, orange, and purple, some with beautifully variegated leaves.

■ **Blushing bromeliads** *(Neoregelia)* produce large rosettes of thick, shiny leaves with somewhat spiny edges. They are tank bromeliads that usually grow as epiphytes. The most common is *N. carolinae*. It reaches a diameter of 30 inches and produces lavender-blue flowers that appear to float on the water in the tank. Just before flowering, the young leaves in the center turn bright red. *N. carolinae* 'Tricolor' is a variegated form with cream-striped leaves. *N. spectabilis* features green leaves with red-tipped ends, inspiring the name painted-fingernail plant. Both species bear pups near the mother plant, but some of the smaller cultivars, such as 'Fireball', produce numerous outstretched stolons bearing pups at their tips, which then bear more pups. In a hanging basket, they

The leaves in the center of variegated *Neoregelia carolinae* 'Tricolor' turn bright red just before the lavender-blue flowers appear.

quickly form an intricate aerial colony of considerable beauty. 'Fireball' is so-called because its otherwise green leaves turn coppery red in full sun.

■ Bird's-nest bromeliad

(*Nidularium*) is a generally epiphytic tank bromeliad with spiny-edged leaves. Both the common and Latin names refer to the bracts that form in a nestlike cluster just above the rosette at flowering time. It changes color, often to bright red, many weeks before the white flowers appear. Foliage color and patterns vary according to species. Among the most popular is *N. innocentii*, with green leaves and small red bracts cradling white flowers. It needs bright light to bloom.

Tillandsia ionantha **is an air plant that has colorful, arching foliage and upright purple bracts.**

■ Air plants (*Tillandsia*) comprise

the largest and most varied genus of bromeliads, with some 400 mostly epiphytic species. The spineless leaves may be broad, straplike, and green, forming a tank, in which case their culture and appearance are much like *Guzmania* or *Vriesea*. More often, though, the leaves are thick and pointed, and covered with gray scales, giving the whole plant a silvery appearance. Such plants have no central tank for water storage, generally few roots, and absorb all their moisture and nutrients through their leaves. The more silvery the foliage, the more light is required.

Some air plants bear flower stalks composed of sword-shaped bracts, from which peep small violet flowers. Others bear their violet flowers directly from the center of the rosette, which often turns bright red for the occasion.

Most nurseries offer an interesting choice of smaller air plants, often mounted on wood or ceramic figures or sold loose so you can create your own display. *Tillandsia* must have its base exposed to air; it will quickly rot if planted in soil. *T. ionantha*, with miniature silver-gray leaves, is probably the most commonly available. The entire plant turns brilliant red at blooming. Others include *T. caput-medusae*, with silvery twisting leaves and a bulbous base, and *T. argentea*, with strikingly scaly leaves that appear almost white. *T. usneoides* (Spanish moss) produces no roots at all; its tiny curved leaves on branching, wiry stems simply hook over surrounding vegetation. It needs both excellent air circulation and regular misting to thrive indoors.

Grow *T. cyanea* in a pot in regular potting mix. It has a rosette of bright green leaves, deep pink or red bracts, and violet-blue flowers. As its green leaves (without any trace of silver) suggest, it requires only medium light.

'Carly', a flaming-sword (*Vriesea*), has long-lasting red bracts and flattened yellow flowers.

■ Flaming-sword (*Vriesea*) is a

genus of mainly epiphytic species with smooth leaves. The plants are purchased for both their foliage and flowers. When not in bloom, flaming-swords look much like guzmanias, but the flattened flower spikes, often in bright reds or yellows, differentiate them. The bloom will last for several weeks. *V. splendens* is the most popular species, forming a rosette of wide, purple banded leaves. Its swordlike flower spike is made up of red bracts and yellow flowers. It usually produces only one pup from the center of the mother rosette. Several improved selections of this plant are readily available.

Browallia speciosa
bro-AH-lee-a spee-see-OH-sa

Browallia excels in a hanging basket or can be pinched back for a bushier plant. It blooms spring through fall.

BROWALLIA, SAPPHIRE FLOWER

Browallia is a tropical perennial with a woody base. Its popularity as a houseplant is due to its capacity to bloom heavily under only moderate light. It is also used as an annual for the shade garden outdoors.

It produces multiple stems covered with small, elliptic matte leaves. Both the leaves and stems are somewhat sticky to the touch and may even trap small insects. The five-lobed flowers, up to 2 inches in diameter, are violet-blue with a white eye, or all white. Sunken nerves on the lobes give the flowers a velvety texture. Browallia flowers most abundantly spring through fall but will bloom all winter if given adequate light.

Browallia is usually grown in a hanging basket indoors because it tends to trail, but it can be used as a table plant with regular pinching and pruning. Many of the modern cultivars are naturally compact and less trailing. In winter, keep it watered and continue to fertilize lightly until it has finished flowering.

LIGHT: Medium to bright.
WATER: Keep evenly moist.
HUMIDITY: High.
TEMPERATURE: Average.
FERTILIZER: Rich in phosphorous.
DIMENSIONS: 10 to 24 inches tall and 10 to 12 inches wide.
PROPAGATION: From seed or cuttings of nonflowering shoots.
REPOTTING: Annually.
PROBLEMS: Low light may cause spindly growth and poor bloom. Dry air and cold drafts cause leaf scorch. Highly susceptible to whiteflies. Watch for aphids.
TIPS: Pinch regularly for bushy plants. Start anew from cuttings when it becomes too woody. Move browallia outdoors in summer, as it is an excellent plant for container gardening in shade.

Brunfelsia pauciflora
brun-FEL-see-a

***Brunfelsia*'s mildly fragrant purple flowers fade gradually to almost white as they age.**

YESTERDAY-TODAY-AND-TOMORROW

The charming common name for *Brunfelsia* comes from the flowers, which change from dark purple to medium blue to almost white, with all three colors present on the plant at the same time.

Normally a large shrub, you can keep *Brunfelsia* to more modest size by pinching and pruning. The glossy, leathery dark green leaves are attractive in their own right, looking much like those of a coffee plant (*Coffea arabica*, page 135) when not in flower. The mildly fragrant, broad, wavy, 2-inch flowers grow in clusters at leaf axils and stem, most abundantly in spring and summer but almost all year long if the plant has plenty of light. Under most home conditions the plant is likely to take a winter break.

LIGHT: Medium to bright.
WATER: Keep evenly moist.
HUMIDITY: Average to high.
TEMPERATURE: Average. Avoid cold drafts.
FERTILIZER: All-purpose during growing period.
DIMENSIONS: About 1 to 3 feet tall and 1 to 2 feet wide indoors.
REPOTTING: Annually.
PROPAGATION: Softwood cuttings.
PROBLEMS: Spindly and weak in low light. Dry soil and excess mineral salts damage roots and cause dieback. Spider mites and mealybugs are possible pests.
TIPS: Prune in early spring, pinching stem tips. Be careful not to remove flower buds.

CACTI

The cactus family is a vast group of more than 2,000 species of mostly New World plants (one species is also found in Madagascar) that evolved to adapt to increasing aridity. As a result, most cacti are succulents, with thickened green stems that have not only taken over the job of photosynthesis but have also become reservoirs for water during times of drought.

However, while most cacti are succulents, not all succulents are cacti. Many different plants from around the world have developed succulent growth habits, with thickened stems and leaves that store water (*Euphorbia, Haworthia*, and *Aloe*, for example). Cacti, however, are a single family. Their specialized growing points, called areoles, usually seen as somewhat fuzzy raised or sunken spots on their stems, separate them from the rest. It is from these areoles that spines, flowers, and new growth appear.

A few of the most popular cacti are described below. They are divided into three categories, according to their cultural requirements: primitive cacti, desert cacti, and epiphytic cacti. You'll find additional information on caring for cacti on pages 86–87.

■ **Primitive cacti** include just a few species, and only one, *Pereskia aculeata*, is commonly grown indoors. These shrubby, treelike, or climbing plants still have the slender stems and broad, thin leaves typical of nonsucculents, and their spines, which are usually used to distinguish cacti, are often hidden by foliage. Some have succulent stems, but others don't. As a consequence, primitive cacti need regular watering year round.

LIGHT: Bright to intense.
WATER: Water thoroughly, then let the medium dry slightly.
HUMIDITY: Average.
TEMPERATURE: Average.
FERTILIZER: All-purpose during growing period. Not heavy feeders.
DIMENSIONS: Prune to maintain at 3 feet tall and wide.
REPOTTING: Occasionally.
PROPAGATION: Stem cuttings.
PROBLEMS: Overwatering leads to root rot. Low light causes spindly growth. Mealybugs and aphids are possible pests.
TIPS: Prune as needed to keep exuberant growth under control, or train it up a trellis or other support.

Barbados gooseberry (*Pereskia aculeata* 'Godseffiana') is a shrubby climbing plant whose abundant leaves hide vicious spines, so be careful when working with it. Its new leaves are peach-colored, becoming yellow with a reddish tinge underneath—the plant's main attraction—as 'Godseffiana' rarely blooms indoors. It may drop its leaves in winter. If so, cut back on watering until new buds appear.

Under the long white hairs of old man cactus are sharp spines. This cactus rarely blooms indoors.

Prickly pear cactus is often called bunny ears because of its growth habit. It grows best in greenhouse conditions.

Pincushion cactus blooms indoors, but be careful: Its spines are sharp.

Barrel cactus tolerates home conditions well and produces yellow flowers.

The exotic blooms of rattail cactus may last up to two months.

■ **Desert cacti** are by far the best known cacti. These are an extremely succulent species, having adapted to severe aridity. They have thick stems designed for water storage and have generally no leaves or only small, short-lived ones. Instead their green stems carry out photosynthesis. An enormous variety of forms, from small and squat to long and rambling to tall and candelabra-like, are available. Most (but not all) bear plentiful spines, and many are so spiny it is hard to see the stems. Some also have attractive woolly areoles or abundant hairs.

Smaller desert cacti tend to bloom well indoors as long as they have a distinct dormant period with little or no water and cold conditions. Winter night temperatures of 40°F to 50°F are necessary to stimulate bloom, which usually only occurs months later, in late spring or summer. Larger desert cacti will usually bloom only at maturity, which can take 20 or more years to attain, so they are grown uniquely for their general form and interesting spines. They still prefer cool to cold dry winters, but adapt well to regular indoor conditions year-round.

LIGHT: Intense.
WATER: Let the soil dry thoroughly after watering. Water infrequently or not at all during dormancy.
HUMIDITY: Low.
TEMPERATURE: Average to high; cool to cold in winter.
FERTILIZER: All-purpose during growing period. Not a heavy feeder.
DIMENSIONS: Highly variable, from a mere inch tall and wide to over 8 feet tall and 4 feet wide.
REPOTTING: Infrequently, in cactus mix.
PROPAGATION: Remove and pot offsets. Set stem cuttings into dry growing mix; withhold water until new growth appears. Some can be grown from seed.
PROBLEMS: Poor drainage and too-frequent watering cause rot. Intense light and cold winters are required for blooming. Mealybugs, root mealybugs, and scale insects are common.
TIPS: Smaller cacti require little grooming. Cut back taller ones that threaten to grow through the roof.

Rattail cactus *(Aporocactus flagelliformis)* produces narrow stems 1 inch wide and up to 6 feet long. Its aerial roots grip onto rock faces in the wild. For indoor culture, let the plant dangle from a hanging basket and occasionally remove the old brown stems. Purple-red flowers appear along the stems in summer.

Bishop's-caps or star cactus *(Astrophytum)* have thick green to reddish stems. Their globular forms vary in shape, accounting for the common names. Many cultivars are spineless. Most are small plants, but some grow to 3 feet. Yellow flowers appear on the top of the plant after a cold winter.

Old man cactus *(Cephalocereus senilis)* can reach a height of 10 feet and a diameter of 8 to 10 inches. Its upright, cylindrical gray-green body is covered with soft white wool while still immature, but beware of the sharp spines it hides. The funnel-shaped rose-colored flowers rarely bloom indoors. It grows very slowly and is a good plant to place on a windowsill when young.

Peruvian apple or curiosity-plant *(Cereus)* generally has deeply ribbed blue-green stems and few spines. Specialty cultivars, such as *C. peruvianus* 'Monstrosus', are noted for the numerous deformed growths that cover the plant. Large flowers open at night but are rarely produced indoors.

Peanut cactus *(Chamaecereus sylvestri)* is sometimes classified with *Lobivia* or *Echinopsis*. It has short, clustering green stems that grow to 6 inches long. They are ribbed and covered with short, bristly spines. Vivid scarlet red flowers appear in the summer along the stems after a winter dormant period of cool temperatures and drought. Even young plants bloom readily.

Scarlet-bugler or silver-torch (*Cleistocactus*) has cylindrical green clustering stems that can grow to 3 inches in diameter and 2 to 3 feet tall. They have many ribs and spines, which vary from white to brown and dense to sparse. Tubular scarlet or orange flowers are borne along the length of the stems during the summer on mature plants. The flowers barely open at the tip, giving them their Latin name (*cleisto* means cloistered or closed). Most common is *C. straussi* (silver-torch), with stems entirely covered in dense snowy-white bristles.

Golden barrel (*Echinocactus grusonii*) is a popular globe-shaped cactus with yellow spines prominently borne on its stem ribs. It requires bright to intense light and grows very slowly but can reach 3 feet in diameter. Yellow bell-shaped flowers are borne on the top central ring in the summer on mature plants.

Hedgehog cacti (*Echinocereus*) are generally upright, cylindrical plants that form self-branching clumps of stems. Spines and colors vary among the cultivars. The pink, purple, or whitish flowers appear near the tops of the stems in late spring or summer.

Urchin cactus or Easter-lily cactus (*Echinopsis*) is best known for its abundant large night-blooming funnel-shaped flowers, which range from white to pink and sometimes reach 8 inches long. They are intensely fragrant. Its gray-green, globular to oval stems grow singly at first, eventually forming clusters. They are distinctly ribbed and have clusters of spines along the ribs. For better bloom, remove most of the offsets. Most varieties sold are complex hybrids based on *E. multiplex*.

Barrel cactus or fishhook cactus (*Ferocactus*) species are big plants, globular to columnar with blue-green to green stems. They have approximately 10 to 20 ribs, often

very broad spines that range from yellow to red, and yellow to red-purple flowers that appear at the top of mature plants in summer.

Chin cactus (*Gymnocalycium*) has globular 8- to 12-inch-thick stems that grow in clusters or singly, depending on the species. They usually bear thick spines, but some are nearly spineless. The bell-shaped, white to pale rose flowers are borne near the top of the plant in spring and summer. They tend to bloom readily from an early age and don't require cool winter conditions in order to do so. The most common chin cactus is *G. mihanovichii*, with distinct ribs and a dark reddish-green coloration, and its brilliant red cultivar, 'Hibotan'. The latter lacks chlorophyll and can be grown only by grafting onto another cactus.

Lobivia or cob cacti (*Lobivia*) are small and often grown in clumps in a wide, flat container. They bloom more easily than many other cacti even when they aren't exposed to cool winters. The large yellow, red,

The highly fragrant trumpet-shaped flowers of urchin cactus bloom at night.

or purple flowers appear in spring and summer and generally last a long time. Most nurseries offer only unnamed hybrids.

Grow blooming ball cactus (*Notocactus eugeniae*) for quick satisfaction. It flowers while still young.

Crown cactus (Rebutia kupperiana) is native to Bolivia.

Pincushion cactus *(Mammillaria)*, also called snowball cactus, little candles cactus, silver cluster cactus, and rose pincushion, is a numerous and diverse genus that includes globular and cylindrical forms. They range from tiny individual heads, only a few inches wide, to massive clumps. The tiny flowers form a ring around the top of the plant and are often followed by red berries. They are comparatively easy plants to bloom, but do prefer cool, dry conditions in winter.

Snowball cactus *(M. bocasana)* has hooked, yellowish spines and bell-shaped yellow flowers. It has given rise to several mutations, including 'Fred', a nearly spineless version with lumpy, unequal growths. *M. prolifera* (little candles or silver cluster cactus) is a small, globe-shaped species with bristly, white spines and yellow flowers. *M. zeilmanniana* (rose pincushion) has a solitary stem topped with a ring of purple flowers.

Ball cactus *(Notocactus)* has dark green spines and bell-shaped yellow

flowers. *N. leninghausii*, one of the largest species, can reach 3 feet tall. This plant is a good choice for beginners, as it blooms while young.

Opuntia *(Opuntia)*, often called bunny-ears or beavertail cactus, usually bears a flattened stem resembling a pad. Opuntias bear two types of spines: long visible ones and glochids, small tufts of shorter, hooked spines that break off when touched and penetrate the skin. Bunny-ears *(O. microdasys)* has only glochids. They can be reddish, yellow, or white and create a dotted pattern over the surface of the plant. These cacti require minimal care but rarely bloom indoors. Some opuntias can be difficult to grow indoors, yet some grow outdoors even in cold-winter regions.

Rebutia or crown cactus *(Rebutia)* is a small, glove-shaped cactus similar to *Lobivia*, covered with small, warty tubercles. The short spines range from white to dark brown. Surprisingly large yellow, orange, red, or purple flowers appear at the base of the plant during the summer. It flowers readily from an early age.

■ **Epiphytic cacti** went in a different evolutionary direction than the desert cacti: They moved up into the trees, using aerial roots to cling to their support. Though they still store water, their stems are much thinner than those of desert cacti. Likewise, they are rarely as spiny. Some only have a few hairs where their ancestors' spines used to be.

Coming from a more shaded environment than most desert cacti, epiphytic cacti require protection from harsh sun, plus more frequent watering and feeding, and a soil that is rich in humus. They often bloom best when slightly to severely potbound. Most need a cool, dry dormant period in the winter to bloom well the following summer. Most look best in hanging baskets.

LIGHT: Medium to bright.

WATER: Water thoroughly, then let the medium dry slightly. Water sparingly in winter.

HUMIDITY: Average.

TEMPERATURE: Average; cool in winter. Avoid cold drafts.

FERTILIZER: All-purpose during growing period.

DIMENSIONS: Depending on the variety, 1 to 3 feet tall and 1 to 6 feet wide.

REPOTTING: Infrequently. Use a very light growing mix for good drainage.

PROPAGATION: From stem cuttings or by division. Some can be grown from seed.

PROBLEMS: Low light causes spindly growth and poor bloom. Overwatering causes stem rot. Mealybugs are possible pests.

TIP: Prune out damaged stems.

Orchid cacti *(×Epicactus)* include a wide variety of plants, mostly complex hybrids among the genera *Epiphyllum*, *Nopalxochia*, *Heliocereus*, and others. They are called orchid cacti because of the

Flowers of Echinocereus viridiflorus open during the day and close at night.

extreme beauty of the flowers. The typical orchid cactus is grown indoors in a hanging basket. Its branches are flat and leaflike and arch outward. It is grown primarily for its large, showy flowers, which appear in spring and early summer. Hybrids are available in reds, yellows, oranges, or white.

Easter cactus (*Rhipsalidopsis gaertneri*) is often confused with *Schlumbergera*, but its spring blooms distinguish it. The scarlet flowers are also more symmetrical. *R. rosea* is similar but has smaller, rose-pink flowers. Cultivars are available in shades of pink and red.

Mistletoe cacti or chain cacti (*Rhipsalis*) have jointed, branching, leafless stems that cascade or climb in their native habitat, making them particularly suitable for hanging pots and baskets. They have aerial roots on their flattened or cylindrical green stems. Flower shape, color, and size vary greatly within the genus, but most have tiny flowers and attractive, long-lasting berries. The best known species is probably *R. baccifera*, with dangling spaghetti-like stems, small white flowers, and white translucent berries. It is the only cactus native to both the Old and New worlds.

Christmas cactus (*Schlumbergera*), also called Thanksgiving cactus or holiday cactus, has arching spineless bright green stems. *S. ×buckleyi* (Christmas cactus) has scalloped stems that bear tubular flowers in a wide range of colors in mid- to late December. *S. truncata* (Thanksgiving cactus) flowers earlier in winter. Its stem joints are longer and narrower. The 3-inch-long flowers, borne at the ends of the stems, are shades of white and red. Hybrids between the two offer the widest range of colors, including white, pink, magenta, red, and yellow. They tend to flower between Thanksgiving Day and New Year's Day.

Schlumbergera requires a rich, porous soil kept moist but not soggy

'Madonga' often blooms in December.

and weekly fertilizer when the plant is growing. It does well in front of a cool, bright window. During the summer, you can move it outdoors into partial shade. Budding is brought on by the short days

of autumn or by a cold shock. To promote flowering, move it outdoors during cool fall weather. After it has flowered, keep it drier and withhold fertilizer. It often blooms again later in winter.

Easter cactus blooms in spring and sometimes again in early autumn. Its flowers are more upright than those on other *Schlumbergera* species.

CALADIUM, ELEPHANT'S EAR

Caladium bicolor
ka-LAY-dee-um BY-kuh-ler

Caladium 'Candidum' has green veins and white interveinal areas.

Caladiums, with their dozens of different leaf patterns and colors, create a display to rival that of any flowering plant. Masses of exquisite, paper-thin leaves, 12 to 24 inches long, are borne on long stalks. They come with spots and veins in shades of white, pink, red, green, and mixed colors. Most leaves are heart- or arrow-shaped, but some are lance-shaped. The thin leaves are translucent; light shining through them creates a glowing effect.

Caladium does bloom, but the flowers are of little interest: Dull green or greenish white, they are much like those of a Jack-in-the-pulpit. They're usually removed so as not to drain the tuber's energy.

In spring and early summer, you'll find caladiums in nurseries already in full growth and ready to take home. However, you can save considerable money by purchasing tubers in spring. Just plant three per 8-inch pot, covering the tubers with 1 inch of potting mix, then water.

At the end of the summer or after six or seven months of growth, caladiums begin to look tired. Stop watering and put them in the shade. When the leaves die back, cut them off. Store the tubers either loose, in peat moss or vermiculite, or leave them in their pots. Keep them at room temperature or slightly cooler (never less than 50°F) for the winter. When new sprouts appear in spring, repot and begin watering again.

C. bicolor (*C.* ×*hortulanum*) is the most commonly grown species and hundreds of cultivars are available. These include 'Candidum', with pure white foliage veined dark green; 'Fanny Munson', with pale pink leaves with green margins and veins and deep pink midribs; 'Little Miss Muffet', a dwarf variety rarely much more than 12 inches tall, with arrow-shaped lime-green leaves with burgundy speckles and bright red veins; 'Pink Beauty', with pink leaves bordered green with pink speckles and red veins; and 'Red Flash', with dark green leaves spotted white, deep red veins and wide green margins. *C. humboldtii* is a miniature species with dark green leaves splotched with white.

LIGHT: Medium.

WATER: Keep evenly moist; allow to dry during winter dormancy.

HUMIDITY: High.

TEMPERATURE: Average.

FERTILIZER: Rich in phosphorous.

DIMENSIONS: 9 to 24 inches by 9 to 24 inches.

REPOTTING: Each spring, at the end of dormancy.

PROPAGATION: By division of tubercles and offsets.

PROBLEMS: Low light causes spindly growth. Dry air and cool drafts cause leaf dieback. Aphids and spider mites are possible pests.

TIPS: Remove flowers. Remove dead leaves at dormancy. If you plant the tubers upside down, they'll grow larger quantities of much smaller leaves, creating a beautiful effect. You have to turn them upside down each spring to get the same effect.

'Pink Beauty'

'Rose Bud'

'Red Flash'

CALATHEA, PEACOCK PLANT, CATHEDRAL WINDOWS

Calathea
ka-LAH-thee-a

Calatheas are among the most beautiful of all the foliage plants for indoor growing. Their shiny, elliptic, long-stemmed leaves are exquisitely marbled with silver or pink patterns, and most are reddish or purplish underneath. Often the paler parts are translucent, looking like stained glass when lit from behind and giving the plant one of its several common names: cathedral windows. Most calatheas are grown for their attractive foliage and rarely bloom indoors. The flowers of those few that do bloom are usually removed to encourage new leaves.

Calatheas are clump-forming plants, spreading over time as they root underground. Some have small tubers on their roots and are able to take drier conditions, but most prefer even moisture throughout their growing season. During the winter, they have a semidormant period that must be respected. Let the potting mix go a bit drier, but not to any extremes, then begin regular watering again in spring.

There are more than 300 species of *Calathea*, many of them potential ornamentals for indoor growing. Here are just a few of the more common varieties:

Peacock plant, or cathedral windows (*C. mackoyana*), is perhaps the most popular species. The leaf is essentially pale silver-green on the top, with oblong patches and fine lines of dark green along the veins and the margin. Below it is purplish red, a color that shows through when lighted from behind. It has tuberous roots to store water but is less forgiving of overwatering than the others.

C. louisae has dark green leaves overlaid with olive-green patches and purple underneath. Flowers, if they appear, are white. The leaves of *C. picturata* 'Argentea' are entirely silver above except for a green margin. They're red below. *C. majestica* 'Roseo-Lineata' (*C. ornata* 'Roseo-Lineata') is dark olive-green with pinkish red stripes on either side of the lateral veins of young leaves. They become white on mature leaves. The plant can reach up to 6 feet tall at maturity. Also large is *C. zebrina* (zebra plant). It has velvety dark green leaves with yellow-green veins and margins and purplish-red undersides. In addition to these species, an increasing variety of hybrid calatheas, such as *C. burle-marxii* 'Ice Blue', are grown more for their flowers than their foliage.

LIGHT: Medium. Tolerates low light.
WATER: Evenly moist.
HUMIDITY: High to very high.
TEMPERATURE: Average to high.
FERTILIZER: All-purpose during growing period.
DIMENSIONS: Depending on variety, 12 to 60 inches tall by 12 to 36 inches wide.
REPOTTING: As needed to maintain even growth.

Calatheas thrive in medium light and high humidity.

PROPAGATION: By division.
PROBLEMS: Excess mineral salts cause leaf tip burn and stem dieback. Overwatering causes crown rot. Dry air causes leaf dieback. Spider mites, mealybugs, and aphids are possible pests.
TIPS: Keep evenly moist, never wet or dry. Pick off yellowing leaves.

The dramatic coloration of peacock plant is best appreciated when lighted from behind. Blooms are usually pinched off to encourage new foliage.

Calceolaria herbeohybrida
kal-kee-oh-LAR-ee-a herb-ee-o-HYE-bri-da

Calceolaria is biennial, so enjoy its unusual pouch-shaped blooms, then discard the plant when flowering ends.

CALCEOLARIA, POCKETBOOK FLOWER, SLIPPER FLOWER

Calceolaria is best purchased as a temporary plant, to be enjoyed while the blooms last. It is a biennial, so after it has bloomed, it sets seed and dies. The flowers are an unusual pouch form and come in a wide range of brilliant colors, including red, pink, maroon, and yellow, and most have purple or brown markings on the petals. The plant nearly covers itself in flowers.

You can grow calceolarias from seed, but they are sensitive to improper watering and fertilizing. Also, they like cool nights. A barely heated greenhouse or cool windowsill is perfect. Among the best varieties for home-growing is the Anytime Series, which is less heat-sensitive than most and blooms more quickly.

LIGHT: Medium for homegrown plants. Place blooming temporary plants anywhere.
WATER: Keep evenly moist.
HUMIDITY: High.
TEMPERATURE: Cool to cold, to prolong bloom.
FERTILIZER: All-purpose. No need to fertilize temporary plants.
DIMENSIONS: 8 to 18 inches tall and 6 to 12 inches wide.
REPOTTING: Transplant seedlings several times.
PROPAGATION: From seed.
PROBLEMS: Overwatering causes crown rot. Low light causes spindly growth and weak plants. Dry air causes leaf dieback. Whiteflies, spider mites, and aphids are possible pests.
TIPS: Discard after flowering. If growing from seed, regularly pinch back seedlings to form bushy plants.

Capsicum annuum
KAP-see-kum AN-ew-um

Although the fruits are edible (and hot), ornamental peppers are usually grown just for their bright colors.

ORNAMENTAL PEPPER, CHRISTMAS CHERRY

Ornamental pepper is simply an ornamental selection of the same chile pepper that many gardeners grow in their vegetable beds. Ornamental types have denser growth and numerous small fruits in bright colors. Leaves can be green, purple, or variegated. The fruits are edible but fiery hot. Even handling the fruits causes a burning sensation. This is a different plant than Jerusalem cherry (page 202), which is poisonous.

Ornamental pepper is usually sold as a gift plant already in full fruit, so simply compost it after the fruits begin to dry up. Harsh pruning can revive it, but young plants give better results. Give seedlings the brightest light possible; place them outside in full sun during the summer. Outdoors, insects pollinate the flowers. Indoors, mist blooms daily to spread the pollen.

LIGHT: Bright.
WATER: Keep evenly moist.
HUMIDITY: Average.
TEMPERATURE: Average.
FERTILIZER: All-purpose during growing period. No need to fertilize temporary plants.
DIMENSIONS: 6 to 30 inches tall and 6 to 24 inches wide.
REPOTTING: Repot seedlings as needed.
PROPAGATION: From seed.
PROBLEMS: Low light causes spindly growth, and poor bloom and fruit. Irregular watering causes leaf drop. Overwatering causes root rot. Whiteflies, aphids, and spider mites are possible pests.
TIPS: Keep fruits out of reach of children. Harvest seed from the healthiest plants for sowing the following season.

Carissa grandiflora
kah-RISS-uh grand-ih-FLOR-uh

Dwarf cultivars of natal plum (syn *C. macrocarpa*) have twisting, spiny branches and shiny leaves that make near-perfect bonsai. The taller forms make nice floor plants. In spring, both types produce abundant waxy white flowers that look and smell like jasmine (page 162). They may bloom sporadically through summer and fall in intense light, followed by plumlike purple to dark red fruits. Almost all parts of this plant are poisonous, including the seeds.

Standard-size natal plums are large shrubs up to 10 feet tall and so will need regular pruning to maintain them indefinitely at about 2 to 3 feet tall and wide. Many dwarf cultivars also are available.

LIGHT: Bright.
WATER: Keep evenly moist.
HUMIDITY: Average.

NATAL PLUM

TEMPERATURE: Average; cool to cold in winter.
FERTILIZER: All-purpose during growing period.
DIMENSIONS: 10 inches to 10 feet tall and wide.
REPOTTING: As needed in late winter or early spring.
PROPAGATION: By stem cuttings.
PROBLEM: Spindly and weak in low light.
TIPS: A summer outside helps stimulate bloom. Keep away from children because of spiny branches and poisonous seeds.

Natal plum has fragrant flowers and attractive but poisonous fruits.

Chirita sinensis
kee-REE-tuh sih-NEN-sis

This relative of the African violet looks much like its cousin but has thicker, shinier, almost succulent leaves. It bears funnel-shaped lavender flowers with an orange flush to the throat on sturdy, upright stems. The opposite, or whorled, leaves on short, thick petioles form a rosette. It's a low-growing plant, ideal for light benches or windowsills.

Some plants have dark green leaves with deeply set veins, but in most popular varieties the veins are heavily marked with silver. Leaves can be almost lance-shaped or very broad and have nearly smooth edges or deep-cut teeth. *C. sinensis* prefers cool growing conditions indoors and may fail to flower under constant warmth. The flowers, slow to open, are not as interesting as the silver filigree patterns of the leaves. The

CHIRITA

thick leaves store considerable water, so water thoroughly, then let the plant dry out before watering again.

'Hisako', with deeply toothed leaves and a fine silvery pattern, and 'Augustifolia', with narrower leaves less heavily marked in silver, are two popular cultivars.

LIGHT: Medium to bright.
WATER: Let potting mix dry slightly between waterings.
HUMIDITY: Average.
TEMPERATURE: Average; cool to cold in winter.
FERTILIZER: Rich in phosphorous.
DIMENSIONS: 5 inches tall and 14 inches wide.
REPOTTING: As needed.
PROPAGATION: From leaf cuttings, offsets, or seed.
PROBLEMS: Poor bloom under low light or high temperatures. Avoid spraying leaves to prevent leaf spots.
TIPS: Remove faded flowers and leaves to encourage new growth.

The unusual foliage of this African violet relative is more appealing than its flowers, which are slow to open.

Chlorophytum comosum
klo-RO-fi-tum ko-MO-sum

Spider Plant

Spider plants are well-known for their wiry stolons up to 6 feet long, with plantlets at their tips. The stolons rise from among grassy green arching leaves often striped with yellow or white, making this plant perfect for hanging baskets. The hanging stems also produce small white flowers.

The spider plant produces dense masses of carrot-like roots that quickly fill up most pots and make watering difficult: Water often flows right out without sinking in. It is therefore best to soak the pot in a sink of tepid water, then drain the excess.

You can remove the plantlets for propagation. You can also layer the plants by attaching a plantlet to a neighboring pot. Plants will survive but not bloom under very low light.

Green-leaved spider plants are comparatively rare. Much more common is 'Vittatum', with white to cream central stripes. 'Variegatum' has the reverse variegation: cream leaves with a green central stripe.

LIGHT: Low to bright.
WATER: Keep evenly moist. Soaking is best.
HUMIDITY: Average.
TEMPERATURE: Average to cool.
FERTILIZER: All-purpose during growing period.
DIMENSIONS: 1 foot tall and 2 feet wide; can trail to 6 feet.
REPOTTING: As needed.
PROPAGATION: From offsets or by layering. Growing from seed results in all-green plants.
PROBLEMS: Leaf tips brown due to excess mineral salts and fluoride, so repot or leach frequently. Dry soil also causes browning.
TIPS: Root plantlets in late spring for use in a shady summer border: They make great edging plants.

Spider plants thrive in average household conditions and are easily propagated from plantlets.

Chrysanthemum ×morifolium
kris-ANTH-uh-mum mo-ri-FO-lee-um

Florist's Mum

Florist's chrysanthemum (*C. ×morifolium*, syn. *Dendranthema grandiflora*) is a popular gift plant. After blooming, you can try transplanting it into the outdoor garden, but florist's mums are not as hardy as garden mums.

Mums normally bloom in fall, but commercial greenhouses can obtain flowers at any season by giving them short days. The flowers come in every color of bloom except blue and also in a wide range of forms (pompon, quill, anemone, etc.) and sizes.

Look for plants with fresh but mostly open flowers; even buds showing color don't always mature indoors. Place the plant in a cool room on a windowsill where it will receive about 4 hours of direct sun daily. Morning or evening sun is best. It should bloom continuously for 3 to 4 weeks.

LIGHT: Bright, with some direct sun. Tolerates low light for short periods.
WATER: Keep evenly moist.
HUMIDITY: Average.
TEMPERATURE: Cool to cold temperatures, if possible. Hot temperatures cause flowers to fade prematurely.
FERTILIZER: No need to fertilize temporary plants. If you're growing them yourself, apply all-purpose fertilizer during the growing period.
DIMENSIONS: Depending on variety, 5 to 36 inches tall and 6 to 36 inches wide.
REPOTTING: Not usually needed.
PROPAGATION: From stem cuttings of nonflowering shoots.
PROBLEMS: Plants decline rapidly under hot temperatures or when insufficiently watered. Spider mites, whiteflies, leaf miners, and mildew are possible pests.
TIPS: Discard or plant outdoors after blooming. Flowering plants may need water more than once a week.

Florist's mums bloom for up to two months if located in a cool room where they can receive direct sun each day.

CISSUS, GRAPE IVY

The genus *Cissus* includes more than 350 species of mostly climbing plants and is closely related to *Vitis* (the common grape), which shares the same vining habit. Cissus climbs by means of tendrils and can reach incredible heights in the wild but is easily kept under control indoors through regularly pinching and pruning. Although young stems are green and pliable, old growth eventually becomes woody. Generally it is grown in hanging baskets or trained up trellises. Cissus does not usually bloom or produce fruit indoors.

Indoor ivy is popular in commercial settings. The plants also grow rapidly at home and acclimate easily to low light and infrequent watering. With care, you can maintain plants for many months in adverse conditions, but they will not flourish unless they are given medium or bright light and kept moderately moist and well-fertilized.

LIGHT: Medium to bright. Tolerates low light for long periods.

WATER: Let potting mix dry slightly between waterings.

HUMIDITY: Average to high. A humidifier may be necessary for some species.

TEMPERATURE: Average.

FERTILIZER: All-purpose during growing period.

DIMENSIONS: Easily maintained under 36 inches tall and wide, if required.

REPOTTING: As needed to maintain healthy growth.

PROPAGATION: From softwood cuttings.

PROBLEMS: Low light causes spindly growth. Excess mineral salts cause brown leaf tips, so repot or leach frequently. Whiteflies, mealybugs, spider mites, and downy and powdery mildew are possible.

TIPS: Pinch and prune regularly to control excess growth. Drops of sap naturally form on the underside of the leaves, a phenomenon called guttation. This is not harmful.

Pink cissus *(Cissus adenopoda)* is a lesser-known tuberous-rooted species with rapidly growing stems bearing coppery green trifoliate leaves lightly covered with purple hair. This is rarely found in nurseries; starts are shared with family or friends. It thrives under ordinary growing conditions.

Kangaroo ivy or kangaroo vine *(C. antarctica)* is a vigorous indoor climber. It is usually trained onto a trellis, string, or post, but you can use it in hanging baskets. The toothed single leaves are large and shiny but may be sparse if the plant is not in good light. Train or wrap several vines together to make the foliage look denser. The common name refers to its Australian origin.

Begonia-treebine *(C. discolor)* is a vigorous vine with stupendous foliage. The leaves resemble those of a rex begonia, velvety with toothed edges and deep red veins with a purple reverse. In ample light, pink and silvery colorations appear. It's an ideal choice for a humid greenhouse but less well-adapted to home culture.

Winged grape *(C. quadrangularis)* has thick, distinctly winged green stems that constrict at the nodes. The small, dark green maple-like leaves are generally short-lived, giving the plant a cactus-like appearance when they fall. A true succulent, this ivy needs intense light and thorough but infrequent watering.

Grape ivy or oakleaf ivy *(C. rhombifolia)* grows wild in the West Indies and South America. Its stems and buds are brown and have reddish hairs, and its shiny, three-lobed leaves are similar to those of poison ivy. Its two cultivars, 'Mandaiana' and 'Ellen Danica', are more widely available than the species. It tolerates a wide range of growing conditions and grows

Grow cissus in a hanging basket or on a trellis to show off its vining habit.

Kangaroo ivy has large, shiny leaves. It needs good light to thrive.

Begonia-treebine's dramatic foliage does best in a humid greenhouse.

'Ellen Danica' grape ivy tolerates typical indoor growing conditions.

rapidly even in medium light.

Succulent grape or wax cissus *(C. rotundifolia)* has thick green stems and round, waxy, lilypad-like leaves in glossy green to olive. Very easy to grow, it needs intense light and thorough but infrequent watering.

CITRUS

If you want homegrown lemons that look like those you buy at the grocery, try *Citrus limon* 'Meyer'.

Citrus plants have something for all seasons: shiny dark green foliage; sweetly scented white flowers that appear intermittently throughout the year; and colorful, long-lasting fruits. The fruits range in color from green to yellow or orange, depending on the species and the maturity of the fruit. Fruits at various stages of development and color are often found on the plant at the same time.

All citruses are shrubby plants that normally become large with time, but you can keep them in check with regular pruning. Avoid trimming off branches with flowers or buds, though, if you want to see fruit. Some citruses bear numerous thorns; others have few or none.

Citrus fruits produced indoors tend to be sour or bitter and aren't eaten fresh. You can, however, use them in marmalades, candies, and other foods. To ensure fruit production indoors, pass pollen from flower to flower with a small paintbrush or a cotton swab.

Growing a citrus plant from store-bought fruit is a popular pastime. Sow the seeds in small pots in a moist growing mix, and cover with plastic wrap. Place the pots in a warm, brightly lit spot. The seedlings will appear in 2 to 3 weeks and become attractive, long-lived foliage plants. It is unlikely that plants raised from store-bought fruit will ever flower or produce fruit indoors, as the parent plants were selected for outdoor conditions. For good fruit production, take stem cuttings of selections that bloom well indoors or buy plants that are already in bloom. The latter can be expensive, but they give quick results; young cuttings can be years away from flowering.

The best choice for indoor growing is the calamondin or miniature orange (×*Citrofortunella mitis)*, a cross between *Citrus reticulata* (mandarin orange) and *Fortunella*. It is widely available and blooms and produces fruit year-round. It also remains compact with only minimal pruning.

Citrus limon 'Meyer' (Meyer lemon) is also productive indoors, bearing yellow fruits identical to store-bought lemons. Also try *C. limon* 'Ponderosa' (Ponderosa lemon), which has enormous fruits with thick, tough rinds. *C. sinensis* cultivars (sweet oranges) sometimes are available. They require ideal conditions to produce fruit indoors.

Another citrus that's fun to grow at home is *Fortunella margarita* (kumquat). It has small orange-yellow, oblong fruits.

Most citruses offer variegated forms, which bloom and fruit as readily as the all-green ones, but tend to be more expensive.

LIGHT: Bright to intense.
WATER: Let potting mix dry slightly between waterings.
HUMIDITY: Average.
TEMPERATURE: Average.
FERTILIZER: Acid-based with added trace elements.
DIMENSIONS: 1 to 10 feet tall and 1 to 6 feet wide.
REPOTTING: Infrequently.
PROPAGATION: From softwood cuttings.
PROBLEMS: May not bloom in poor light. Overly dry or wet soil may cause leaf drop. Mealybugs, scale insects, whiteflies, and spider mites are possible pests. Lack of iron causes leaf yellowing.
TIP: Prune as needed to maintain the desired size and shape.

Miniature orange trees are easier to grow than full-size cultivars, and they bloom all year long.

CLERODENDRUM, GLORYBOWER, BLEEDING HEART

Clerodendrum
kle-ro-DEN-drum

Nearly 400 species of clerodendrum exist, but most are too large to consider as houseplants. Only one species is generally available: glorybower (*C. thompsoniae*). Another form of this plant is *C. thompsoniae* 'Variegatum', with cream-margined leaves.

Clerodendrum is sometimes called "bleeding heart" because of its intricate flowers borne in clusters of bell-shaped white calyxes that last for a month or more. From among these appear brilliant red flowers with extended stamens. Flowering occurs mainly in spring but can be sporadic throughout the year under ideal conditions. The heart-shaped dark green leaves are attractive, and the plant can double as a foliage plant when it is between blooms.

Glorybower is a climber in the wild but is usually grown indoors as a trailer or pruned into a shrub form. Either way, it will need regular pinching or pruning, best done immediately after the flowers have faded so as not to remove new flower buds.

Provide high humidity and very bright light year-round, and this plant should thrive indoors.
LIGHT: Bright.
WATER: Keep evenly moist while the plant is in bloom, somewhat drier at other times.
HUMIDITY: High.
TEMPERATURE: Average.
FERTILIZER: Rich in phosphorous.
DIMENSIONS: 1 to 15 feet tall and 1 to 10 feet wide.
REPOTTING: Infrequently.
PROPAGATION: From softwood cuttings.
PROBLEMS: Overwatering causes crown rot. Whiteflies, mealybugs, and aphids are possible pests.
TIP: Prune after flowering.

The "bleeding hearts" of Clerodendrum are the red flowers that flow from the plant's white calyxes.

CLIVIA

Clivia miniata
KLYE-vee-a min-ee-AII-ta

Thick stems 12 to 18 inches tall emerge from a crown of leathery, strap-shaped dark green leaves and support large clusters of trumpet-shaped orange flowers with yellow throats. Some cultivars have yellow flowers and variegated leaves. After the flowers fade in late spring, ornamental red berries form and add a touch of lasting color.

This winter bloomer does well in a room that receives plenty of bright light in summer. Crowded roots left undisturbed for years produce the best blooms; repotting is rarely necessary unless the pot starts to split open. Repotting or dividing clivia can cause it to remain flowerless for a year or two, until its pot fills up with roots again.

Offsets may bloom within only a year or so, but seeds can take seven years or more to bloom. Seeds must be fresh and can take several months to germinate.
LIGHT: Medium to bright.
WATER: Keep evenly moist; water sparingly in winter.
HUMIDITY: Average.
TEMPERATURE: Average; cool to cold in winter.
FERTILIZER: All-purpose during growing period.
DIMENSIONS: 18 inches tall and 12 inches wide.
REPOTTING: Infrequently.
PROPAGATION: Remove and root offsets. Seed is available but germinates slowly.
PROBLEMS: Overwatering causes crown rot. Short, stubby flower stems result from excess heat or water during the winter months. Low light or immaturity causes lack of blooms.
TIPS: Pull off yellowing leaves. Leave flower stalks after they bloom in order to get the attractive red berries.

Let clivia's roots become pot-bound in order to get the best blooms. Repot only If the container splits open.

Codiaeum variegatum pictum
ko-dee-EYE-um var-ee-GA-tum PIK-tum

CROTON

The varied leaf shapes and exotic colors of the croton make it an especially attractive indoor plant. It produces shiny, leathery leaves that can reach from 3 to 18 inches long. Foliage colors vary endlessly with spots, splotches, stripes, and irregular bands in red, pink, orange, brown, white, and green. Color markings vary even among leaves on the same plant.

Leaves are often most brightly colored when young, then darken as they mature. Leaves can be elliptic, linear, lobed, or even corkscrew. Mature crotons flower quite readily, with arching stems of fuzzy, ball-shaped flowers appearing mostly in summer.

C. variegatum pictum is a shrub that reaches over 6 feet in height outdoors, but you can prune it to a more amenable 3 or 4 feet for use indoors. It is usually grown several stems per pot to give it a fuller appearance. Regular pinching (wear gloves, as the sticky white sap is slightly toxic) helps a single-stemmed specimen fill out.

Crotons have the reputation of being finicky, and that is certainly true of mature specimens fresh off the truck. They tend to react badly if moved from their usual growing location, losing leaves by the dozens and often dying outright. Young plants, however, tend to be fairly adaptable. You can move them to the most unlikely spots, including into fairly low light or dry air, and they still thrive. Once settled, they'll reach full height over time. Low-light plants are not nearly as colorful as plants grown in bright light, tending toward darker leaf colors.

If you buy a full-size specimen, ask for a well-acclimatized plant that has been in a local greenhouse for at least two months. Many crotons sold in stores throughout much of North America are taken from sunny southern states, packed in trucks, and shipped to stores where they are immediately put on sale. If your home's environment does not resemble Florida's, buy a small plant.

LIGHT: Bright to intense; young plants can adapt to low light.
WATER: Keep potting mix evenly moist.

Crotons grown in bright light have more colorful foliage than low-light specimens. They darken as they mature.

HUMIDITY: High.
TEMPERATURE: Average to high. Avoid cold drafts.
FERTILIZER: All-purpose during growing period. Not a heavy feeder.
DIMENSIONS: 1 to 6 feet tall and 1 to 5 feet wide.
REPOTTING: As needed.
PROPAGATION: From softwood cuttings, using rooting hormone, or by air layering.
PROBLEMS: Low light or dry air causes spindly growth and leaf loss, as does soggy or dry soil. Spider mites, mealybugs, and scale insects are possible pests.
TIPS: To prevent spider mites, give the plant a monthly shower. This also keeps leaves shiny and dust-free. Pinch occasionally to stimulate branching. Crotons are slightly poisonous, so keep them out of reach of children.

Crotons are usually grown potted in multiples in order to create a bushier shape.

Coffea arabica
KOF-ee-a a-RA-bi-ka

COFFEE PLANT

Growing your own coffee indoors is a refreshing idea, but it's best to view coffee plants as foliage plants that might one day surprise you with flowers, and later, fruit. Coffee plants make attractive, bushy shrubs up to 3 or more feet in height. The dark green elliptic leaves with wavy margins are attractive and their growth is slow but steady. Keep them pruned for a bushy look.

Most plants sold are seedlings about 6 to 8 years from blooming. Only at maturity will they begin to produce clusters of highly fragrant white flowers that give way to green berries that eventually turn bright red, then darken. At this point, you can harvest them, extract the seeds ("coffee beans"), roast them, and make ... a few spoonfuls of coffee.

You can also grow your own coffee plants from fresh, unroasted coffee beans. They germinate quite readily and produce fine-looking young plants within a year.

LIGHT: Bright.
WATER: Let potting mix dry slightly between waterings.
HUMIDITY: High.
TEMPERATURE: Average.
FERTILIZER: All-purpose during growing period.
DIMENSIONS: Usually under 3 feet tall and 2 feet wide indoors.
REPOTTING: Annually.
PROPAGATION: From seed or cuttings.
PROBLEMS: Lack of bloom may be due to immaturity, but could be caused by poor growing conditions. Plants may lose leaves due to over- or underwatering or dry air. Spider mites are possible pests.
TIPS: If possible, purchase a mature specimen already in flower or fruit. Pinch stems regularly to stimulate branching. Remove yellowed leaves.

Coffee arabica is grown for its glossy dark green leaves, but mature plants also produce fragrant blooms.

Columnea
ko-LUM-nee-a

COLUMNEA, GOLDFISH PLANT

More than 150 different species of columnea exist, along with numerous hybrids. Because they tend to be trailing or only semi-upright, they look especially good in hanging baskets.

The stems can be hairy or smooth and produce pairs of elliptic leaves that range in size from no bigger than a shirt button to over 5 inches long. They can be smooth or hairy, thin or thick and waxy, dark or light green, and can even be bronze or have variegated markings.

The brightly colored, tubular flowers open into four lobes: The upper one forms a hood that projects forward, and the other three angle outward, giving the flowers a fishlike shape. Flowers come in orange, red, or yellow. Bloom is usually in spring and summer, but some hybrids, such as 'Early Bird' (yellow with orange tips) and 'Mary Ann' (deep pink), bloom continuously throughout the year. Flowers range in length from ½ to 4 inches, depending on the variety.

LIGHT: Medium to bright.
WATER: Keep evenly moist.
HUMIDITY: Average.
TEMPERATURE: Average. A short period of cold temperatures (down to 50°F) in the fall may stimulate new blooms.
FERTILIZER: Rich in phosphorous.
DIMENSIONS: Depending on variety, 6 to 14 inches tall and 12 to 36 inches wide. May trail several feet.
REPOTTING: Infrequently.
PROPAGATION: From softwood cuttings or seed.
PROBLEMS: Low light causes spindly, weak growth. Spider mites and aphids are possible pests.
TIPS: Remove yellowed leaves and faded flowers. Prune as needed to produce even growth.

The trailing stems and tubular flowers of Columnea look particularly striking in hanging baskets.

Cordyline fruticosa
kor-DY-li-nee froo-ti-KO-sa

Cordyline terminalis 'Lilliput' thrives in bright light and high humidity. Use a humidifier or humidity tray indoors.

TI PLANT

The ti plant (*C. fruticosa*, syn. *C. terminalis*) is touted as the "good luck plant" and frequently sold as "ti logs" (sections of stem) at flower exhibitions and agricultural shows. The "logs" root quite readily: Simply plant them on their sides and half cover them with potting mix.

Popular indoor cultivars grow to 3 feet or more indoors and have green or red foliage with pink or white variegations or margins. Flowers are rarely produced indoors. Although ti plants tolerate low light, foliage color will not develop well under such conditions. In fact, they are difficult plants to grow to perfection indoors because they need extremely humid air. Keep the humidifier running during the winter months and whenever air is dry.

Since ti plants branch little if at all, even after pruning, use several plants to a pot for a fuller look.

LIGHT: Medium to bright.

WATER: Let potting mix dry slightly between waterings.

HUMIDITY: Very high.

TEMPERATURE: Average to high. Avoid cold drafts.

FERTILIZER: All-purpose during growing period.

DIMENSIONS: 1 foot to 15 feet tall and 1 foot to 8 feet wide.

REPOTTING: As needed.

PROPAGATION: From softwood cuttings or by air layering.

PROBLEMS: Excess mineral salts and fluoride cause leaf-tip burn, so leach frequently. Dry air causes leaf dieback and invites spider mites. Mealybugs and scale insects also are possible pests.

TIPS: Ti plants need high humidity, especially during winter months, or their health quickly goes downhill. Remove any yellowed lower leaves.

Costus speciosus 'Variegatus'
KOHST-us spee-see-OH-sus

Variegated crepe ginger derives its common name from the white margins on its leaves.

VARIEGATED CREPE GINGER, SPIRAL GINGER

Costus speciosus 'Variegatus', variegated crepe ginger, also called variegated spiral ginger or variegated stepladder plant, sends up thick reddish stems from underground rhizomes, forming a dense clump over time. Around the stems twist 8- to 12-inch, thick, green leaves, fuzzy underneath, with a distinct white margin. This spiral arrangement is quite unique, giving the plant two of its common names: spiral ginger and stepladder plant. At the end of the summer or in fall, if conditions are particularly good, a conelike reddish spike may appear at the tip of the stem and open into spectacular, large white to pink flowers with yellow centers and creped edges, but this rarely happens if indoor air is dry.

C. speciosus, with all green leaves, is sometimes available, as are other spiral gingers, such as *C. igneus*, with yellow flowers; *C. malorticaeanus*, with orchid-like flowers in yellow with red bands; and the much smaller *Monocostus uniflorus*, only 20 inches tall, bearing crepelike yellow flowers much of the year.

LIGHT: Medium to bright.

WATER: Keep evenly moist.

HUMIDITY: High.

TEMPERATURE: Average to high. Avoid cold drafts.

FERTILIZER: All-purpose during growing period.

DIMENSIONS: 3 to 6 feet tall and 1 foot to 3 feet wide.

REPOTTING: Annually, in acidic growing mix. Grows best with ample root space.

PROPAGATION: Divide in spring. Will sometimes sprout from stem cuttings.

PROBLEMS: Dry or cold air causes spindly growth and leaf dieback. Susceptible to spider mites.

TIPS: Cut out old stems. Keep air humid to ensure bloom.

Crassula ovata
KRAS-ew-la oh-VAH-ta

The jade plant (*C. ovata*, syn. *C. arborescens*, *C. argentea* and *C. portulacea*) is one of the most familiar houseplants. Generations of gardeners have watched it produce its thick branches and succulent, spoon-shaped dark green leaves that turn reddish on the edges in full sun.

Jade is an adaptable plant, putting up with both low and intense light and dry to moist soil. The plant will be healthiest in bright to intense light and when allowed to dry out between waterings. Mature plants bloom, bearing hundreds of star-shaped white to pale pink blossoms in winter at the tips of the stems.

Stems root readily and even leaves that fall onto the potting mix often root and form new plants. Stem cuttings are required to reproduce variegated varieties; leaf cuttings produce all-green plants.

JADE PLANT

Jade plant has also given rise to several cultivars, including 'Hobbit' and 'Gollum', with curiously congested leaves. Look for more information on growing succulents on pages 86–87.

LIGHT: Bright to intense but tolerates low light for long periods.
WATER: Let potting mix dry thoroughly between waterings.
HUMIDITY: Low to average.
TEMPERATURE: Cool to hot.
FERTILIZER: All-purpose during growing period. Not a heavy feeder.
DIMENSIONS: 1 foot to 6 feet tall and 1 foot to 3 feet wide.
REPOTTING: Repot infrequently into well-drained, weighty mix.
PROPAGATION: From stem or leaf cuttings, depending on variety.
PROBLEMS: Overwatering leads to stem rot. Mealybugs and scale insects are possible pests.
TIP: Tends to be top-heavy, so pot in clay pots rather than plastic.

Jade plants thrive in bright light and well-draining soil. Mature plants may bloom if light is intense enough.

Crinum
KREE-num

This relative of the amaryllis (*Hippeastrum*, page 157) looks much like its cousin but has solid stems and much more arching, straplike leaves up to 4 feet long. The funnel-shaped pink, red, or white flowers are fragrant and sometimes 6 inches across. They are borne in clusters on top of a 3- to 5-foot stalk. Bloom is usually in late spring or summer but may repeat into fall.

Plant with the bulb tip exposed in a comparatively small pot; it blooms best when pot-bound. In nature, this plant grows in swamps, so it prefers abundant moisture, although it adapts well to drier conditions.

Crinum is a magnificent plant and needs a lot of room for its spreading leaves. Give it a moderately dry resting period during winter. Most varieties lose their leaves at that time, then start to grow anew in spring, but a few are evergreen.

CRINUM LILY, BENGAL LILY, MILK-AND-WINE LILY

LIGHT: Medium to bright.
WATER: Keep evenly moist. Water sparingly in winter.
HUMIDITY: Average.
TEMPERATURE: Average.
FERTILIZER: Rich in potassium.
DIMENSIONS: 3 to 5 feet tall and 18 inches wide.
REPOTTING: Blooms best when pot-bound, but pot seedlings into larger pots as they grow.
PROPAGATION: By division, or remove and pot the bulblets that develop beside the parent.
PROBLEMS: No significant problems.
TIPS: Remove old leaves when the plant goes dormant. Keep it away from foot traffic, as its leaves are easily damaged. Its sap is somewhat toxic, so wear gloves when handling crinum lily and keep it out of reach of children.

Crinum lily's fragrant flowers bloom in late spring or summer. Like its cousin, the amaryllis, it needs a rest period.

Crossandra infundibuliformis
kros-AN-dra in-fun-dib-ew-lee-FORM-is

Modern cultivars of firecracker flower come in shades of orange, coral, red, and yellow.

FIRECRACKER FLOWER

This colorful houseplant is almost never without bloom, even in midwinter. Modern firecracker flower hybrids are dense, low-growing plants that branch readily and bear numerous glossy, often wavy-edged medium-green leaves. Four-sided green spikes that bear the fan-shaped flowers appear at the tips of the stems. The original species had salmon-red flowers, but many modern cultivars come in orange, yellow, and red. The Florida series is especially popular: 'Florida Summer' (yellow), 'Florida Flame' (red), 'Florida Passion' (coral), and 'Florida Sunset' (orange). They adapt more readily to seasonal changes and cooler winter temperatures than previous varieties.

Give firecracker flower abundant moisture and plentiful light, not to mention high humidity, and it will perform wonderfully. After the last flower in any individual spike fades, clip off the spike. This will stimulate branching and more flowers. It is not a long-lived plant, however. When bloom becomes sparse and the plant no longer looks its best, start it over from cuttings or raise more plants from seed. Seed-grown plants tend to be more floriferous than those grown from cuttings.

LIGHT: Bright.
WATER: Keep evenly moist.
HUMIDITY: High.
TEMPERATURE: Average.
FERTILIZER: Rich in phosphorous.
DIMENSIONS: 1 foot to 3 feet tall and 1 foot to 2 feet wide.
REPOTTING: Annually.
PROPAGATION: Semi-ripe cuttings. Easily grown from seed.
PROBLEMS: Irregular watering causes root rot. Aphids, whiteflies, and thrips are possible pests.
TIPS: Prune regularly to maintain an attractive shape.

Cuphea hyssopifolia
KEW-fee-a hi-sop-i-FO-lee-a

Mexican heather is a small shrub that blooms best when pot-bound.

Cigarplant flowers resemble small cigars with ashes at their tips.

ELFIN HERB, MEXICAN HEATHER

This small shrub is elfin in proportion, with its slender stems, tiny dark green needle-like leaves, and ½-inch flowers. It blooms spring through fall, sometimes in winter, with numerous pink, white, or pinkish-purple flowers.

Mexican heather is a fairly tough houseplant: As long as it gets enough light and moisture, it does well. If it begins to flag, either prune it harshly or take a few stem cuttings and start it again.

Numerous other *Cuphea* species and hybrids exist, few of which have been thoroughly tested as houseplants. One that has, though, is cigarplant *(C. ignea,* syn. *C. platycentra).* A bushy plant with narrow leaves much like elfin herb, it produces an abundance of narrow, tubular bright red blooms tipped with a white rim and two tiny black-purple petals. As the name implies, they do look like tiny cigars with ashes at their tips. Cigarplants also come with pink or white flowers.

LIGHT: Bright.
WATER: Keep evenly moist.
HUMIDITY: Average. *C. ignea* needs high humidity.
TEMPERATURE: Average.
FERTILIZER: All-purpose during growing period.
DIMENSIONS: 6 to 24 inches tall and 8 to 22 inches wide.
REPOTTING: Blooms best when slightly pot-bound.
PROPAGATION: From softwood cuttings. *C. ignea* grows from seed.
PROBLEMS: Low light causes spindly and weak growth. Whiteflies and aphids are possible pests.
TIPS: Pinch as needed. Elfin herb makes an interesting indoor bonsai.

Curcuma alismatifolia
kur-KYEW-muh al-iss-mat-uh-FOH-lee-uh

Siam tulip is often sold in bloom as a gift plant, but you can save money by purchasing and potting rhizomes in the spring and covering them with an inch or so of growing mix. They sprout quickly in warm soil, producing arching, strap-shaped leaves followed by an 8-inch inflorescence composed of pink bracts, with greenish tips, that last up to 3 months. Smaller violet flowers appear among the bracts.

Other species and hybrids of Siam tulip range in color from pink to purple, orange, yellow, red, and white. The leaves are highly variable in form: Some are strap-shaped like those of *C. alismatifolia*, others heart-shaped, and yet others are more like those of cannas.

During the growing season, keep the soil evenly moist and supply

SIAM TULIP

bright to intense light. In fall, let the plant dry out gradually, then store the rhizomes in peat moss or vermiculite or in their pot, in a cool, dry spot for the winter. In spring, start the cycle anew.

LIGHT: Medium to bright.
WATER: Keep evenly moist. Dries out and goes dormant in fall.
HUMIDITY: Average to high.
TEMPERATURE: Average.
FERTILIZER: All-purpose during growing period.
DIMENSIONS: 20 to 35 inches tall and 10 to 14 inches wide.
REPOTTING: In spring, as rhizomes come out of dormancy.
PROPAGATION: Divide in spring.
PROBLEMS: Low light causes spindly and weak growth. Siam tulip rots in winter unless kept nearly dry. It has few insect problems.
TIP: Remove faded leaves and flowers.

Siam tulip's flowers are actually bracts. Species and hybrids bloom in white, pink, red, purple, orange, or yellow.

Cycas revoluta
SEE-kas re-vo-LOO-ta

Although it resembles a palm tree, sago palm is more closely related to modern conifers. Its pinnate fronds are shiny and extremely stiff. They appear tough but are actually quite easily damaged, and because the plant produces only one new set of leaves each year, any damage remains visible for a long time. The plant forms a thick, rough trunk like a palm trunk after many years. Offsets are produced only on very mature specimens.

The huge seeds are sometimes offered for sale but can take a year to germinate, and even then produce only a single leaf the first year. If you want a plant with a visible trunk, buy one that has already reached that stage. Young plants are sometimes used for bonsai, but will eventually outgrow that use.

SAGO PALM

Other types of cycads occasionally grown indoors include *Ceratozamia*, *Dioon*, *Encephalartos*, and *Zamia*.

LIGHT: Medium to bright.
WATER: Let the potting mix dry slightly between waterings.
HUMIDITY: Average to high.
TEMPERATURE: Average.
FERTILIZER: All-purpose during growing period. Not a heavy feeder.
REPOTTING: Repot infrequently.
DIMENSIONS: 1 foot to 6 feet or more in height and width.
PROPAGATION: Older specimens can produce offsets. Grows slowly from seed.
PROBLEM: Spider mites can be a problem in dry air.
TIP: The plant is toxic and spiny, so keep out of reach of children.

Sago palm is not really a palm but can be grown like one in average indoor light, humidity, and temperature.

Cyclamen persicum
SIK-la-men PER-si-cum

With careful culture it is possible to keep cyclamens growing after they have finished blooming.

FLORIST'S CYCLAMEN

The heart-shaped dark green, silver-mottled leaves of cyclamen form a rosette topped with upright butterfly-like blossoms from mid-autumn until mid-spring. Cyclamen does best in a cool room with good air circulation but no drafts.

Many people discard cyclamen after blooming, but you can keep it growing with special care. When blooming ceases and the foliage dies back, put the plant in a cool spot and let the soil dry. In midsummer, repot the corm with new soil in a small pot, and place it in a warm area to encourage root growth. As it grows, gradually return the plant to a cool location (55°F) to induce blooming.

Cyclamen seed is available but very difficult to germinate and grow to flowering size under average home conditions.

LIGHT: Bright; intense in winter.
WATER: Keep evenly moist, watering from below; keep dry during summer dormancy.
HUMIDITY: Average.
TEMPERATURE: Cool to cold.
FERTILIZER: All-purpose during growing period.
DIMENSIONS: 4 to 12 inches tall and 6 to 24 inches wide.
REPOTTING: Keep pot-bound.
PROPAGATION: From seed.
PROBLEMS: Subject to rot if water accumulates in the depression at the top of the corm (always water from below). Cyclamen will not bloom or will stop blooming if night temperatures are too warm. Spider mites and cyclamen mites are possible pests.
TIPS: Pull off faded leaves and flowers. Miniature cultivars are more heat-resistant than the larger, old-fashioned florist's varieties. Some may even bloom during the summer, skipping the dormant period.

Cyperus alternifolius
SY-pe-rus al-ter-ni-FO-lee-us

This is one plant you can't overwater. Umbrella plant is semiaquatic, so double-pot it and let it stand in water.

UMBRELLA PLANT, DWARF PAPYRUS

This popular indoor plant is ideal for gardeners who love to water. Since it is semiaquatic, it actually prefers to stand in water. Just slip the pot into a larger cachepot and keep it soaking in water at all times. You can submerge the entire root ball in up to 1 inch of water.

Umbrella plant forms a spreading clump of upright green stems, each topped off by a whorl of narrow, grasslike green "leaves" (in fact, bracts). In summer, small greenish to brown flowers form among the bracts and the plant may even self-sow into surrounding pots, if they are kept moist at all times.

Plant height is variable and depends on lighting conditions. Taller plants may require staking.

LIGHT: Bright.
WATER: Very moist at all times. Prefers to stand in water.
HUMIDITY: High.
TEMPERATURE: Average. Avoid cold drafts.
FERTILIZER: All-purpose during growing period. Not a heavy feeder.
DIMENSIONS: 18 to 36 inches tall and 16 inches wide.
REPOTTING: As needed.
PROPAGATION: By division or from seed or tip cuttings.
PROBLEMS: Will die if allowed to dry out. Leaf dieback and spider mites are problems in dry air.
TIPS: Cut out dead stems. To propagate the umbrella plant rapidly, cut off the top of a stem and set the resulting cluster of bracts in water. It will readily root, even if placed upside down. Prune back the roots of mature plants occasionally, or they can clog up their container.

DIEFFENBACHIA, DUMB CANE

Dieffenbachia seguine
dee-fan-BAHK-ee-a say-GWEE-nay

Dieffenbachia usually features a single thick, green, canelike stem marked by the scars of fallen leaves. Arching oblong pointed leaves, 10 to 12 inches long, often marbled white or cream, spiral around the "trunk." Dieffenbachias are often planted several to a pot to give a denser appearance. Mature plants eventually reach ceiling height, then are cut back or air layered. Even leafless stem sections just 3 inches long will form new plants if placed on their sides and half-covered in growing mix.

The nomenclature of the genus *Dieffenbachia* can be confusing. Plants sold as *D. amoena*, *D. maculata*, or *D. picta* are now considered variations of a single species, *D. seguine*.

Older cultivars are treelike in habit, but newer hybrids are clump-forming. They develop multiple shoots at the base and stay compact longer than the older varieties.

Ingested sap from the cane stems of dieffenbachia causes temporary speechlessness and much pain, hence the name dumb cane.

LIGHT: Medium. Tolerates low light.
WATER: Let the potting mix dry slightly between waterings.
HUMIDITY: Average.
TEMPERATURE: Average.
FERTILIZER: All-purpose during growing period.
DIMENSIONS: Depending on variety, 2 to 10 feet tall and 2 feet wide.
REPOTTING: Repot infrequently.
PROPAGATION: From stem cuttings or by air layering.
PROBLEMS: Poor drainage, too-frequent watering, and standing in water cause root rot. Spider mites, aphids, mealybugs, and scale insects are possible pests.
TIPS: Remove faded leaves. Cut off any inflorescences that appear. Rolled-up "leaves" that don't open may in fact be flowers; if so, prune them out.

Plant several dieffenbachias together in one pot to disguise their stems and create a shrubbier appearance.

VENUS FLYTRAP

Dionaia muscipula
dee-on-EYE-a mus-KIP-ew-la

Venus flytrap is a carnivorous plant bearing traps that close on flies and other small insects. It does not need to be fed indoors, but you can supply the occasional insect. Never give it red meat of any kind. These interesting plants die after only a few meals, so resist the urge to stimulate the traps too often, and do not use red meat as bait.

Venus flytrap is a small plant, with a rosette of 3-inch winged leaves. The tip of each mature leaf ends in a hinged trap with soft teeth. In summer, tall stalks bearing small white flowers appear. Blooms weaken the plant, so pinch them off if you want to keep it growing.

Venus flytrap is fairly easy to grow for short periods indoors, preferably in a terrarium. It goes into dormancy in winter and requires cool to cold conditions at that time.

LIGHT: Bright to intense.
WATER: Keep evenly moist except during dormancy. Use only rain or distilled water.
HUMIDITY: Very high. Grows best in a terrarium.
TEMPERATURE: Average to cool. Keep cold during dormancy.
FERTILIZER: Do not fertilize.
DIMENSIONS: About 6 inches tall (18 inches when in bloom) and 6 inches wide.
REPOTTING: Each spring, into pure sphagnum moss.
PROPAGATION: By division or from leaf cuttings in spring, but doing so is not practical except under greenhouse or nursery conditions.
PROBLEMS: Subject to crown rot if conditions are too warm. Venus flytrap may die if mineralized (tap or bottled) water is applied.
TIPS: Pick off blackened leaves. Does best outdoors in bog gardens in Zones 8 through 10.

The winged leaves of carnivorous Venus flytrap close around its prey. It does not need food indoors.

DRACAENA

Dracaena
dra-KYE-na

Highly popular as indoor foliage plants, most dracaenas have tall stems like palm trees, with tufts of narrow, swordlike leaves near the top. Many grow into large plants, often 10 feet or more in height. To offset their natural tendency for tall, leggy growth, stems of different heights are often planted together in the same pot. Many indoor gardeners air layer plants to reduce their height. The canes that are left after the air layers are removed will sprout new leafy growth.

Many species and cultivars are available. Most are selected for their foliage and form, and often are used for large-scale architectural plantings indoors. Some have narrow, spiky foliage; others have wider, more arching leaves. Most of the popular cultivars are variegated.

If conditioned properly, dracaenas tolerate low light and infrequent watering but grow little, if at all.

LIGHT: Medium to bright. Most tolerate low light.

'Warneckii' is the most popular variety of variegated dracaena, although many other cultivars are more colorful.

WATER: Let potting mix dry slightly between waterings.
HUMIDITY: Average.
TEMPERATURE: Average. Keep dracaenas out of cold drafts.
FERTILIZER: All-purpose during growing season. Do not fertilize plants growing in low light.
DIMENSIONS: Depending on variety, 1 foot to 10 feet tall and 1 foot to 5 feet wide.
REPOTTING: Repot infrequently.
PROPAGATION: From stem cuttings or by air layering.
PROBLEMS: Excess mineral salts and fluoride buildup cause brown leaf tips, so leach frequently. Soil kept too wet or too dry causes leaf drop. Spider mites, mealybugs, and scale insects are possible pests.
TIPS: Pick off yellowed leaves. Trim brown leaf tips.

Deremensis dracaena (*D. deremensis*) comes in a wide range of colors and leaf patterns. All normally grow as single-stemmed plants. Most have long, narrow leaves arching outward all along the stem. It is common to cluster several plants of differing heights in one pot for more visual interest. They remain attractive for many years, as their leaves are long-lived, until they lose their lower foliage. When that happens, start them over again from cuttings or air layer them. They are easily maintained at under 6 feet in height. 'Janet Craig' has very dark green, shiny leaves. 'Janet Craig Compacta' is the same color but has much shorter, upward-pointing leaves, creating the impression of a thick green bottlebrush. 'Warneckii' is the most common variety. It has narrower leaves with thin white stripes along the edges. It has given birth to numerous cultivars, all with varying degrees and colors of variegation in the leaves. These include 'Gold Star', with broad yellow bands on each side of the leaf, and others with self-explanatory names such as 'Lemon Lime',

Madagascar dragontree has narrow, red-margined leaves. 'Colorama' thrives in bright light and high humidity.

'Yellow Stripe', and 'White Stripe'.

Corn plant (*D. fragrans*) has leaves that are longer and broader than those of *D. deremensis*. The plant is grown two ways: as a single stem with leaves reaching outward all along the trunk, in which case it truly looks like a corn plant, or as a series of bare, woody stems that have been topped to produce clusters of foliage on stalks that sprout from just below the cuts. In ample light, the corn plant may occasionally produce sprays of white flowers that are extremely fragrant, although only at night. The scent is delicious but overpowering, so you may find it necessary to remove the flower stalks. This plant easily reaches 20 feet tall, so it must be cut back occasionally. *D. fragrans* 'Massangeana,' with a yellow stripe down the center, is the most common cultivar. Under low light, the stripe turns lime green or may even disappear altogether. 'Victoriae' has the opposite pattern: The center of the leaf is green and the margins are yellow.

D. reflexa 'Variegata', variegated Song of India, needs regular pruning to maintain a pleasing shape.

D. reflexa, Song of India, has a shrubby habit and narrow, upward-pointing dark green leaves.

Madagascar dragontree, or red-margined dracaena *(D. marginata)*, has narrow leaves with a red margin that grow in tufts at the top of gray woody stems. This dracaena is often sold with bent and twisted stems, caused by growing the plants on their sides in the greenhouse until their stems bend upward, then setting them upright again. Like most dracaenas, it eventually gets too tall for indoor use and has to be cut back or rerooted. Several cultivars, such as 'Colorama', with extra wide red bands, and 'Tricolor', whose leaves are striped lengthwise in pink and cream, are available. They generally need more light and higher humidity than the species to do well indoors.

Pleomele *(D. reflexa)*, until recently classified as *Pleomele reflexa*, grows into a large plant with narrow leaves closely set along canelike stems. Several variegated cultivars exist, of which the best known is 'Song of India', with cream-edged leaves. It tends to grow at odd angles and must be pruned to keep it under control. It will grow to the size of a tree if you let it; to keep it within bounds, you'll have to do some artful trimming.

Lucky bamboo, also called ribbon-plant and Sander's dracaena *(D. sanderiana)*, has an upright growth habit with leaves well spaced on lanky stems. It will grow to 5 feet in time, but it is usually sold as a small plant, less than a foot tall. The leathery, narrow leaves may be all green or abundantly striped in white. It does well in a dish garden or terrarium. If the plant gets too leggy or spindly, take cuttings and replant.

The visual effect of lucky bamboo is achieved by removing all its leaves to reveal its bamboo-like stem, then rooting the stem in water or in water and stones. The stems are sometimes trained into a corkscrew pattern or braided together. Surprisingly, lucky bamboo can survive for years in water alone.

Golddust dracaena *(D. surculosa)* is small and shrubby, with a very different habit than other dracaenas, featuring broad, oval leaves on thin, branching stems. The leaves are brilliantly spotted with yellow or cream markings. 'Florida Beauty' is even more abundantly spotted than the species. Golddust dracaena must have good light and you must keep it constantly moist. It is slow-growing and will rarely reach more than 2 feet tall, even in ample light.

The ribbon-like stems of lucky bamboo (D. sanderiana) can be trained to spiral. The plant is often grown in water only.

POTHOS, DEVIL'S IVY

Epipremnum aureum
e-pi-PREM-num OW-ree-um

Pothos (*Epipremnum aureum*, syn. *Scindapsus aureus* or *Pothos aureus*) is a common indoor plant, both in homes and commercial interiors. Itis generally used as a vining groundcover or as a cascading accent plant, often in a hanging basket. It also may grow, as it does in the wild, as a climber. Its aerial roots cling to all but the smoothest surfaces, even on interior walls.

Pothos's heart-shaped, leathery leaves look somewhat like the heart-leaf philodendron's (page 184), but they are irregularly marbled yellow, with better color in good light. *E. aureum* 'Golden Queen' is similar, but with more yellow than green in the leaf. *E. aureum* 'Marble Queen' is just as heavily mottled but with white and gray-green.

Pothos is popular for its marbled foliage and vining habit. It is easy to grow in almost any conditions.

Silver or satin pothos (*E. pictum* 'Argyreum', syn. *Scindapsus pictum* 'Argyreus'*)*, with silver markings on a satiny, heart-shaped leaf and narrower stems less densely clothed in foliage, is also available.

LIGHT: Low to bright.
WATER: Keep evenly moist.
HUMIDITY: Average.
TEMPERATURE: Average.
FERTILIZER: All-purpose during growing period. Not a heavy feeder.
DIMENSIONS: Can be maintained at any height or width desired.
REPOTTING: As needed.
PROPAGATION: Stem cuttings or layering.
PROBLEMS: Extremely low light causes spindly growth. Overwatering leads to root rot. Spider mites and scale insects are possible pests.
TIPS: Remove yellowed leaves. Pinch as needed to maintain the desired size and shape.

EPISCIA, FLAME VIOLET

Episcia
e-PIS-kee-a

Episcias offer both attractive flowers and distinctive foliage.

Episcias resemble their cousin, the African violet (*Saintpaulia*, page 195), with short-stemmed rosettes of large, shiny, slightly downy leaves. However, unlike African violets, they also produce numerous trailing or hanging stolons along which appear smaller plants (offsets). In a hanging basket, plants can thus trail 4 feet or more. Indeed, episcias are generally used in hanging baskets or as groundcover in well-lit terrariums and dish gardens. They produce small red, yellow, orange, pink, lavender, or white flowers.

Several species and hundreds of cultivars exist, each with distinctive foliage texture and coloration. Leaves can have a green, copper, purple, or pink base overlaid with all sorts of metallic colors.

Alsobia is a vining plant that may produce fringed white blossoms.

Alsobia dianthiflora, or laceflower vine (syn. *E. dianthiflora)*, produces much smaller rosettes and velvety, dark green leaves. It readily sends a mass of greenery cascading down from hanging baskets. Heavily fringed white flowers with purple spotting appear intermittently.

LIGHT: Medium to bright. Does well under fluorescent lights.
WATER: Keep evenly moist.
HUMIDITY: High.
TEMPERATURE: Average. Avoid cold.
FERTILIZER: All-purpose during growing period.
DIMENSIONS: 6 inches tall.
REPOTTING: As needed.
PROPAGATION: By division or from leaf cuttings. Remove and root offsets or layer them.
PROBLEMS: Leaf edges roll or die back in dry air. Overwatering leads to crown rot. Low light causes spindly and weak growth. Mealybugs and aphids are possible pests.

HEATH, HEATHER

Erica
e-REE-ka

Heaths are most often grown outdoors in cool northern landscapes. A few cultivars are also commercially grown for cut flowers, but the northern species do not make good houseplants. Numerous species of subtropical heaths from South Africa, however, are offered as gift plants during the winter months.

This group includes mostly smaller types, such as *E. gracilis* and *E. ×hiemalis*. They do well indoors in bright light and cool temperatures year-round. The bell-shaped to tubular blooms are of varying colors and usually quite fragrant. The plants are bushy and produce dense branches and tiny, narrow leaves that are easily pruned or clipped.

Heaths are very sensitive to soluble salts from excessive fertilizer or hard tap water. Where possible, use distilled or rain water.

LIGHT: Bright.
WATER: Water evenly with distilled or rain water.
HUMIDITY: High.
TEMPERATURE: Cool to cold; average for short periods.
FERTILIZER: No need to feed temporary plants.
DIMENSIONS: 8 to 24 inches tall and 8 to 24 inches wide.
REPOTTING: In a peat-based mix.
PROPAGATION: Impractical under most indoor conditions.
PROBLEMS: Short-lived in average temperatures. Spindly and weak in low light. Sensitive to excess mineral salts, so leach frequently or repot annually into acidic growing mix. Powdery mildew is common.
TIPS: Best considered a temporary plant to be enjoyed as a living bouquet, then composted when it finishes flowering.

Smaller heathers, such as *Erica gracilis*, grow well indoors in bright light and cool temperatures.

JAPANESE EUONYMUS

Euonymus japonicus
ew-ON-i-mus ja-PON-ee-kus

Japanese euonymus (*E. japonicus*) is a woody plant that does fairly well indoors if given ample light, although it grows best in cool temperatures. The glossy, dark green toothed foliage is tiny, only about half an inch long. Most varieties available are variegated. Keep these plants constantly moist and do not allow them to become pot bound. Stress makes them susceptible to spider mites and other pests.

Wintercreeper (*E. fortunei*) does best in a cool location, such as an entranceway. The trailing stems eventually climb and attach themselves to vertical surfaces. Unless cool temperatures can be maintained year-round, though, wintercreeper is unlikely to live long enough to have time to cling to any surface. Both species are generally used in dish gardens and terrariums.

LIGHT: Bright.
WATER: Keep evenly moist.
HUMIDITY: Average.
TEMPERATURE: Cool to cold. Tolerates average temperatures if grown in a terrarium.
FERTILIZER: All-purpose during growing period. Not a heavy feeder.
DIMENSIONS: Best maintained by pruning to less than 1 foot high and wide.
REPOTTING: Infrequently.
PROPAGATION: From softwood cuttings.
PROBLEMS: Excess heat causes spindly growth. Overwatering leads to crown rot or leaf drop. Euonymus may not recover if allowed to dry out. Spider mites, leaf miners, aphids, mealybugs, and scale insects are possible pests.
TIPS: Pick off yellowed leaves. Prune at any time to control size.

Euonymus fortunei 'Ivory Jade', also called wintercreeper, thrives in a bright but cool location.

Euphorbia pulcherrima
ew-FOR-bee-a pul-KEH-ri-ma

POINSETTIA

The poinsettia has become the most popular living winter holiday gift in North America. The large white, pink, red, yellow, lime green, or bicolor flowers are actually groups of bracts (colored leaves) that surround clusters of small, inconspicuous true flowers. The plants produce ovate to lance-shaped bracts that are 6 to 12 inches long and frequently lobed or toothed. The leaves on the stems below are identical in shape and usually dark green, sometimes with reddish petioles or veins or with various shades of variegation.

With proper care, poinsettias continue to bloom for several months, into April or May. While blooming, the plants simply need plenty of bright light and protection from drafts and sudden changes in temperature, plus basic watering.

Home gardeners have a choice to make with poinsettias, though, as they are not easy to get to bloom a second time. Are you satisfied with

'Silverstar Marble' (left) and 'Monet' (right) are just two of the many variegated poinsettias available. It's hard to let go of such beauty! To encourage reblooming, treat poinsettias as short-day plants (see page 25).

your plant's long blooming period and ready to let it go after that? If so, simply compost it once it has lost any semblance of beauty. That's the easy way out and the most logical one. After all, perfectly healthy and beautifully formed poinsettias will be available next December at very reasonable prices. And a poinsettia without flowers does not make a particularly attractive houseplant. Besides, getting poinsettias to bloom again is complicated. If you do decide to treat your poinsettia as a temporary plant, it will need no fertilizing or repotting, only watering.

To get poinsettias to bloom again, treat them as short-day plants. You'll find information on this technique on page 25. Even the best of care, though, rarely produces plants as dense and lovely as those sold in nurseries, as the latter are treated with growth retardant products that create especially dense bloom, and such products are not available to home gardeners.

Poinsettias will continue to grow with no special treatment, becoming green foliage plants that are unlikely to bloom.

LIGHT: Temporary plants tolerate all light conditions but need bright light for reblooming.
WATER: Keep evenly moist.
HUMIDITY: Average.
TEMPERATURE: Cool to average. Avoid cold drafts.
FERTILIZER: Not needed if grown as a temporary plant. Use all-purpose fertilizer during the summer growing season for plants being kept.
DIMENSIONS: Usually under 3 feet tall and wide indoors.
REPOTTING: As needed. Not needed if grown as a temporary plant.
PROPAGATION: From softwood cuttings.
PROBLEMS: Cold temperatures can cause leaf and flower damage; make sure plants are well-wrapped for the trip home in winter. Overwatering or underwatering leads to rapid leaf drop, while extreme overwatering can cause root rot. Spider mites and mealybugs are possible pests.
TIPS: Remove faded bracts and leaves. Prune as needed to keep plants dense. Unwrap plants as soon as you get them home: Ethylene gas can build up under the wrapper and cause defoliation.

Bracts, and not true flowers, provide the dramatic colors for which poinsettias are grown.

Exacum affine
EKS-a-kum a-FFF-nee

PERSIAN VIOLET

LIGHT: Bright.
WATER: Keep evenly moist.
HUMIDITY: High.
TEMPERATURE: Average. Avoid cold drafts.
FERTILIZER: Rich in phosphorous
DIMENSIONS: 5 to 12 inches tall and wide.
REPOTTING: Rarely needed with mature plants. Repot seedlings as they grow.
PROPAGATION: From seed. Sow in a small pot and transplant as needed. Stem cuttings do not produce as fine a plant as one grown from seed.
PROBLEMS: Low light causes spindly and weak growth. Excess mineral salts cause leaf-tip burn and stem dieback, so leach frequently. Dry soil damages roots and causes dieback. Overwatering leads to crown rot. Whiteflies are possible pests.
TIP: Best discarded after blooming.

Persian violets are popular because they bloom so abundantly in small pots. They are generally sold in full bloom as gift plants, especially during the winter and spring. Plants are covered with tiny, delightfully scented blue, rose-pink, or white flowers with yellow centers.

Persian violet is in fact a short-lived perennial but is most easily grown as an annual. It has a dense, bushy habit and bears small, shiny, ovate leaves on green to purplish four-angled stems. Buds begin to appear on plants that are only a few months old and flowering can continue nonstop for months. When flowering begins to falter, prune back harshly; sometimes this will produce another flush of bloom. If not, it's time to compost the plant.

Persian violet is covered with sweetly scented flowers for months at a time. When flowering stops, prune or discard.

Fatsia japonica
FAT-see-a ja-PON-i-ka

JAPANESE ARALIA

aralia *(Fatsia japonica)*, a very unlikely mixture, as English ivy is a small-leaved climber and Japanese aralia a large-leaved shrub.
LIGHT: Bright if possible.
WATER: Keep evenly moist.
HUMIDITY: High.
TEMPERATURE: Cool to cold; tolerates average.
FERTILIZER: All-purpose during growing period.
DIMENSIONS: 5 to 12 feet tall and wide outdoors, but easily maintained by pruning to 3 to 4 feet tall and wide indoors.
REPOTTING: As needed.
PROPAGATION: From softwood cuttings or seed, or by air layering.
PROBLEMS: Overwatering leads to root rot. Spider mites, whiteflies, mealybugs, and scale insects are possible pests.
TIPS: Prune as needed to keep growth under control. This plant needs plenty of room.

Japanese aralia is a handsome evergreen plant with bold, lobed leaves of shiny green, occasionally variegated with white. It is fast growing, durable, and tolerant of many environments. It is particularly easy to grow in a cool, well-ventilated location with bright light but adapts to average temperatures. Wash and mist the leaves regularly and feed every 2 weeks during the growing season; otherwise the leaves may yellow from lack of nitrogen.

In winter, move Japanese aralia to a cool spot and water much less frequently than usual. If it begins to look gangly or has misshapen leaves, trim it back severely.

Tree-ivy *(×Fatshedera lizei)* is similar, with smaller leaves and weak stems that need support. It was created by crossing English ivy *(Hedera helix)* with Japanese

Japanese aralia (above) and tree-ivy (below) grow quickly.

FERNS

Maidenhair fern (Adiantum pedatum)

Ferns are primitive plants, popular in households for their delicate, airy appearance. They fail to produce flowers or seed but have sporangia (spore-producing organs), usually in the form of dusty bumps on the underside of the fronds.

Most common indoor ferns produce multiple crowns that you can divide. Cuttings can be made of surface rhizomes. Others have solitary crowns but occasionally produce offsets that you can pot. A few, however, can be reproduced only by spores. See pages 58–59 for more information on spores.

LIGHT: Medium.
WATER: Keep evenly moist.
HUMIDITY: High to very high. A terrarium may be necessary.
TEMPERATURE: Average to cool.

Staghorn fern (Platycerium bifurcatum)

Bird's-nest fern (Asplenium nidus)

FERTILIZER: All-purpose during growing period. Not heavy feeders.
DIMENSIONS: Depending on species, 6 inches to 10 feet tall and 6 inches to 7 feet wide.
REPOTTING: As needed.
PROPAGATION: By division or rhizome cuttings, or from spores.
PROBLEMS: Leaves may die back in dry air or when exposed to drafts. Excess mineral salts cause leaf-tip burn and stem dieback, so leach frequently. Overwatering leads to root rot. Dry soil can be fatal. Mealybugs and scale insects are possible pests.

Rabbit's-foot fern (Davallia)

Boston fern (Nephrolepis exaltata 'Bostoniensis') has arching fronds.

TIPS: Remove yellowed fronds. Rejuvenate tired plants by pruning to soil level and repotting.

Maidenhair fern (*Adiantum pedatum*) has striking black hairlike stalks and leaflets that are broad but frilled. Common varieties include *A. hispidulum*, *A. raddianum*, and *A. tenerum*. They require high humidity, so a terrarium is ideal.

Mother fern (*A. bulbiferum*) has finely divided fronds that arch outward from the crown. The fronds carry tiny plantlets that you can use for propagation, hence the common name. High humidity is a must.

Bird's-nest fern (*Asplenium nidus*) has graceful, outward-arching, undivided fronds that emerge from a fuzzy dark crown that looks like a bird's nest. The plant is easy to grow indoors but difficult to propagate.

Brazilian tree fern (*Blechnum*

Silver tree fern (Cyathea dealbata)

gibbum) forms a neat, ground-hugging rosette of deeply lobed fronds, reaching a diameter of 3 feet. New fronds are an attractive red. As it ages, it forms a narrow, black trunk up to 3 feet tall. This fern must never dry out entirely.

Tree fern *(Cyathea)* grows slowly indoors. The finely divided fronds, which emerge from the top of a 3- or 4-foot-high trunk, may reach 10 feet long, although 2 to 4 feet is more likely in the drier atmosphere of the average home. Purchase a fairly large plant so you can enjoy its tree stature without delay. Keep the soil wet. Place in a humid spot that's protected from drafts. Several *Cyathea* species are available, as well as relatives *Cibotium chamissoi* and *Dicksonia squarrosa.*

Japanese holly fern *(Cyrtomium falcatum)* is perhaps the most tolerant of indoor environments. It is a slow-growing plant that may reach 2 feet wide in time. The fronds are divided into large leaflets 3 to 5 inches long and up to 2 inches wide. They are a glistening green as if covered in wax: An extra-thick cuticle helps protect them from dry air. The cultivar 'Rochfordianum', with more numerous and more deeply cut leaflets, is the most common form.

Rabbit's-foot fern *(Davallia)*, also called squirrel's-foot fern or deer's-foot fern, is noted for its finely divided fronds and furry rhizomes, which creep over and down the sides of the growing container and resemble animal feet. *Davallia* is attractive in a hanging basket as the "feet" cascade or creep downward. You can cut off surplus rhizomes and root them for fast propagation.

Boston fern *(Nephrolepis exaltata* 'Bostoniensis')*, also called sword fern or Dallas fern, is tolerant of indoor conditions. Its arching form and long, dangling fronds make it especially useful for hanging baskets. Some cultivars, such as 'Fluffy

Brake fern (*Pteris* spp.) is also commonly known as table fern.

Ruffles', are small plants with finely divided fronds. *N. exaltata* 'Dallasii' (Dallas fern) and *N. obliterata* 'Kimberley Queen' tolerate dry air. Boston ferns produce thin, snaky, fuzzy green stolons, forming new plants at their tips. Cut them off if you find them unattractive.

Button fern *(Pellaea rotundifolia)* has shiny round leaflets borne on ground-hugging black stems, making the plant look more like a groundcover than a fern. It's ideal for the high humidity of a terrarium.

Staghorn fern *(Platycerium bifurcatum)* is an epiphyte that can grow on a bark slab. Growth is slow, but eventually it develops massive fronds that resemble the antlers of a large animal. Plantlets eventually form at the base of the parent plant and emerge between the large, flat basal fronds. To water staghorn ferns, soak them in a bucket or sink.

Bear's-paw fern *(Phlebodium aureum* syn. *Polypodium aureum)*, also called hare's-foot fern or golden

Japanese holly fern (*Cyrtomium falcatum*) grows well indoors.

polypody fern, got its common names from the furry golden rhizomes that grow along the surface of the soil. The tough blue-green fronds are divided into a few large lobes. The most popular cultivar is *P. aureum* 'Mandaianum', with more deeply cut fronds than the species. All are easy to grow.

Dwarf leatherleaf fern *(Polystichum tsus-simense)* is a slow-growing plant ideally suited to terrariums and dish gardens. The shiny, deep green fronds are deeply cut and tolerant of dry air.

Table fern *(Pteris)*, also called brake fern, fan table fern, or silverleaf fern, comes in a wide variety of frond styles that are variegated and divided in different ways. *P. cretica* 'Albo-lineata' (variegated table fern) bears abroad band of creamy white down each slightly wavy leaflet, and *P. ensiformis* 'Victoriae' (silverleaf fern) has finely divided fronds with a silver band down the middle.

Tree fern (*Dicksonia antarctica*)

Button fern (*Pellaea rotundifolia*)

Ficus
FEE-kus

FIG

Figs make up a large, diverse family of more than 800 tropical trees, shrubs, and vines. It includes not only *F. carica* (edible fig) but also a number of ornamental plants for indoor gardening. Some favorites are listed here.

Figs will do well if they have good light, rich soil kept evenly moist, and frequent feeding. Guard against overwatering, and protect against cold drafts, dry heat, and any sudden changes in environment. Weeping fig (*F. benjamina*), for example, is famous for dropping nearly all of its leaves when moved to lower light conditions. Try to obtain an acclimatized plant—one that has been kept in half shade for several months—so less leaf loss will occur when you bring it home. Or cover a newly purchased fig in a large transparent plastic bag to increase humidity for the first few weeks, until it has adapted to the lower light in your home.

LIGHT: Medium to bright.

WATER: Let potting mix dry slightly between waterings.

HUMIDITY: Average to high.

TEMPERATURE: Average.

FERTILIZER: All-purpose during the growing period.

DIMENSIONS: Depending on the species, 6 inches to 12 feet tall and 6 inches to 10 feet wide. Easily kept at desired dimensions by pruning.

REPOTTING: Repot infrequently.

PROPAGATION: From semi-ripe cuttings, using rooting hormone, or by air layering.

PROBLEMS: Figs are sensitive to excess mineral salts, which cause brown leaf tips and leaf drop, so leach their pots frequently. Sudden changes in lighting may cause massive leaf drop. Spider mites, mealybugs, thrips, and scale insects are possible pests.

TIPS: Prune to shape as required. Wear gloves when handling figs, as the sap causes skin and eye irritation and some people develop allergies to it. It is also slightly toxic, so keep plants out of reach of children.

Creeping fig (*Ficus pumila*)

■ **Shrubby figs** naturally form compact shrubs. They normally don't become much larger than 3 or 4 feet tall; you can keep them considerably smaller by judicious pruning. Some make excellent indoor bonsai.

Mistletoe fig (*F. deltoidea*, also known as *F. diversifolia*) is an interesting indoor shrub. It bears spreading branches covered with small, rounded to wedge-shaped leaves and many tiny (but inedible) green figs that turn red in bright sun.

Left to right: India rubber tree, weeping fig, fiddle-leaf fig

Triangleleaf fig (*F. triangularis*) resembles a large mistletoe fig, but it has larger leaves that have a distinctly triangular outline and rounded edges. Like the mistletoe fig, it produces numerous tiny but inedible figs.

■ **Tree-size figs** are forest giants in the wild but can be kept under 3 to 8 feet or so indoors. Some are sold with braided trunks, giving them extra support. You can prune the smaller-leaved varieties for use as indoor shrubs.

Weeping fig (*F. benjamina*) holds a prominent position among container plants because so many designers favor it. It has pale brown bark, like birch bark, and graceful, arching branches loaded with glossy pointed leaves. It grows from 2 to 18 feet tall. Several variegated forms, with leaves speckled or splotched in white or yellow and others with dark green, nearly black leaves, are also available. This plant often loses most of its leaves when moved to a new location. It requires a period of adjustment, but with care, will flourish again. *F. stricta* is similar to *F. benjamina,* but has larger, less pointed leaves. It is often listed as *F. benjamina* var. *nuda*.

Rubber tree (*F. elastica*) and the larger-leaved *F. elastica* 'Decora' are old favorites. They have bold, deep green leaves on stems 2 to 10 feet tall. 'Variegata' has leaves that make rippling patterns of grass green, metallic gray, and creamy yellow. When a rubber plant becomes too lanky, cut off the top and select a side branch to form a new main shoot, or air layer the plant. This species tolerates low light for several months but needs very bright light to thrive.

Fiddle-leaf fig (*F. lyrata*, also known as *F. pandurata*) is a striking container plant. It has durable, papery, deep green leaves shaped like fiddles and adapts well to moderate light. The plant grows 5 to 10 feet tall or more.

Alii fig (*F. maclellandii* 'Alii') is a more recent introduction, with long, narrow, pointed leaves that give it a bamboo appearance. It makes a striking specimen plant and is more tolerant of being moved than *F. benjamina*.

Indian-laurel (*F. microphylla*, often listed as *F. retusa* or *F. retusa nitida*) is similar to weeping fig but has a slightly larger leaf and a more upright habit. Indian-laurels are commonly seen in commercial interiors. Grow it as a single-stemmed shrub when it is small. As it grows, gradually prune it into a tree form. 'Green Island' is a denser, smaller selection with extra-thick leaves. It's a popular bonsai subject.

■ **Climbing figs** scale great heights into treetops and up walls and cliff faces. Indoors, they rarely produce the clinging aerial roots that would allow them to climb, unless they are in a humid greenhouse. However, they can be trained up trellises, used as groundcovers, or grown as hanging plants. Their thin leaves are more sensitive to dry air than those of other figs.

Creeping fig (*F. pumila*) has tiny, heart-shaped leaves. It's a fast-growing trailer that looks especially attractive in a hanging basket or cascading from a shelf. It also makes an excellent groundcover in terrariums. Variegated and oakleaf versions are available. Remove all-green branches on variegated figs.

Variegated rooting fig (*F. sagittata* 'Variegata', also sold as *F. radicans* 'Variegata') bears thin, pointed, 2- to 4-inch leaves heavily marked with creamy white. It makes an elegant hanging plant. Brown patches in the variegated areas are due to too much cold or sun.

The straplike leaves of Alii fig may be up to a foot long.

Ficus benjamina **'Too Little' grows more slowly than the straight species.**

Fittonia verschaffeltii
fi-TON-ee-a vair-shaf-FELT-ee-eye

Fittonia is popular for its attractive foliage. Pinch out flower spikes and prune regularly to encourage growth.

NERVE PLANT, MOSAIC PLANT

The intricately veined, oval leaves of fittonia grow semi-upright at first, then spread over the soil surface and trail over the sides of the container. They bear small green spikes of tiny white to reddish white flowers that are scarcely noticed. Fittonia's charm comes from its striking green leaves overlaid with an intricate pattern of contrasting veins.

Only one species of *Fittonia* is commonly grown: *F. verschaffeltii*. It has produced numerous clones, all with red, pink or white veins. Some have large leaves, 2 to 4 inches long, while others, such as *F. verschaffeltii argyroneura* 'Minima', with white veins, have especially small ones.

Fittonias are wonderful terrarium plants. The smaller-leaved varieties, with their more restrained growth, look good in smaller terrariums.

LIGHT: Medium.
WATER: Keep evenly moist.
HUMIDITY: High. ('Minima' tolerates average humidity levels).
TEMPERATURE: Average.
FERTILIZER: All-purpose during growing period. Not a heavy feeder.
DIMENSIONS: 6 inches tall and an unlimited spread.
REPOTTING: As needed.
PROPAGATION: From stem cuttings. Stems self-layer.
PROBLEMS: Dry air causes leaf drop or kills the plant outright. Low light causes spindly growth. Overwatering leads to root rot. Aphids, mealybugs, and scale insects are possible pests.
TIPS: Prune occasionally to stimulate even growth. Water carefully: Soil must remain at least slightly moist or the plant will die.

Fuchsia ×hybrida
FUKS-ee-a HY-bri-da

Fuchsias are perfect for hanging baskets. Move them outdoors to a cool, shady spot during summer.

FUCHSIA, LADY'S EARDROPS

The pendant flowers of fuchsias have brightly hued sepals that flare open to reveal petals in often contrasting colors. Colors range from white to pink, red, lavender, violet, and purple. Many plants have double flowers.

Some 8,000 cultivars of fuchsia exist in a great number of shapes and sizes, with green, bronze, or variegated leaves. Many cultivars have pendulous branches and are therefore excellent subjects for hanging baskets.

During summer, keep fuchsias in moderate light, but avoid burning sun or stifling heat and humidity. They're often best moved outdoors to a cool, shaded spot. While they are in bloom, feed frequently and always keep the soil moist.
LIGHT: Bright.
WATER: Keep evenly moist. Water sparingly in winter.
HUMIDITY: Average.

TEMPERATURE: Average to cool; cool to cold in winter.
FERTILIZER: All-purpose during growing period.
DIMENSIONS: Depending on cultivar, 10 inches to 10 feet tall and 10 inches to 5 feet wide.
REPOTTING: Annually in spring.
PROPAGATION: From softwood or semi-ripe cuttings (may need rooting hormone), or from seed.
PROBLEMS: Soil that is too moist or too dry causes leaf drop. Summer heat causes dieback. Fuchsias are highly susceptible to whiteflies; check plants for pests before bringing them indoors in the fall. Spider mites, thrips, mealybugs, and scale insects also are possible pests.
TIPS: Keep in bright light for bloom all winter. Otherwise let it go dormant, pruning back harshly and keeping its growing mix just barely moist. When dormant, it can be stored in a cold room without light.

GARDENIA, CAPE JASMINE

Gardenia augusta
gar-DEN-ee-a ow-GUS-ta

The common gardenia (*G. augusta*, formerly *G. jasminoides*) is the type most often grown indoors. It's a spectacular plant in bloom and its creamy, spiraling blossoms emit a heady aroma.

G. *augusta* has large, glossy, dark green leaves and produces an abundance of large white flowers that turn cream-colored after a few days. Most have double flowers. Gardenias bloom regularly from spring through fall and sometimes throughout the year.

Gardenias can be difficult to grow indoors. The secret is to provide the proper night temperature: The plant will not set flower buds when temperatures exceed 65°F. Gardenias kept indoors also need high humidity and plenty of sunlight but never searing heat. They are best suited to a cool greenhouse.

LIGHT: Bright to intense.
WATER: Keep evenly moist.
HUMIDITY: High.
TEMPERATURE: Cool.
FERTILIZER: Acid with added trace elements.
DIMENSIONS: Usually 1 to 5 feet tall and 1 to 3 feet wide indoors.
REPOTTING: Infrequently. Use an acid growing mix.
PROPAGATION: From softwood or semi-ripe cuttings; use rooting hormone.
PROBLEMS: Bud drop is frequent and caused by overly dry air, high temperatures, or a sudden change in environment. Plants purchased in bud, for example, often drop their buds when brought home. If soil is too wet or too dry, leaves drop too. Poor light may prevent blooms. Whiteflies, mealybugs, and mildew are possible.
TIPS: Prune in early spring. Pinch back tips of young or regrowing plants to improve form, but be careful not to remove flower buds when pruning.

Gardenias bloom indoors if nighttime temperatures are cool. They need bright light and high humidity.

VELVET PLANT, PURPLE PASSION PLANT

Gynura aurantiaca 'Purple Passion'
gin-EW-ra ow-ran-ti-AH-ka

Velvet plant is a trailing species with lobed leaves densely coated in purple hairs, formerly sold as *G. sarmentosa*. New leaves are particularly colorful.

'Purple Passion' is easy to grow and attractive in a hanging basket if pruned. With enough light, the plant produces clusters of tiny flowers with dingy white petals and orange-yellow centers. It is best to pick these off quickly, however, because they have an unpleasant odor and will produce a mess of dropping petals and seedpods. Low light may prevent flowering.

There is also a variegated form called *G. aurantiaca* 'Aureo-variegata' that appears pink and purple from a distance, although the actual leaf variegation is yellowish. It is just as attractive and easy to grow as 'Purple Passion'.

LIGHT: Bright.
WATER: Keep evenly moist.
HUMIDITY: Average.
TEMPERATURE: Average.
FERTILIZER: All-purpose during growing period.
DIMENSIONS: 10 to 24 inches tall and 10 to 48 inches wide.
REPOTTING: As needed.
PROPAGATION: Stem cuttings.
PROBLEMS: Excess mineral salts cause leaf-tip burn and stem dieback, so leach frequently. Low light causes spindly growth. Spider mites, whiteflies, and aphids are possible pests.
TIPS: Prune to shape. It's often best to start this plant over again from cuttings after a year or so, as older plants become woody and unproductive.

Velvet plant's flowers are messy and foul-smelling. Picking them off when they appear encourages the foliage.

Hedera
HEH-de-ra

IVY

HUMIDITY: Average.

TEMPERATURE: Cool to cold are best, but it adapts readily to average temperatures.

FERTILIZER: All-purpose during growing period.

DIMENSIONS: Unlimited height and spread; but you can control it by pruning. Trailing types can dangle 6 feet or more.

REPOTTING: Repot as needed.

PROPAGATION: From softwood cuttings.

PROBLEMS: Spider mites can be a major problem, especially in dry air, which also causes brown leaf tips. Small leaves spaced far apart and variegated leaves that turn green indicate poor light. Aphids, mealybugs, and scale insects are possible pests.

TIPS: Prune to control and direct growth. Pinch branch tips on cultivars that don't self-branch to make them denser.

Canary Island ivy (*Hedera canariensis*), also called Algerian ivy, is a fast-growing plant with large, brilliantly glossy leaves. You can grow it in a basket or train it on a trellis. The most popular cultivar, *H. canariensis* 'Variegata' (also known as 'Gloire-de-Marengo'), has green leaves with white variegation.

Canary Island ivy differs from other ivies in that it needs some warmth. Of subtropical origin, it does best with average temperatures year round.

English ivy (*Hedera helix*) is the original ivy. Other climbing plants (German ivy, Swedish ivy, grape ivy, etc.) are called ivies because their growth habit is similar to *Hedera* species. Countless varieties of this trailing and climbing plant are available. 'Merion Beauty' has small leaves in the characteristic star-shaped English ivy form. 'Itsy Bitsy' is a tiny variety. Others have leaves that are curled, waved, or crinkled. 'Curlilocks' is an example. Still others have color variegation, such as the yellow-gold 'Gold Dust' and white-marked 'Glacier'.

Wild ivies rarely branch, producing long stems with well-spaced leaves instead. This is also true of many older cultivars. As these trail downward, they take on a light, airy look. Many modern cultivars, though, are self-branching and produce full stems with numerous secondary growths, giving them a naturally fuller appearance. Both forms are attractive in their own right, so choose according to your own tastes.

Fast-growing Algerian ivy thrives in warm household temperatures.

The genus *Hedera* is a small one, with only 8 to 12 species, but that doesn't stop it from being among the most popular houseplants in the world. The two species most commonly grown indoors offer hundreds of varieties to choose from. Combine that with a general ease of culture and good adaptability to home conditions, and *Hedera* comes out a winner.

Ivies are climbers with 3- to 5-lobed evergreen leaves. In the wild, they use clinging aerial roots to climb up walls, trunks, and rocks. Indoors, they are usually used as trailing plants for hanging baskets, although you also can train them to climb a trellis. Or let them climb rough surfaces, like a brick fireplace wall, for example. You can also use them in large planters as a groundcover. Ivies never bloom indoors.

LIGHT: Medium to bright. Tolerates low light if all other needs are met.

WATER: Keep evenly moist.

English ivy 'Shamrock' is just one of dozens of *Hedera* species. Choose from a variety of foliage types and sizes as well as green or variegated varieties. All trail or climb and grow well in cool indoor conditions.

Hedychium coronarium
hay-DY-kee-um ko-ro-NAH-ree-um

Ginger lily is a tall plant with long, lance-shaped glossy green leaves on either side of a tall, slender, slightly arching, reedlike stem. The white flowers with yellow markings are produced in terminal clusters in late summer to fall and may last for several weeks.

Grow ginger lily in containers. You can put it outside for the summer, if you wish, but be sure to bring it indoors before evenings become cool. When the stems start to deteriorate, usually in December, stop watering, then cut them back to near ground level and store the rhizomes nearly dry in a cool spot until new sprouts appear in spring.

LIGHT: Bright; intense in winter if maintained in growth.
WATER: Keep evenly moist, even soaking wet; allow to dry during dormancy.

White Ginger Lily, Garland Flower

HUMIDITY: High.
TEMPERATURE: Average to high; cool when dormant. Keep it out of cold drafts.
FERTILIZER: All-purpose during growing period.
DIMENSIONS: 4 to 6 feet tall and 3 feet wide indoors.
REPOTTING: In late winter or early spring.
PROPAGATION: Division of rhizomes at repotting.
PROBLEMS: Dry air, poor light, or irregular watering causes failure to bloom. Weak stems that need staking indicate a lack of light. Leaves may dry out along the edges in dry air. Spider mites and aphids are possible pests.
TIP: If you provide bright light, even warmth, and high humidity in winter, this plant will grow, and even bloom, sporadically throughout the year.

Ginger lily blooms in late summer, so move it outdoors where you can enjoy it on your patio or balcony.

Heliconia
hay-lee-KON-ee-a

Lobster claws are creeping, rhizomatous plants. Their upright green or bronze leaves are paddle-like or spoon-shaped, rising directly from the ground.

Flower stalks bear brilliantly colored boat-shaped bracts in two opposite rows (or sometimes in a spiral) usually in the summer but also sporadically throughout the year. Bract colors include red, pink, orange, and yellow; bracts can remain in top shape for months. The inflorescence can be upright or pendant. The actual flowers poke up from the bracts and can be green, red, orange, yellow, or white, often blooming in a hue strikingly different from that of the bracts.

Most heliconias, though, are far too large for pot culture. Look instead for the new dwarf heliconias, mostly hybrids of *H. psittacorum*, the parrot flower heliconia. Keeping

Dwarf Heliconia, Lobster Claw

them underpotted helps maintain a smaller size.
LIGHT: Intense.
WATER: Keep evenly moist.
HUMIDITY: High.
TEMPERATURE: Average to high. Avoid cold drafts.
FERTILIZER: All-purpose during growing period.
DIMENSIONS: Depending on variety, 2 to 10 feet tall and 3 feet wide.
REPOTTING: As needed.
PROPAGATION: By division of rhizomes in spring.
PROBLEMS: Grows weakly at cool temperatures; must have heat to do well.

Brown leaf edges indicate dry air. Spider mites are a problem when the air is too dry.
TIP: Although lobster claws grow from rhizomes, like many indoor bulbs they remain green all year long and will dry out and die if their rhizomes are left exposed to the air for more than a day or so.

Heliconia is a banana relative. Add a few stems of 'Belize' to give cut-flower arrangements a tropical touch.

Heliotropium arborescens
hay-lee-o-TRO-pee-um ar-bo-RES-enz

H. arborescens 'Marine' has highly fragrant purple flowers.

HELIOTROPE, CHERRY PIE

Heliotrope is a bushy, woody shrub often grown as an annual, as it grows from seed to bloom in only a few short months. Most modern varieties are dwarfs and many remain under 12 inches tall even without pruning.

The rough, wrinkled, dark green oval leaves of heliotrope often have a purple tinge and seem to beg to be touched, but some people find the sap irritating to the skin and eyes. Instead, just bring your nose to within smelling range of the dense clusters of tiny flowers. Heavenly! Many hybrids are available with purple, blue, or white flowers. Some paler shades seem to be the most highly scented.

Helios was the Greek god of the sun, so it's no surprise the heliotrope is a sun-lover. Where light is low, it may bloom only sporadically, but where there is plenty of light, expect bloom from spring through fall.

LIGHT: Intense.
WATER: Keep evenly moist.
HUMIDITY: High.
TEMPERATURE: Average; cool in winter.
FERTILIZER: Balanced.
DIMENSIONS: 10 to 18 inches tall and wide.
REPOTTING: As needed.
PROPAGATION: From softwood cuttings or seed.
PROBLEMS: Low light causes spindly and weak growth. Overwatering or underwatering causes leaf drop. Whiteflies are often a serious pest problem.
TIPS: Prune after flowering. Discard older plants when they become less productive; start new ones from cuttings. Heliotrope is slightly toxic, so keep out of reach of children.

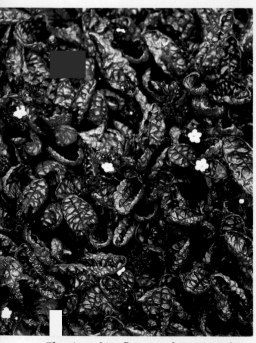

Hemigraphis alternata
hay-mi-GRAF-is al-ter-NAH-ta

The tiny white flowers of *Hemigraphis alternata* 'Metallica Crispa' stand out against its colorful foliage.

RED-IVY, RED-FLAME IVY

Red-ivy (*Hemigraphis alternata*, syn. *H. colorata*) is a creeping plant with oval to heart-shaped scalloped leaves that display an attractive combination of metallic violet above and wine red underneath. New growth is upright at first, then bends at the base, rooting as it creeps. As a result, red-ivy looks best in a hanging basket where its stems arch downward and hide the container. With regular pinching, you can create a perfect sphere of shiny purple foliage.

Short-lived but numerous tubular five-lobed white flowers appear on terminal spikes during spring and summer. The flowers are tiny but show up beautifully against the shiny metallic purple background.

The only other variety grown is the purple waffle plant (*H.* 'Exotica'). It produces larger, puckered leaves with a purple sheen. They are deep red underneath and give the whole plant a deep purplish-red coloration. Like red-ivy, it produces tubular five-lobed white flowers in the spring and summer, and looks best in a hanging basket.

LIGHT: Medium to bright.
WATER: Let potting mix dry slightly between waterings.
HUMIDITY: High.
TEMPERATURE: Average. Keep plants away from cold drafts.
FERTILIZER: All-purpose during growing period. Not a heavy feeder.
DIMENSIONS: 6 inches tall and 18 inches wide.
REPOTTING: As needed.
PROPAGATION: From stem cuttings.
PROBLEMS: Low light causes spindly, pale growth. Overwatering leads to crown rot. Whiteflies are possible pests.
TIP: Prune regularly for a full, well-balanced appearance.

CHINESE HIBISCUS

Hibiscus rosa-sinensis
hi-BIS-kus RO-sa-si-NEN-sis

A woody shrub, hibiscus bears huge saucer-shaped single or double flower blooms in pink, red, yellow, orange, or white. Individual hibiscus flowers last only one day (two for double types), but the plant may bloom throughout the year. The shiny dark green leaves vary from heart-shaped to deeply lobed and maple-shaped. Several cultivars, like the red-flowered 'Cooperi', have leaves marbled with green, white, and sometimes pink, but they don't bloom well.

Chinese hibiscus loves sun. The more it gets, especially in winter, the better it blooms. Water regularly as hot sun leads to desiccation. Fertilize regularly for best bloom. This plant is usually treated before purchase with a growth retardant to keep it dense and compact. When the effect wears off, the plant becomes more open and requires trimming.

LIGHT: Bright to intense.
WATER: Keep evenly moist.
HUMIDITY: High.
TEMPERATURE: Average to high.
FERTILIZER: Rich in phosphorous.
DIMENSIONS: Prune to maintain 2 to 5 feet tall and wide.
REPOTTING: As needed.
PROPAGATION: From softwood or semi-ripe cuttings, with rooting hormone.
PROBLEMS: Lack of bloom in poor light. Spider mites are a serious problem in dry air, causing leaves and buds to yellow and drop off. Whiteflies, aphids, mealybugs, and scale insects are possible pests.
TIPS: Keep well pruned. A weekly shower keeps spider mites at bay.

Although Chinese hibiscus flowers last only a day or two, the plant will bloom year-round in bright to intense light.

AMARYLLIS

Hippeastrum
hi-pee-AS-trum

The 1- to 2-foot amaryllis stems bear clusters of trumpet flowers 8 to 10 inches wide. They come in both single and double blooms and a wide array of colors—reds, purples, pinks, whites, yellows, and more. The straplike leaves emerge as, or after, the flowers bloom.

Pot bulbs in mid-autumn, leaving the top one-third exposed. When a flower stem appears, move to a well lit location. After flowering, the foliage will grow for several months. Keep it well watered, well fertilized, and in the brightest light possible during this period: This is when it stores up the energy it will need to flower the following winter. By late summer, when foliage looks a bit ragged, allow the plant to dry out and become dormant, then cut off the yellowed leaves. Start watering again about 2 months later or when new flower buds appear.

LIGHT: Bright.
WATER: Keep evenly moist; dry during fall dormancy.
HUMIDITY: Average.
TEMPERATURE: Average.
FERTILIZER: Rich in potassium when plant is in leaf.
DIMENSIONS: 12 to 24 inches tall and 12 inches wide.
REPOTTING: Every three or four years; blooms best when pot-bound.
PROPAGATION: By division, from bulblets that appear next to the parent, or from seed.
PROBLEMS: Symptoms of insufficient light include lack of bloom; long, pale green leaves; and a bulb that shrinks in size. Overwatering leads to root rot. Rotting, hollow bulbs indicate narcissus fly infestation.
TIPS: Remove yellowed leaves. *Hippeastrum* is toxic, so keep out of reach of children.

Hippeastrum bulbs come in a great variety of colors, but 'Red Lion' is one of the most popular.

Homalomena rubescens
ho-mah-lo-MEE-na roo-BES-senz

HEART-LEAF HOMALOMENA

These philodendron relatives are native to deep shade in the forests of South America, a situation much like a north window in a home, and have shown themselves very amenable to indoor growing. They even survive in dark corners indoors, a place few other plants tolerate, although they do grow better with moderate light.

The main species marketed today is *H. rubescens*, with 4- to 6-inch heart-shaped leaves on sturdy petioles. The leaves are dark green and have a waxy appearance. It blooms readily indoors, but the greenish spathes are of little interest. 'Emerald Gem' has dark green leaves and is perhaps the most widely

Homalomena species like this 'Emerald Gem' grow slowly but are tolerant of even low light indoors.

grown cultivar. 'Queen of Hearts' has leaves with a distinct reddish tinge, and 'King of Spades' has nearly black-green leaves, much darker than the others. Silver shield (*H. wallisii*) has thick, oblong, dark green leaves mottled with yellow. It needs very high humidity.

LIGHT: Low to medium.
WATER: Keep evenly moist.
HUMIDITY: Average to high.
TEMPERATURE: Average to high.
FERTILIZER: All-purpose during growing period. Not a heavy feeder.
DIMENSIONS: 18 inches tall and 24 inches wide.
REPOTTING: As needed.
PROPAGATION: Divide offsets.
PROBLEMS: Generally problem-free. Long, weak petioles indicate poorer-than-desirable light. Thrips and whiteflies are possible pests.
TIPS: Slow to mature, so buy a plant large enough for your immediate needs. Remove yellowed leaves.

Hoya carnosa
HOY-a kar-NO-sa

HOYA, WAX PLANT

Hoyas are slow-growing, vining plants with thick leaves. Given enough light (medium light often will do), they produce clusters of extremely fragrant, waxy, star-shaped flowers in summer or fall, depending on the cultivar. Most hoyas are perfumed only at night. The flowers form on the same spur year after year, so be careful not to prune off these leafless vine extensions. Train the plants on a trellis or use them in a hanging basket. The vines get quite long, but you can double them back to give the plant a denser appearance.

The most common plants are varieties of *H. carnosa*. It has smooth, shiny, dark green leaves and pinkish white flowers with dark red crowns. It has given rise to numerous cultivars with variously variegated or even crinkled leaves. *H. bella* is a small-leaved species that is also popular. Rather than climbing,

its branches hang down, making it attractive in a hanging basket. It also produces its clusters of sweetly scented starry white flowers at the stem tips.

LIGHT: Medium to bright.
WATER: Keep evenly moist.
HUMIDITY: Average.
TEMPERATURE: Average to high.
FERTILIZER: Rich in phosphorous.
DIMENSIONS: Essentially unlimited in height and spread. Will grow to cover its trellis or other support.
REPOTTING: Repot infrequently; blooms best when pot-bound.
PROPAGATION: From softwood cuttings.
PROBLEMS: Inadequate light causes lack of bloom. Mealybugs and scale insects are possible pests.
TIPS: Hoyas tend to become straggly with time and will need some serious trimming.

Wax plant produces clusters of star-shaped flowers along its vines. Most blooms are fragrant only at night.

FLORIST'S HYDRANGEA, HORTENSIA

Hydrangea macrophylla
hye-DRAIN-gee-a mak-ro-FIL-la

Hydrangeas produce immense clusters 8 to 10 inches in diameter made up of ½- to 1-inch flowers. Shiny, oval leaves 6 inches long set off the flowers. The blooms are pink, red, white, blue, or mauve.

Purchase in bloom during the spring or summer and use for temporary decoration. The blooms last up to 6 weeks if the plant is kept in a cool location and if the soil is never allowed to dry out. Since florist's hydrangea transpires abundantly, it may need daily watering during flowering.

Under most circumstances, you should consider florist's hydrangea only a temporary visitor to the average home. In Zones 5 through 9, though, you can plant hydrangea outdoors for summer blooms.

LIGHT: Bright.

WATER: Keep very moist. Hydrangea may need several waterings a week when in bloom.

HUMIDITY: Average.

TEMPERATURE: Cool to cold; tolerates average temperatures.

FERTILIZER: No need to fertilize temporary plants. Otherwise, all-purpose during growing period.

DIMENSIONS: Usually 1 to 3 feet tall and wide for indoor plants.

REPOTTING: Not required unless you're keeping florist's hydrangea indoors year-round.

PROPAGATION: From softwood and semi-ripe cuttings.

PROBLEMS: The plant withers rapidly when its roots lack water and does not always recover when watered again. Leaves and flowers desiccate in dry air. It's sensitive to mineral salts, so leach frequently.

TIPS: Buy this plant in full bloom. Buds that don't show color may fail to open indoors. Prune harshly after blooms fade.

Florist's hydrangea is typically used as a temporary houseplant and needs ample watering while it is in bloom.

POLKA-DOT PLANT, FRECKLE-FACE

Hypoestes phyllostachya
hi-po-ES-teez fil-lo-STAK-ee-a

It's hard to believe the beautifully marbled leaves of the modern polka-dot plant were once only medium-green leaves modestly spotted with tiny specks of the palest pink. Recent hybrids have bold speckles of bright pink, red, or white, sometimes covering more than half the leaf's surface. Even the rangy, open habit of the wild plant has been tamed: Today's cultivars are dense, thick plants entirely covered with foliage.

The common names for *Hypoestes* come from the unusual pink spots on its leaves (its botanical name formerly was *H. sanguinolenta*). It's a bushy, herbaceous plant that grows rapidly in good light. Terminal spikes of tiny magenta to lilac flowers appear from late summer to winter but are of little interest and can simply be pinched off.

You can start seed for polka-dot plant at any season. Simply sow the seeds on the surface of a sterile seed bed and lightly cover with soil.

LIGHT: Bright.

WATER: Keep evenly moist.

HUMIDITY: High.

TEMPERATURE: Average.

FERTILIZER: All-purpose during growing period.

REPOTTING: As needed.

DIMENSIONS: 9 to 18 inches tall and 9 to 12 inches wide.

PROPAGATION: From softwood cuttings or seed.

PROBLEMS: Spindly growth in low light. Short-lived. Powdery mildew can be a problem.

TIPS: Prune regularly to keep the plant dense. Older plants tend to become weak and unattractive; start over with fresh cuttings or new seed.

Prune often and pinch out flower spikes to keep polka-dot plant bushy.

IMPATIENS, BUSY LIZZIE

Impatiens walleriana
im-PAT-ee-enz wo-la-ree-AH-na

Long before anyone considered growing *Impatiens walleriana* outdoors, it was a popular indoor plant, handed down from generation to generation. Of course, today it is the most popular garden annual of all, offered in a mind-boggling array of colors—pinks, reds, oranges, purples, whites, and bicolors—and forms—dwarfs, standards, doubles, variegates, and others. The fact that it blooms constantly, year-round, both indoors and out, is a major plus. But it also has a downside: a terrible sensitivity to spider mites.

There are too many specific cultivars to mention. Simply go to your local garden center and pick out whatever plant strikes your fancy. Many gardeners reserve bedding annuals, sold in flats and trays, for the outdoor garden, keeping the prize jewels—double-flowered and variegated cultivars that don't come true from seed and can only be propagated from cuttings—for their indoor gardens.

Although impatiens are true perennials, they are usually grown as summer annuals, a few specimens of which are then overwintered indoors. Either dig up and cut back a garden plant in late summer or take a few cuttings from it (they root readily). You can grow and bloom impatiens all year long indoors.

The New Guinea hybrids (*I. hawkeri*) were developed from a number of species native to that country. These plants are also perennials grown as annuals and are well-suited to container culture. The flowers are large and brilliantly colored in pink, red, orange, lavender, or purple. Their green or bronze foliage is often variegated with bright patches of yellow or white. New Guinea hybrids need plenty of water and fertilizer and more light than other impatiens. They also grow best in cooler temperatures.

Plant collectors enjoy the curious "Congo cockatoo," *I. niamniamensis*. This is an upright, shrubby, succulent impatiens up to 3 feet tall with large, broad leaves. Bright yellow with a rolled-up red spur and an apple-green corolla, the flower is impressive. The plant tends to lose its lower leaves over time. When there is more bare stalk than bloom, take cuttings and start it anew.

LIGHT: Bright; intense in winter.
WATER: Keep evenly moist.
HUMIDITY: Average; high humidity helps prevent spider mites.
TEMPERATURE: Average.
FERTILIZER: All-purpose, year-round.
DIMENSIONS: Depending on the cultivar, 8 to 24 inches tall and wide.
REPOTTING: Pot seedlings several times. Plants that are slightly pot-bound bloom more profusely.
PROPAGATION: From stem cuttings or seed.
PROBLEMS: Very susceptible to spider mites in dry air. Overly dry or moist soil causes leaf drop. Poor light prevents bloom. If you bring an impatiens in from the garden in fall, be sure it is free of pests, particularly whiteflies and spider mites.
TIPS: Pinch as necessary for compact growth. Spider mites are so common on indoor impatiens that a weekly shower to rinse off the pests should be part of your routine care.

Impatiens walleriana was enjoyed as a houseplant long before it was introduced into the outdoor landscape.

Impatiens hawkeri 'Celebretta Purple' is a New Guinea hybrid with yellow-variegated, dark green leaves.

Iresine herbstii
ee-res-EE-nay HAIRBST-ee-eye

The ornamental foliage of this spectacular plant is an intense, full-bodied red, as its common name bloodleaf suggests. *I. herbstii* has leaves that could be called reverse heart shaped. They're curiously pinched at the tips, an odd appearance that also gives it the old-fashioned name chicken gizzard plant. The leaves are deep purple with red veins, and the stems are pinkish red; when sunlight shines through, the plants appear to be fluorescent cherry red. *I. herbstii* 'Aureo-reticulata' has the same leaf shape but produces green leaves lined with yellow veins and occasional patches of brilliant red. 'Purple Lady' is a newer introduction with almost black leaves.

Just as colorful, *I. lindenii*, also called bloodleaf, has the same coloration—purple leaves with red veins—but its leaves are pointed at

BLOODLEAF, CHICKEN GIZZARD PLANT

the tips. 'Formosa' has green leaves with bright yellow veins. Neither species blooms indoors and the green to whitish flowers are of little interest anyway.

LIGHT: Bright to intense.
WATER: Keep evenly moist.
HUMIDITY: High.
TEMPERATURE: Average.
FERTILIZER: All-purpose during growing period.
DIMENSIONS: 10 inches to 5 feet tall and 8 inches to 3 feet wide.
REPOTTING: As needed.
PROPAGATION: From softwood cuttings. Seeds sometimes available.
PROBLEMS: Low light causes spindly growth. Spider mites and aphids are possible pests.
TIP: Looks better when pinched or pruned regularly to desired height.

Iresine herbstii **'Brilliantissima' has rich crimson leaves veined with cherry red. Pinch regularly to encourage growth.**

Ixora
iks-OH-ra

Ixoras are woody shrubs with simple, untoothed, dark green leaves. They produce dense, rounded clusters of flowers at the stem tips. The individual flowers are actually a trumpet shape, with a narrow tube spreading into four lobes, but they are so densely arranged that you see only the lobes, not the trumpet. The most common species is *I. coccinea*, which has bright red flowers, but modern cultivars are often hybrids with other species and come in a full range of reds, yellows, oranges, and white. Unlike many brightly colored flowers, they are often scented.

Another nice trait of ixora is that it blooms from a very young age. Barely rooted cuttings are often already in flower. Pruning the stems after they bloom stimulates denser growth and more flowers. Shrubs that aren't pruned tend to become leggy and may need staking.

IXORA, FLAME-OF-THE-WOODS

LIGHT: Intense.
WATER: Keep evenly moist.
HUMIDITY: High.
TEMPERATURE: Average.
FERTILIZER: All-purpose during growing season.
DIMENSIONS: 2 to 8 feet tall and 2 to 6 feet wide.
REPOTTING: As needed.
PROPAGATION: From softwood cuttings.
PROBLEMS: Low light causes spindly growth and poor bloom. Aphids and scale insects are possible pests.
TIPS: Prune after blooming. Taller cultivars need considerable pruning to remain a reasonable size indoors, but there are now many dwarf cultivars that naturally remain under 3 feet tall. You can even keep them pruned to less than 12 inches.

Ixora flowers come in many colors and are often scented.

JASMINE

Jasminum
yas-MEEN-um

True jasmines are climbing plants or shrubs that bear numerous white or yellow flowers. Most are highly scented, especially at night. Some are even used in the perfume industry. Their flowering season varies, but the most popular ones are winter or early spring bloomers.

Most jasmines are twining and viny, requiring staking and regular pinching. Even the shrubby types have long branches that lean up against other plants and need support. The foliage, generally feathery, is often shiny, making the plant attractive even when not in bloom.

Among the true jasmines, *J. polyanthum* is probably the most common. A winter bloomer, it bears dozens of scented, star-shaped, narrow-petaled white flowers at a time, even as a small plant. You can grow it as a climber on a trellis or allow it to trail attractively from a hanging basket.

Also popular is *J. officinale affine* (*J. grandiflorum*), called poet's jasmine or French perfume jasmine. It bears highly fragrant pink-tinged white flowers from spring through fall, stopping only in midwinter. It is a vigorous, woody climber and needs a trellis or other support.

J. sambac 'Maid of Orleans' and *J. sambac* 'Grand Duke of Tuscany', known as Arabian jasmines, produce rose-shaped semidouble or double flowers that open a creamy white and fade to purple. Pungently scented, they bloom intermittently throughout the year. Arabian jasmines are shrubbier than most other jasmines and, if carefully pruned on a regular basis, can be grown as bushes.

If you prefer smaller plants with a shrubby habit, try Parker's jasmine (*J. parkeri*). It forms a dome of deep green foliage only 12 inches high and 16 inches across and bears great quantities of fragrant yellow flowers in late winter and spring.

The name jasmine has also been

J. polyanthum is covered with fragrant white flowers in winter.

applied to many other scented plants, especially climbing ones. Among the false jasmines, *Cestrum nocturnum* (night-blooming jasmine) bears greenish-cream flowers from summer to fall, scented only at night. Both *Gelsemium sempervirens* (Carolina jessamine), with scented trumpet-shaped yellow blossoms, and *Trachelospermum jasminoides* (Confederate jasmine), with highly perfumed star-shaped white flowers, bloom in late winter or early spring.

LIGHT: Intense.

WATER: Keep evenly moist. Water sparingly in winter.

HUMIDITY: Average.

TEMPERATURE: Average; cool to cold in winter.

FERTILIZER: Rich in phosphorous.

DIMENSIONS: As climbing plants, most reach over 6 feet tall and wide, depending on their support.

REPOTTING: As needed.

PROPAGATION: From softwood cuttings, or by layering low-growing branches.

PROBLEMS: Low light causes spindly growth and poor bloom. Leaf drop is due to underwatering or overwatering. Spider mites are a problem in dry air. Aphids, mealybugs, and scale insects are also possible pests.

TIPS: For best effect, train jasmines up a trellis or other support. Prune after flowering, being careful not to remove branches with flower buds.

With regular pruning, Arabian jasmines become shrubby plants. Like this 'Maid of Orleans', they bloom off and on throughout the year.

Justicia brandegeeana
jus-TIS-ee-a brand-ee-gee-AH-na

Shrimp plant (*J. brandegeeana*, syn. *Beloperone guttata*) is a woody, branching, evergreen shrub with simple, elliptic, dark green leaves. It is easily maintained under 3 feet tall by regular pruning and pinching. The main attraction is the long-lasting pendant inflorescence, 3 to 4 inches long and covered with scale-shaped bracts in salmon pink. The true flowers are white and protrude from the bracts. Cultivars have different colors: 'Chartreuse' has lime-green bracts and 'Yellow Queen' has glowing yellow ones, for example. 'Variegata' has shrimp-pink bracts and leaves sprinkled with snowy white.

King's crown or Brazilian plume (*J. carnea*) is a much larger, more robust-looking plant with large oval medium-green leaves up to 8 inches long on four angled stems. It bears

SHRIMP PLANT

massive upright terminal spikes of rose-pink flowers held well above the foliage. Blooms usually appear in spring, but if the plant is regularly deadheaded, it will repeat bloom until late fall.

LIGHT: Bright.
WATER: Keep evenly moist.
HUMIDITY: Average for *J. brandegeeana*. High for *J. carnea*.
TEMPERATURE: Average.
FERTILIZER: All-purpose during growing season.
DIMENSIONS: Usually 2 to 3 feet tall and wide; larger if not pruned.
REPOTTING: As needed.
PROPAGATION: From softwood cuttings or seed.
PROBLEMS: Low light causes spindly growth and poor bloom. Spider mites and whiteflies can be pests.
TIP: Prune *J. brandegeeana* carefully because it produces flower buds year-round.

Shrimp plant (*J. brandegeeana*, above) and King's crown (*J. carnea*, below) are grown for their showy flowers.

Lantana camara
lan-TAH-na ka MAH-ra

Lantanas are woody shrubs, bearing clusters of small trumpet-shaped blossoms from late spring to late autumn. The flowers change color as they age, so a cluster usually has a pleasing combination of light and dark flowers. For *L. camara* and its cultivars, the color range includes various shades of red, yellow, and white. Hybrids with *L. montevidensis* produce plants with lilac-pink to violet flowers, sometimes with a yellow eye.

The foliage has a distinctive aroma when crushed or bruised, sometimes lemony but often quite disagreeable, depending on the cultivar. Likewise, some cultivars have green leaves, and others, variegated ones; some have smooth stems, and others, prickly ones.

Indoors, lantanas bloom most profusely in early summer but will

LANTANA

bloom throughout the year if given plenty of light.

LIGHT: Intense.
WATER: Keep evenly moist.
HUMIDITY: High.
TEMPERATURE: Average. May go dormant at temperatures below 50°F.
FERTILIZER: All-purpose during growing period.
DIMENSIONS: 3 to 6 feet high and wide.
REPOTTING: As needed.
PROPAGATION: From softwood cuttings and seed.
PROBLEMS: Low light causes spindly growth and poor bloom. Dry air causes leaf dieback. Whiteflies can be a serious problem; carefully check plants brought in from outdoors. Spider mites, aphids, and mealybugs are other possible pests.
TIP: This plant is poisonous. Mere contact with its foliage causes skin irritation in sensitive individuals. Keep lantana away from children.

***L. camara* 'Confetti' has multicolored blooms that change color as they age, giving the plant a festive appearance.**

Laurus nobilis
LOW-rus NO-bi-lus

SWEET BAY, BAY LAUREL

Sweet bay appears in ancient artwork that depicts people wearing leafy crowns. The leaves are just as decorative today and are also used in cooking. It is one of the few herbs that truly make good long-term houseplants.

Sweet bay is a slow-growing tree in its native Mediterranean region but is readily pruned to size for indoor use. It is generally sold as a dense shrub with thick foliage and can even be trained as a topiary. The simple elliptic leaves are somewhat wavy, dark green, and leathery in texture. It rarely blooms indoors.

Because sweet bay grows slowly, you can prune and train it for indoor use in a location with intense light.

LIGHT: Intense.
WATER: Let the soil dry slightly between waterings.
HUMIDITY: Average.
TEMPERATURE: Average to cool; cool to cold in winter.
FERTILIZER: All-purpose during the growing period. Not a heavy feeder.
DIMENSIONS: Can be maintained indefinitely as a shrub 1 foot to 4 feet tall and wide indoors.
REPOTTING: Infrequently.
PROPAGATION: Not easy to propagate. Semi-ripe cuttings in summer. Rooting hormone required.
PROBLEMS: Overwatering leads to root rot or leaf loss. Leaves also drop if plant is kept too dry. Mealybugs and scale insects are possible pests.
TIPS: Prune lightly at any season to keep to desired height. Try to buy a large plant, since it will take several years to develop its bushy form. Sap sometimes provokes skin irritation; wear gloves when pruning.

Leea coccinea
LEE-ee-uh kahk-SIN-ee-uh

WEST INDIAN HOLLY

West Indian holly (*L. coccinea*, syn. *L. guineensis*) is a stalwart foliage plant that's easy to care for. It is a medium-size shrub in the wild, but unless pruned or pinched occasionally, it tends to branch very little indoors, giving it an upright appearance.

It produces shiny, deep green compound leaves with irregularly toothed margins. New leaves usually have an attractive reddish tinge. The glossy leaflets bear a resemblance to holly leaves, giving it part of its common name.

Although it is considered a foliage plant, mature specimens occasionally bloom indoors. Small but long-lasting berries follow the flattened clusters of pink flowers with yellow stamens.

Although it can reach 8 feet or more in height, West Indian holly is generally kept pruned to 2 or 3 feet. Since pruning stimulates branching,

plants become rounder and fuller as they age.

A purplish-leaved cultivar is sold under the name *L. coccinea* 'Rubra', *L. coccinea* 'Burgundy', or *L. rubra*.
LIGHT: Medium to bright.
WATER: Let potting mix dry slightly between waterings.
HUMIDITY: High.
TEMPERATURE: Average. Keep plants out of cold drafts.
FERTILIZER: All-purpose during growing period.
DIMENSIONS: 2 to 8 feet tall and 2 to 5 feet wide.
REPOTTING: As needed.
PROPAGATION: From semi-ripe cuttings or seed.
PROBLEMS: Spots of black sap may form on the undersides of leaves. They are caused by a natural process called guttation and can be removed with a damp cloth. Spider mites and mealybugs are possible pests.
TIP: Discard yellowing leaves.

Leea is grown indoors for its shiny, holly-like foliage but may bloom in bright light and high humidity.

LIRIOPE, LILYTURF

Liriope
lee-REE-oh-pay

Although well known as a groundcover, lilyturf also makes an attractive houseplant. It is grown for its graceful, dark green, grassy leaves and is popular in dish gardens and terrariums as well as on windowsills.

Under very good conditions, lilyturf may bloom indoors, with narrow spikes of dark blue to purple flowers. Dwarf and variegated cultivars are all suitable for indoor growing. Big blue lilyturf (*L. muscari)* is the most widely available. The species has dark green leaves; its blue flowers, similar to grape hyacinths, bloom in autumn. Some cultivars have white flowers.

Black mondo grass, also called black lilyturf (*Ophiopogon planiscapus* 'Nigrescens'), is a close relative but with much darker, purple-black leaves. Pinkish white bell-shaped flowers appear on short stems in the summer.

LIGHT: Bright.
WATER: Let potting mix dry slightly between waterings.
HUMIDITY: Average.
TEMPERATURE: Average; cool to cold in winter.
FERTILIZER: All-purpose during growing period. Not a heavy feeder.
DIMENSIONS: 10 to 12 inches tall and 12 inches wide. Dwarf varieties are much smaller.
REPOTTING: Looks best when pot-bound.
PROPAGATION: Divide in spring.
PROBLEMS: Dry air causes leaf dieback. Thrips are possible pests.
TIPS: Old specimens accumulate yellow leaves and removing them individually can be time-consuming. Instead, prune the whole plant back to the soil in late winter and it will put on a flush of new growth.

Lilyturf is well-known as a landscape perennial in warm climates but also blooms indoors in bright light.

MANDEVILLA, DIPLADENIA

Mandevilla
man da-VIL-la

Mandevilla was long known as *Dipladenia*. It's a woody-stemmed climber with twining stems and elliptic, lustrous, bright green leaves. Up to 3 inches across, the trumpet-shaped, five-petaled flowers are pink, red, rose, or white with orange to yellow throats. Most are single, but a few double-flowered cultivars are available. Several species exist, including *M. sanderi* and *M. speciosa*, but most plants grown today are hybrids. The flowers bloom spring through autumn.

Mandevilla does a wonderful job of twining around a support, or you can trim back the rampant growth to give the plant a shrubby appearance. Flowers appear on new growth, so heavy pruning helps stimulate new blooms.

A close relative, *Allamanda cathartica*, extends the range of "trumpet climbers" into bright yellow. It, too, offers a range of cultivars, including double forms, and requires the same care and maintenance as mandevilla.

LIGHT: Bright.
WATER: Keep evenly moist.
HUMIDITY: Average.
TEMPERATURE: Average.
DIMENSIONS: Will grow approximately to the dimensions of its trellis.
FERTILIZER: All-purpose during growing period.
REPOTTING: Annually, in spring.
PROPAGATION: From softwood cuttings. Use a rooting hormone. It might need bottom heat.
PROBLEMS: Spider mites, whiteflies, mealybugs, and scale insects are possible pests.
TIPS: All parts of this plant are toxic. Keep out of reach of children. Wear gloves when handling as the milky sap can cause skin irritation.

You can train *Mandevilla* 'Alice du Pont' up a trellis or other support, or prune it regularly for a shrubbier shape.

Manettia luteorubra
ma-NET-ee-a loo-tay-oh-ROO-bra

BRAZILIAN FIRECRACKER

Brazilian firecracker (*M. luteorubra*, syn. *M. bicolor* and *M. inflata*) is a fast-growing twiner that quickly covers a trellis. Its sticky, hairy stems help it cling to its support. The ovate to lance-shaped leaves are dark green; when not in bloom, the plant is a mass of green. Then, from fall through spring, the entire plant is dotted with flowers. Tubular and bright red, with an inflated base and vivid yellow lobes at the tip, the 1- to 2-inch blooms look like lighted firecrackers.

Brazilian firecracker is usually trained onto a small trellis or even allowed to climb up a piece of cord from the floor to the ceiling. Unlike many vines, it doesn't make a very good hanging basket plant, as the

Manettia luteorubra quickly covers a trellis and displays its fireworks from autumn through spring.

stems twist around each other rather than stretching outward and downward in a desirable manner. It is possible to prune it regularly into a rounded bush, but that requires a lot of pinching, as each cut doubles the number of stems and the plant grows back quickly.

LIGHT: Bright.
WATER: Keep evenly moist.
HUMIDITY: Average.
TEMPERATURE: Average.
FERTILIZER: All-purpose during growing season.
DIMENSIONS: Climbs to 12 feet or more but is easily maintained at less than 3 feet tall and wide.
REPOTTING: As needed.
PROPAGATION: From softwood cuttings.
PROBLEMS: Low light causes spindly growth and poor bloom. Whiteflies are possible pests.
TIP: Prune or pinch at any time to keep the plant under control.

Maranta leuconeura
ma-RAN-ta loo-ko-NEWR-ra

PRAYER PLANT

The name prayer plant comes from this plant's curious growth habit. In the daytime its satiny foliage lies flat, but at night the leaves turn upward like praying hands.

Prayer plant is closely related to *Calathea* and shares the same

M. leuconeura 'Erythorneura' is popular for its colorful foliage and suitability for a hanging basket.

paddle leaf shape. It grows outward and somewhat downward, and so looks good in a hanging basket. It blooms quite readily indoors, but the small two-lipped white to pink flowers are of only minor interest.

Four cultivars are commonly grown. *M. leuconeura* 'Erythroneura' has velvety black-green leaves, paler toward the margin, with bright red veins and yellow green markings along the midrib. 'Kerchoveana', has pale gray-green leaves with dark brown marks on either side of the pale green midrib. 'Kerchoveana Variegata' is similar but marbled white. 'Massangeana' has blackish-green

leaves, purple underneath, that are feathered silvery gray along the midrib and veins.

LIGHT: Medium to bright.
WATER: Keep evenly moist.
HUMIDITY: High.
TEMPERATURE: Average. Keep plants out of cold drafts.
FERTILIZER: All-purpose during growing period. Not a heavy feeder.
DIMENSIONS: 12 inches tall and wide.
REPOTTING: Repot infrequently.
PROPAGATION: By division.
PROBLEMS: Leaf edges turn brown or entire leaves dry up in dry air or excess sun. Overwatering leads to root rot, especially in winter. This plant must have a semidormant period. Spider mites and mealybugs are possible pests.
TIPS: Discard yellowed leaves. Start new plants to replace old specimens when they get weak

Medinilla magnifica
me-di-NI-la mahg-NI-fi-ka

Medinilla magnifica is a well-chosen name for this plant, for it is indeed magnificent when in bloom. The drooping flower stalks, measuring up to 16 inches long, are composed of vivid pink bracts and clusters of bell-shaped carmine flowers. The plant itself is striking, with woody, four-sided stems and large leathery leaves with prominent veins.

Medinilla is, however, one of the most difficult houseplants to grow well. It tolerates less-than-ideal conditions (at least if the air remains reasonably warm) and can remain in bloom for months, from spring right through much of summer, but then tends to enter into a long decline that ends in the compost pile.

Most of all, this plant needs extremely high humidity. It fares well in a tropical greenhouse where water condenses on the glass, but

MEDINILLA

indoors, you may need to use a humidifier and a humidity tray. It will not tolerate temperatures much below 60°F.

LIGHT: Bright.
WATER: Keep evenly moist during the growing season.
HUMIDITY: Very high.
TEMPERATURE: Average.
FERTILIZER: All-purpose during growing period.
DIMENSIONS: 3 feet tall and wide on average; can reach twice that under ideal conditions.
REPOTTING: Annually.
PROPAGATION: From softwood cuttings or by air layering.
PROBLEMS: Low light causes spindly growth and poor bloom. Dry air causes leaf dieback and gradual decline. Spider mites and scale insects are possible pests.
TIPS: Remove yellowed leaves and faded flowers. Prune after flowering.

M. magnifica thrives in the bright light and high temperature and humidity of a steamy greenhouse.

Mikania ternata
mih-KAY-nee-uh ter-NAH-ta

Lovers of purple foliage will adore this rapidly growing foliage plant. It produces long trailing stems covered with felty hairs and 1½-inch maple-shaped, five-lobed leaves that are deep purple underneath, dark copper green above, and covered with fuzzy white hairs on the top, giving the overall purple, plushy appearance suggested by its common names. Insignificant flower heads may appear in fall when the plant is grown outdoors but are rarely seen on houseplants.

In nature, this is a creeping groundcover and often is used as such in tropical countries. Indoors, it is primarily used in hanging baskets where its trailing stems are put to best use. It can be used to decorate trellises but will need a helping hand, as it does not climb readily on its own. It also makes a

PLUSH VINE, PURPLE PLUSH

lovely addition to summer container gardens outdoors. You can then bring cuttings indoors in the fall.

LIGHT: Medium to bright.
WATER: Let potting mix dry slightly between waterings.
HUMIDITY: High.
TEMPERATURE: Average.
FERTILIZER: All-purpose during growing period.
REPOTTING: As needed.
DIMENSIONS: 12 inches tall; can trail to 4 feet or more.
PROPAGATION: From softwood cuttings. Will self-layer if stems contact the soil.
PROBLEMS: Low light causes spindly growth. Avoid spraying leaves to prevent leaf spots. Aphids, mealybugs, and scale insects are possible pests.
TIPS: Pinch and prune as needed to control growth. Older plants tend to decline; restart from new cuttings.

Plush vine is a tropical groundcover that grows well in hanging baskets indoors and in container gardens outdoors.

Mimosa pudica
mee-MO-sa puh-DEE-ka

SENSITIVE PLANT

Here's one plant that is grown simply for the sheer fun of stroking it. It is not particularly pretty in either flower or leaf and rarely survives more than 10 or 12 months, but its fascinating habit of closing its leaves when they are touched make it a pleasure for both young and old alike. The finely divided leaflets of sensitive plant fold together in just a few seconds when touched.

Sensitive plants are often sold as small plants in nurseries but are easily and rapidly grown from seed as annuals. For faster germination, pour boiling water over the flat seeds or singe them with a match. The plants will be at their peak size in only three or four months.

Children enjoy stroking sensitive plant's unusual leaves, which quickly fold together when touched.

Sensitive plant flowers readily, with small pink, fuzzy flower heads. Keep the plant warm and in good light.

LIGHT: Bright, direct sun in winter.
WATER: Keep evenly moist.
HUMIDITY: Average.
TEMPERATURE: Average to high.
FERTILIZER: All-purpose during growing period.
DIMENSIONS: 12 to 30 inches tall and 16 to 36 inches wide.
REPOTTING: Rarely required. Pot seedlings as they increase in size.
PROPAGATION: From seed.
PROBLEMS: Poor drainage, too-frequent watering, or standing in water causes root rot. Low light causes spindly and weak growth. Drafts and dry air cause leaf scorch. Spider mites are possible pests.
TIP: When your sensitive plant begins to look unattractive, it's best to compost it and start new plants from seed.

Monstera deliciosa
mon-STEH-ra day-li-kee-OH-sa

SPLIT-LEAF PHILODENDRON, SWISS-CHEESE PLANT

Most split-leaf philodendrons are sold with relatively small leaves only lightly cut along the edges, and they become even smaller and less deeply cut in the home. That's because they are too often grown in low light. Give them bright light, and something to grow on, and the leaves will increase in size.

At full maturity, the split-leaf philodendron may even produce large white spathes followed by corncob-like fruits that turn red at maturity. They are edible and taste like pineapple.

Also offered is *M. friedrichsthalii*, popular in hanging baskets. Its leaves are small with wavy edges and are perforated on either side of the midrib.

LIGHT: Medium to bright.
WATER: Let potting mix dry slightly between waterings.

HUMIDITY: Average.
TEMPERATURE: Average.
FERTILIZER: All-purpose during growing season.
DIMENSIONS: 3 to 7 feet tall and 2 to 5 feet wide.
REPOTTING: Repot infrequently.
PROPAGATION: From stem cuttings or by air layering. Can be grown from seed but takes years to mature.
PROBLEMS: Declines in low light. Dry air gives leaves brown, brittle edges. Brown edges on yellowed leaves are a symptom of overwatering. Spider mites and mealybugs are possible.
TIP: All parts of this plant are toxic except the ripe fruit; even its sap causes dermatitis in sensitive individuals. Keep plants out of the reach of children.

Split-leaf philodendrons thrive, and may even bloom, if given bright light and a strong trellis to climb.

A fully mature *Monstera deliciosa* produces dark green, leathery, heart-shaped leaves 3 feet across with multiple perforations and deep slashes. Its aerial roots attach to supports to help it climb.

Murraya paniculata
mur-RAY-uh pan-ih-kyew-LAY-tuh

This close relative of citrus is truly a dual-purpose plant. It makes a fine foliage plant, forming a dense bush composed of pale brown branches and covered with shiny, dark green pinnate leaves with seven to nine oval to diamond-shaped 2-inch-long leaflets. You also can grow it as a small tree if you prune to remove the lower branches.

Murraya paniculata blooms beautifully and abundantly. The waxy white five-petaled flowers are not only attractive and long-lasting but also intensely fragrant, smelling of orange blossoms with just a hint of jasmine. It flowers not only in late summer and fall but often again in spring and sporadically throughout the year. A mature plant produces attractive red berries.

Mock orange seems perfectly adapted to most household

ORANGE-JASMINE, MOCK ORANGE

conditions, even low light, although it prefers medium to bright light. Regular home temperatures and air humidity are fine as well. Few other houseplants have so much to offer.

LIGHT: Medium to bright. Tolerates low light but will not bloom.
WATER: Keep evenly moist.
HUMIDITY: Average.
TEMPERATURE: Average, cool to cold in winter.
FERTILIZER: All-purpose during growing period.
DIMENSIONS: 3 to 10 feet tall and 3 to 6 feet wide.
REPOTTING: Annually in late winter or early spring for best growth.
PROPAGATION: From softwood cuttings.
PROBLEMS: Lack of bloom in poor light. Spider mites, mealybugs, and scale insects are possible pests.
TIPS: Remove yellowed leaves. Prune as needed after flowering.

Mock orange grows well in average household conditions, and its blooms are fragrant and long-lasting.

Musa acuminata
MOO-suh a-kyew min-AY-tuh

You can successfully grow a few banana plants of moderate size indoors. Their huge paddle-shaped leaves make quite an impact. Fruits, though, are unlikely indoors. Bananas simply find the average home too cool and too dry to fruit readily.

Bananas are not trees, but rather very tall, treelike herbaceous plants. Their "trunk" is actually composed of leaf bases wrapped tightly together like a cigar. And unlike true trees, once a banana has fruited, it dies and is replaced by one of its offsets.

The banana plants sold as houseplants are usually dwarf varieties of the common banana, *M. acuminata*. The shortest variety is probably 'Novak', sold as Super Dwarf Banana. It rarely attains more than 4 to 5 feet in height. Its foliage may be green or bear red spots, especially under strong light.

DWARF BANANA

It produces yellow, seedless, edible bananas, if it fruits.
LIGHT: Medium to bright.
WATER: Very moist at all times.
HUMIDITY: High.
TEMPERATURE: Average to high. Avoid cold drafts.
FERTILIZER: All-purpose during growing season.
DIMENSIONS: 3 to 10 feet tall and 3 to 6 feet wide.
REPOTTING: As needed.
PROPAGATION: By division or offsets. Banana seed is available but not for *M. acuminata*.
PROBLEMS: Low light or low temperature causes failure to bloom. Drafts and dry air cause burnt leaf edges. Spider mites, aphids, and mealybugs are possible pests.
TIP: Grow banana plants for the pleasure and challenge without expectation of fruit.

Compact varieties of the common banana plant, such as 'Dwarf Cavendish', are unlikely to fruit indoors.

Nematanthus
nay-ma-TAN-thus

Guppy plant's unusual flowers often bloom off and on throughout the year. The foliage is appealing too.

GUPPY PLANT

Guppy plant gets its name from the pudgy ventral pouch of its tubular flowers, much like the bulging stomach of a female guppy. The tiny opening at the tip resembles the fish's mouth.

The orange, red, or yellow flowers, sometimes striped in contrasting colors, are carried up tight near the stem or in long hanging stalks that drip down like dangling fishing lines with a goldfish at each tip. Equally colorful calyxes often accompany the flowers. Guppy plant often blooms sporadically throughout the year, sometimes massively in summer.

The leaves are generally thick, waxy, and very shiny, often with a bright red patch underneath. Some have purple tints and others are variegated. The leaves are produced along stems that usually arch upward and outward, eventually becoming trailing, making the plant a natural for hanging baskets. A few species and hybrids, though, have a more upright rounded habit and are better suited to tabletop use.

LIGHT: Bright.
WATER: Keep evenly moist.
HUMIDITY: Average.
TEMPERATURE: Average.
FERTILIZER: Rich in phosphorous.
DIMENSIONS: 8 to 24 inches tall and 8 to 36 inches wide.
REPOTTING: Infrequently.
PROPAGATION: From softwood cuttings.
PROBLEMS: Low light causes spindly growth and poor bloom. It is sensitive to excess mineral salts, which cause leaf-tip burn and stem dieback, so leach frequently. Spider mites and aphids are possible pests.
TIPS: Prune in early spring. Pinch back stem tips of young or growing plants to improve overall form. Be careful not to remove flower buds when pruning.

Neomarica gracilis
nee-oh-ma-REE-ka gra-KEE-lis

Apostle plant's fragrant flowers look just like iris blooms. Its plantlets are easily layered or cut and repotted.

APOSTLE PLANT, WALKING IRIS

Apostle plant is essentially a tropical iris. It has the same fan of flattened, elongated, lance-shaped leaves, and the flower is the spitting image of a garden iris. It is called apostle plant because it was once believed each fan had to have 12 leaves before it would bloom.

The common name walking iris comes from the unusual way it reproduces in the wild. After blooming, plantlets form at the tops of the flower stems, which then bend over to the ground, where the plantlets take root and form new plants. The plantlets also can be layered into neighboring pots or removed and rooted.

This all occurs in winter, when the plant produces attractive, scented flowers on top of flattened, leaflike stems. The blooms are white with a chocolate brown center and curling blue petals. Flowers open in the morning and bloom for only one day, but are replaced by others.

LIGHT: Bright.
WATER: Keep evenly moist.
HUMIDITY: Average.
TEMPERATURE: Average to cool, especially in winter.
FERTILIZER: All-purpose during growing season.
DIMENSIONS: 16 inches tall and 24 inches wide.
REPOTTING: Infrequently.
PROPAGATION: Remove and root plantlets or layer into neighboring pots. Divide crowded adult plants.
PROBLEM: Poor bloom in low light. Rarely subject to pests or diseases.
TIP: Keep it somewhat pot-bound, as it blooms best when its roots are compressed.

TROPICAL PITCHER PLANT, MONKEY CUP

Nepenthes
nay-PEN-theez

These unusual carnivorous plants produce a twisting tendril at the tips of their otherwise unremarkable leaves. At the tip of each tendril forms an incredible hanging pitcher, with a rolled rim and even a lid to keep out excess rain. The rim secretes sweet nectar, attracting insects to their doom, as they slip down inside the trap and are digested. The small flowers are insignificant by comparison.

More than 70 species of *Nepenthes* and hundreds of hybrids exist, varying most notably in the size and appearance of their pitchers, some of which are tiny while others are large enough to trap small birds. Pitchers may be green, reddish, purple, or mottled.

High humidity is absolutely crucial; otherwise, they are quite adaptable. Most grow best in very well-drained potting mix.

LIGHT: Bright.
WATER: Keep evenly moist.
HUMIDITY: High.
TEMPERATURE: Average. Highland pitchers need cool temperatures.
FERTILIZER: Rich in nitrogen but highly diluted.
DIMENSIONS: Keep to 1 to 3 feet tall and wide by pruning.
REPOTTING: As needed, using a well-aerated potting mix, such as sphagnum moss or orchid mix.
PROPAGATION: From stem cuttings or seed, or by air layering.
PROBLEMS: Low light causes spindly growth and an absence of pitchers. Excess mineral salts cause leaf-tip burn and stem dieback, so leach frequently. Dry air causes leaf dieback. Mealybugs can be pests.
TIPS: Keep this plant pruned or it becomes ungainly. As old traps fade, cut the stems back to near the base to encourage fresh sprouts.

Carnivorous pitcher plants must have bright light and high humidity to put on their remarkable show.

OLEANDER

Nerium oleander
NAY ree-um o-lee-AN-der

Oleander bears narrow, glossy, willow-like leaves on upward-growing branches. Clusters of often highly scented, white, yellow, pink, or red flowers bloom in summer. Both single and double forms are available, and some varieties have yellow variegated leaves. Dwarf varieties are especially popular. Although they readily reach 6 feet tall indoors, you can keep them to 3 to 4 feet tall by pruning.

The secret to success with oleander is summer heat and winter cold. It pays to set oleanders outside for the summer, then move them to a barely heated garage for the winter and greatly reduce watering.

All parts of this plant are extremely poisonous, and you should not grow them where small children or pets have access. Always wear gloves when pruning and

taking cuttings, to make sure you don't accidentally ingest the sap. Wash your tools and your hands afterward. Even smoke from the burning of its wood is toxic.
LIGHT: Bright.
WATER: Let potting mix dry slightly between waterings.
HUMIDITY: Average.
TEMPERATURE: Average; cool to cold in winter.
FERTILIZER: All-purpose during growing period.
DIMENSIONS: Usually maintained at 3 to 8 feet tall and 3 to 5 feet wide when grown indoors.
REPOTTING: Annually, in spring for best growth.
PROPAGATION: From softwood cuttings or seed.
PROBLEMS: Low light causes spindly growth and poor blooming. Plants are susceptible to mealybugs outdoors. Spider mites and aphids also are possible pests.

TIP: Prune severely after blooming, wearing gloves, goggles, and a mask.

Move oleander outdoors for the summer and to a cold area during winter and it will bloom profusely.

ORCHIDS

Some people regard growing exquisite orchids as the supreme gardening achievement. But in fact, some species of orchids grow so well indoors they require less routine care than many other houseplants. In addition, improved breeding techniques have significantly increased the availability and lowered the cost of many cultivars. Placed on a windowsill in the living room, an orchid is sure to be the center of attention.

Orchids may have striking flowers, but their foliage is generally unattractive. They often have wrinkled, lumpy pseudobulbs at the base of the leaves and bear thick, aerial roots that many people find objectionable. Some indoor gardeners grow orchids among other houseplants, where their less attractive features are not so noticeable, then move them to a more visible spot when they are in bloom.

Orchids are an extremely varied group of plants, and their cultural requirements vary considerably, not only from one genus to another but from one species to another. This diversity makes it hard to give a general summary of orchid care, but it also means there is an orchid that adapts to just about every indoor situation. Always check on the cultural needs of an orchid before purchasing it; it is far easier to find an orchid that suits your conditions than to change your conditions to suit a particular species. For more information, see "Growing Orchids" on pages 84–85.

LIGHT: Most orchids fall into one of two categories: those requiring intense light and those preferring medium to bright light. Give the first group full sun throughout the winter months, preferably in a south-facing window, with some shading from direct midday sun in summer. If they take on a light green tinge, all is well; if their foliage is dark green, they need more light. This group may need supplemental artificial light during the winter. The orchids that prefer medium to bright light are suited to either east or west windows or curtain-filtered bright windows year-round. They also do well under fluorescent lights.

WATER: Water varieties with thick leaves and large pseudobulbs thoroughly, then allow them to dry out before the next watering. Those with thin roots and no pseudobulbs generally need water as soon as the potting mix starts to dry. Most orchids need a short period of dry conditions in autumn to stimulate new flowers.

Cymbidium hybrids are well-suited for use as houseplants. Their blooms are long-lasting.

HUMIDITY: Although some orchids tolerate average humidity, it's best to offer them high humidity indoors. A humidifier may be necessary during the winter months. You also can grow orchids on a humidity tray.

TEMPERATURE: Average indoor temperatures are generally acceptable throughout much of the year. A night temperature up to 15°F cooler is best. An annual period of cool to cold temperatures (down to 50°F), combined with reduced watering, induces flowering in many orchids.

FERTILIZER: Fertilize year-round, more heavily in summer. Special orchid fertilizers are available, although standard fertilizers generally give excellent results. In general, orchids grown in bark mixtures need fertilizers rich in nitrogen, as bark uses up much nitrogen as it decomposes. Those grown on more stable media, such as osmunda fiber,

Cattleya 'Nacouchee' is a relative of the orchids used in corsages.

Dendrobrium 'Stardust' will produce its vibrant flowers if grown in a location with plenty of direct sun.

need balanced fertilizers. Or you can alternate between the two types.

DIMENSIONS: Highly variable, but most indoor orchids range from 5 inches to 3 feet tall and 3 inches to 2 feet wide.

REPOTTING: Allow roots to extend beyond the pot as long as the plant continues to grow well. When growth is inhibited, repot into a larger container using an appropriate orchid potting mix (see page 45). Very few orchids grow well in regular potting mixes, since those mixes don't allow sufficient air circulation to the roots. Use a special orchid mix (generally a mixture of bark, perlite, sphagnum moss, and other bulky products). Many orchids also grow on bark or on pieces of osmunda fiber. Tie them solidly to the support until they are well rooted. For more information on repotting orchids or growing them on bark slabs, see page 85.

PROPAGATION: You can divide most orchids every few years, but leave at least three pseudobulbs in each pot. Some orchids also produce keikis, or plantlets, at the bases or on the flower stalks. You can remove and pot these once they have produced roots. For more information on dividing orchids, see page 51. Growing orchids from seed is generally done in a test tube and is a delicate and very slow technique best left to specialists.

PROBLEMS: Limp leaves or flowers are caused mainly by insufficient light but can also be due to improper watering (usually overwatering). If leaves are old or the plant is deciduous, you can expect yellowing leaves. Otherwise yellowing results from overwatering or sunburn. Brown spots are due to too much sun or leaf spot disease. Orchids are sensitive to excess mineral salts that cause leaf-tip burn and stunted growth, so leach frequently. Spider mites, aphids, mealybugs, and scale insects are possible pests.

TIPS: Remove yellowed leaves and cut back flower stalks to the nearest green joint after blooming. Purchase mature, blooming orchids, as young plants often take years to flower.

Some of the orchids that grow well under average indoor conditions are listed here.

■ **Foxtail orchid** (*Aerides*) is a summer-flowering epiphyte of moderate size. Given intense sun, this orchid blooms profusely with fragrant flowers in red, pink, or white on long stalks that arch outward from the plant. *A. odorata* is particularly fragrant and popular with indoor orchid growers.

■ **Comet orchids** (*Angraecum*) are small plants well-suited to indoor gardens. *A. eburneum* (syn. *A. superbum*), which is larger than most, bears waxy, greenish white flowers and strap-shaped leaves that are fragrant at night. Like most comet orchids, it flowers in winter. The plants need brightness and even moisture but are tolerant of cool night temperatures and average household humidity.

Jewel orchid (Ludisia discolor) is grown more for its dark purple, variegated foliage than for its flowers.

Paphiopedilum H. S. Vander Sluis 'Charlotte' is a hybrid lady's slipper orchid with long-lasting flowers.

■ **Lady of the night** *(Brassavola)* is a popular plant for beginners, since it blooms readily even under adverse conditions. The flowers are usually quite large for the size of the plant and greenish in color. Their most notable characteristic is that they are intensely fragrant, but only at night, which gives the group its common name. Best known are *B. nodosa* and *B. digbyana* (the latter is more properly classified as *Rhyncholaelia digbyana)*. Brassavolas require abundant watering and full sun when in active growth.

■ **Spider orchids** *(Brassia)* bear flowers with long, narrow sepals that give rise to their common name. The plants are fairly large, with 15-inch flower spikes and leaves that grow to 10 inches long. They generally bloom in fall or winter if given sufficient sunlight. Most varieties popularly sold are hybrids.

■ **Bulbophyllums** *(Bulbophyllum)* are the largest and most varied genus in the orchid family. Some are large plants with equally large flowers, but the most popular are

Moth orchids, such as *Phalaenopsis* 'Kaleidoscope', adapt easily to average indoor conditions.

dwarf or even miniature plants, which fit easily on a narrow windowsill. Cultural requirements vary widely according to their native habitats, but most need warm temperatures, some shade from direct sun, and regular waterings while they are growing actively.

■ **Cattleya** *(Cattleya)* is not nearly as popular as the numerous hybrid genera derived from crosses between it and related orchids, such as *Rhyncholaelia, Laelia,* and *Sophronitis*. These breeder-made genera—among them *Brassolaeliocattleya, Laeliocattleya, Sophrolaeliocattleya,* and *Potinara*— are generally called cattleyas or "catts" by orchid fanciers. Cattleyas in the large sense include both the old-fashioned corsage orchids and an increasingly popular range of miniature hybrids with smaller blooms. The vigorous plants produce gorgeous flowers when they receive plenty of sun.

■ **Cymbidium** *(Cymbidium)* "miniature" orchids are especially well-suited for many indoor gardens. Even some miniatures are 3 feet tall, so the narrow, arching foliage needs room. Give the plants cool nights to promote flowering, which usually

occurs in winter or spring. Many hybrids are available in a wide variety of colors. The flowers are long-lasting, even as cut flowers.

■ **Dendrobriums** *(Dendrobium)* are mostly epiphytic orchids; both evergreen and deciduous types are available. Large flowers bloom in clusters or in a row along the stem. They last between a week and several months, depending on the species, and need plenty of sun. Numerous hybrids are available. One commonly grown species is *D. nobile*, with club-shaped, upright pseudobulbs and variable flowers, usually rose with a dark center.

■ **Clamshell orchids** *(Encyclia)* are often compact in size and are closely related to *Epidendrum*, but have plump, squat pseudobulbs instead of the canelike stems of the true *Epidendrum*. Flowers are variable in size, color, and shape, but many have curious flowers with a shell-shaped lip and long, dangling sepals.

■ **Buttonhole orchids** *(Epidendrum)* have lengthened, cane-shaped pseudobulbs. Many species are too tall for home conditions, but there are plenty of medium-size and dwarf hybrids that fit. Most of these are suitable indoors on windowsills warmed by the winter sun. Some species may bloom continuously in suitable conditions.

■ **Jewel orchid** *(Ludisia discolor,* also known as *Haemaria discolor dawsoniana)*, is one of several orchids grown more for its exceptional foliage than for its bloom. This plant grows best in regular potting soil. It may reach a height of 8 inches or so on somewhat trailing stems. Its leaves are a velvety, purplish green, nearly black, with a prominent network of red and white veins. Small, white or pinkish flowers grow on long spikes. When given good, indirect light, jewel orchids will bloom in winter.

■ **Tailed orchids** *(Masdevallia)* are grown in cooler temperatures and have curiously un-orchid-like flowers: broad sepals partially joined at the base and pointed at the tips, like a moustache with downturned tips. They like bright light with little direct sun, and high humidity.

■ **Pansy orchid** (*Miltonia*) gets its common name from its flat faced, heavily marbled flowers. The original genus has been subdivided into two closely related ones: *Miltonia* and *Miltoniopsis*. The former, which has two-leaved pseudobulbs, needs warm temperatures year-round. *Miltoniopsis*, which has one-leaved pseudobulbs, needs cooler temperatures. Both require filtered light and high air humidity.

■ **Odontoglossum orchids** (*Odontoglossum*) need the moist air and stable growing conditions of a greenhouse that provides direct sunlight in winter and filtered light in summer. Many species and hybrids are available, most bearing long-lasting, fragrant, large flowers. Many bloom twice a year.

Spider orchid *Brassia Edvah Loo 'Goldilocks'* has distinctive flowers.

■ **Dancing lady oncidiums** (*Oncidium*) are a large group of epiphytic orchids. They generally produce stalks of abundant yellow flowers speckled with brown. Flower size depends on the species but is usually quite small. For the most part, dancing lady requires bright light with protection from direct summer sunlight.

■ **Lady's slipper orchids** (*Paphiopedilum*) have long-lasting flowers with distinctive pouches. Mostly terrestrial, lady's slippers need a more humid, less airy growing mix than other orchids. Simply add extra sphagnum moss to typical orchid mix. Two main groups exist: those with green leaves, which need cool growing conditions, and those with variegated leaves, which adapt well to average growing conditions. All prefer filtered light.

■ **Moth orchids** (*Phalaenopsis*) are probably the best orchids for beginners. They adapt well to average indoor temperatures (about 75°F during the day and 65°F at night), do not require high humidity, and are generally well-suited to the average home. Unlike the many orchids that are grown solely for their blooms, moth orchids often have attractively marbled foliage. They produce sprays of 2- to 3-inch flowers in a wide range of colors. Modern hybrids may bloom throughout much of the year. After blooming, cut back the flower stems to the node just below the last

Pansy orchid (*Miltonia*) needs warm temperatures year-round.

faded flower, and they often will bloom again. Close relatives that require similar care include *Doritis* and the hybrid genus *Doritaenopsis*.

■ **Rodriguezia orchids** (*Rodriguezia*) are mostly miniatures less than a foot tall. The plants bloom abundantly, producing large clusters of small fragrant flowers, usually white or pinkish. Keep these plants moist and in damp air.

■ **Vanda orchids** (*Vanda*) are usually too large for most homes; miniature hybrids are available that are better suited to home culture. *Vanda* needs sunlight from a south window. It also does well in a greenhouse.

Ornithogalum caudatum
or-ni-THO-ga-lum cow-DAH-tum

Pregnant onions are for protected display only: All parts of the plant are toxic, and the leaves are quite fragile.

PREGNANT ONION, FALSE SEA-ONION

Ornithogalum caudatum, now also known as *O. longibracteatum*, is a pass-along plant, rarely seen in nurseries but shared among friends, family, and neighbors since the Victorian era, when it was one of the most common houseplants.

Pregnant onion derives its common name from its aboveground opalescent, pale green, onion-like bulb, which produces offsets just under its semitransparent skin, causing it to bulge outward. Peel off a few layers of skin and break the offsets loose. They root readily when inserted into potting mix.

The leaves are bright green and straplike, arching gracefully away from the bulb. They tend to be very fragile, so keep the plant out of traffic. Pregnant onion readily produces a tall though weak-stemmed flower stalk with numerous star-shaped white flowers with greenish stripes on the outside.

LIGHT: Bright.
WATER: Let potting mix dry between waterings.
HUMIDITY: Average.
TEMPERATURE: Average.
FERTILIZER: All-purpose during growing period. Not a heavy feeder.
DIMENSIONS: 1 foot tall (up to 3 feet when in bloom) and wide.
REPOTTING: After flowering; cover only the base of the bulb with potting mixture.
PROPAGATION: From seed or bulblets.
PROBLEMS: Spider mites, whiteflies, mealybugs, and scale insects are possible pests.
TIPS: To show off the plant's multiple pregnancies, peel off a few layers of drying skin occasionally. All parts of this plant are toxic, so keep out of reach of children.

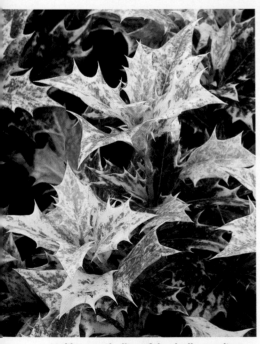

Osmanthus heterophyllus
os-MANTH-us heh-teh-ro-FIL-us

Unlike true hollies, false holly can live a long time inside your home. Decorate it with artificial berries in December.

FALSE HOLLY

Although various holly species *(Ilex)* are offered in December as potted plants decorated with artificial berries, few of them survive more than a few months indoors. An excellent alternative exists, however—a holly look-alike that can live indoors for decades. You can even decorate it like a Christmas tree. All it lacks are bright red berries, but you can always attach artificial ones.

The shiny, evergreen, spine-edged leaves of false holly even have the leathery texture of true holly. The same plant may have both spiny leaves and spineless leaves (*heterophyllus* means "with varied leaves"), but juvenile plants tend to bear only spiny ones. False holly rarely blooms indoors.

Besides the all-green form, there are several variegated types. Fragrant olive or sweet olive (*O. fragrans*) is a dense shrub with narrow, toothless leaves. It is worth trying to grow if you can supply cool winter conditions and high humidity, as its tubular cream flowers, though tiny and often half-hidden, are intensely fragrant like orange blossoms.

LIGHT: Bright.
WATER: Let the potting mix dry slightly between waterings.
HUMIDITY: High.
TEMPERATURE: Average; cool to cold in winter.
FERTILIZER: All-purpose during growing period. Not a heavy feeder.
DIMENSIONS: Usually maintained between 1 and 5 feet tall and wide by pruning.
REPOTTING: Infrequently.
PROPAGATION: From softwood cuttings, with rooting hormone.
PROBLEMS: Dry air causes leaf dieback. Scale insects may be pests.
TIP: Pinch new growth regularly to obtain a bushy form.

Oxalis regnellii
oks-AH-lis rayg-NEL-lee-eye

OXALIS, WOOD SORREL, TROPICAL SHAMROCK

Absolutely the most floriferous houseplant of them all, this plant is essentially always in bloom. Even young plants with a half dozen leaves will bloom steadily.

The most striking characteristic of this species is its three distinctly triangular leaflets. All other oxalis plants have rounded leaflets. In the species, they are dull green on top, sometimes with a silvery overlay, and purplish underneath. The leaves are borne on weak pink to pale green petioles that stand up for a few days, then bend over, giving it a mounded appearance. The flowers are white or pale pink and shaped like an open funnel. They are not individually showy, but their sheer number and consistent blooming make them attractive.

O. regnellii atropurpurea has become more popular than the species. Its leaves are a deep purple, highlighted in some clones by a metallic pink splotch in the center of each leaflet. Its blooms are pink.

LIGHT: Medium to bright.
WATER: Keep evenly moist.
HUMIDITY: Average.
TEMPERATURE: Average to cool.
FERTILIZER: All-purpose during growing period. Not a heavy feeder.
DIMENSIONS: 8 inches tall and 18 inches wide.
REPOTTING: As needed.
PROPAGATION: Dig up and separate the tubers.
PROBLEMS: Overwatering leads to rot. Spider mites, whiteflies, thrips, mealybugs, and scale insects are possible pests.
TIPS: Needs regular grooming. Or simply shear messy plants to the ground; they'll resprout within two weeks.

Tropical shamrock (*O. regnellii atropurpurea*) has triangular purple leaves and continuous blooms.

Pachystachys lutea
pa kee-STA-kis LOO-tee-a

LOLLIPOP-PLANT

Lollipop-plant is a fast-growing shrub with puckered, lance-shaped dark green leaves, slightly wavy along the edges, that reach up to 6 inches long. Its principal attraction, though, is its decorative and long-lasting 4- to 6-inch flower heads that appear at the ends of the branches. They are composed of bright, very long-lived yellow bracts from among which peep tubular, two-lipped flowers. Bloom is most dependable in summer, but in good light it will often bloom sporadically throughout the year.

Its fast rate of growth and tendency to rapidly lose its lower leaves means regular pruning is necessary. Fortunately it responds well to pruning: Essentially, the more you prune, the more stems it produces, and the more stems it produces, the more it flowers. Prune right after the bracts fade to ensure you don't clip off unopened flowers.

LIGHT: Bright.
WATER: Keep evenly moist.
HUMIDITY: High.
TEMPERATURE: Average to high.
FERTILIZER: All-purpose during growing period.
DIMENSIONS: 1 to 3 feet tall and wide (taller if left unpruned).
REPOTTING: As needed.
PROPAGATION: From softwood cuttings.
PROBLEMS: Low light causes spindly growth and poor bloom. Loses lower leaves with age; prune severely or start new plants. Spider mites and whiteflies are possible pests.
TIPS: Prune heavily after flowering to encourage the plant to branch from the base. Most attractive when kept under 3 feet tall. Rejuvenate aging, neglected specimens by cutting to within 6 inches of the soil.

Fast-growing lollipop-plant responds to frequent pruning by producing more stems and more flowers.

Fishtail palm *(Caryota mitis)* **eventually grows to be quite tall.**

Bamboo palm *(Chamaedorea erumpens)* **needs to be divided periodically.**

Areca palm *(Chrysalidocarpus lutescens)* **does best in humid air.**

Palms are consistently popular as houseplants. Their graceful fronds and rich green color give even the coldest northern home a tropical air. They adapt well to the limited light and controlled temperatures of the indoors. You can save money by purchasing small young plants that will grow slowly into large trees, if you don't mind waiting. Many palms flourish for decades in indoor conditions.

Palm leaves are called fronds, and there are two main types: fan-shaped and pinnate (feathery). Most palms grown indoors have a trunk, albeit sometimes a narrow one, but others are stemless. They can be clumping or single-stemmed. Most palms do not bloom indoors and, therefore, do not bear fruit.

Most palms are easy to care for and have uniform growing requirements. During the spring and summer growing season, water plants regularly and fertilize them

lightly. Reduce water and stop feeding them in winter. Protect palms from dry air and direct sunlight, especially if you move them outdoors.

To prune a palm, cut off dead or damaged fronds; never cut off its top. Unlike most plants, palms produce new growth only from the tip, so removing its growing point kills the stem—and the whole plant if it's a single-trunk plant.

LIGHT: Bright. Some tolerate medium or even low light.
WATER: Keep evenly moist.
HUMIDITY: Average to high.
TEMPERATURE: Average to high. Cool for a few species.
FERTILIZER: All-purpose during growing period. Not a heavy feeder.
DIMENSIONS: Highly variable, but usually 3 to 8 feet tall and 2 to 5 feet wide.
REPOTTING: Repot infrequently.
PROPAGATION: From seed. Sow in a small pot and transplant seedlings as needed; both germination and growth are painfully slow. Usually propagated only by professionals. Some palms can be divided.

PROBLEMS: Overwatering leads to stem rot. Spider mites can be a major problem, especially when air is dry. Whiteflies, mealybugs, and scale insects are also possible pests.
TIP: Buy a palm the size you need, as growth is often painfully slow, especially under low light.

■ **Fishtail palm** *(Caryota mitis)* becomes large over time. It has a thick trunk and many spreading fronds, each laden with fans of dark green leaflets. The ribbed texture of the leaflets and their wedge shape account for the common name.

■ **Parlor palm** *(Chamaedorea elegans,* also known as *Neanthe bella)* has handsome, light green fronds. It is a small palm (sometimes seedlings that are only a few inches tall are offered), which eventually grows to a height of only 6 feet. It is very tolerant of low light, which makes it suitable for entryways and living rooms. Generally it is sold with three or more plants to a pot for a fuller appearance, so it looks like a clumping palm, but it never produces offsets. It is one of the rare palms that bloom readily indoors. Given enough light, it will bear open clusters of yellow flowers among the lower leaves. It will only rarely produce fruit, though, as male and female flowers bloom on separate plants. Also commonly available are bamboo palm *(C. erumpens)*, with clusters of drooping fronds, and reed palm *(C. seifrizii)*, with clusters of narrow, feathery fronds. The latter two are clumping palms and produce small thickets, if not divided.

■ **European fan palm**
(Chamaerops humilis) has fan-shaped leaves about a foot wide. The multiple trunks, reaching 4 feet or taller, are rough and black and grow at an angle from the container. Usually only large specimens are sold and used for dramatic effect.

■ **Areca palm or butterfly palm**
(Chrysalidocarpus lutescens) is a cluster of thin yellow canes with arching fronds and strap-shaped, shiny green leaflets. It is a medium-size palm and slow-growing. In dry air, it is extremely subject to spider mites; a weekly shower helps prevent them. Some horticulturists list this plant as *Dypsis lutescens.*

■ **Kentia palm** *(Howea forsteriana)* grows into a very large tree outdoors, but indoors it rarely exceeds 7 or 8 feet and even then only after several decades. Feather-shaped fronds arch outward from a sturdy base and eventually from the trunk, creating a full appearance. It is tolerant of low light but does better in bright light. The leaves scorch easily, so place this plant in the shade if you move it outdoors.

■ **Chinese fan palm** *(Livistona chinensis)* is a large plant with deeply lobed leaves up to 2 feet across. Young plants are trunkless, but older plants produce a rough trunk. The plants eventually grow to 10 feet if given enough room and a large enough container. Keep the soil moist but not soggy, and keep the plants warm at night.

■ **Majesty palm** *(Ravenea rivularis)* is a relative newcomer but already immensely popular, producing a crown of arching,

Pygmy date palm *(Phoenix roebelenii)* grows slowly.

Miniature lady palm *(Rhapis excelsa)* has lance-shaped leaves.

pinnate, bright green fronds around a base that keeps increasing in size, eventually forming an upright trunk. Its growth is quite rapid and it may grow beyond a useful size in four or five years.

■ **Pygmy date palm** *(Phoenix roebelenii)* is a dwarf, rarely reaching more than 4 feet tall indoors. Its arching, narrow-leaved, feathery fronds at the top of a distinct, upright trunk give it the stereotypical palmlike silhouette, making it one of the most popular palms for indoor use.

■ **Lady palm** *(Rhapis excelsa)* features 6- to 12-inch-wide fans of thick, shiny leaflets, four to 10 per fan, that look like they were clipped with pinking shears. The fans grow at the ends of thin leafstalks that arch from a brown, hairy trunk. Popular varieties include *R. humilis* and *R. subtilis.* Variegated cultivars are also available and eagerly sought by collectors.

Fast-growing majesty palm *(Ravenea rivularis)* works well in large spaces. It eventually forms an upright trunk.

Pandanus
PAN-da-nus

SCREWPINE

Screwpine owes its name to its leaves, which spiral upward, corkscrew fashion, forming a rosette. The long, sword-shaped leaves resemble corn leaves but have prickly edges and a row of spines underneath. Even young plants soon develop a distinct trunk, often dotted with offsets. Thick aerial roots grow downward. On the sandy beaches where they grow wild, these roots act like props, holding them upright in the strongest winds. Even the aerial roots are, in most species, covered with small spines. Most screwpines become large trees eventually and either have to be cut back or started anew.

Common varieties include *P. veitchii*, with yellow- and green-striped leaves; its cultivar 'Verde', in which new growth is entirely milky white, then lime green, and finally dark green; *P. sanderii*, which is striped yellow; and *P. utilis*, with burgundy edges. *P. baptistii*, with blue-green leaves lightly striped yellow, is a child-safe pandanus—it has smooth leaf edges.

LIGHT: Medium to bright.
WATER: Keep evenly moist.
HUMIDITY: Average to high.
TEMPERATURE: Average.
FERTILIZER: All-purpose during growing period. Not a heavy feeder.
DIMENSIONS: 1 to 10 feet tall and 1 to 7 feet wide.
REPOTTING: As needed.
PROPAGATION: From offsets, and from seed when available.
PROBLEMS: Usually trouble-free, although spider mites and scale insects are possible. In very dry air, leaf edges may turn brown.
TIPS: Wash foliage from time to time. Train aerial roots into the soil. Keep spiny-leaved plants out of the reach of children.

Screwpine is an easy-to-grow foliage plant, but beware: Most types have spiny leaves.

Passiflora
pa-si-FLO-ra

PASSIONFLOWER

Passionflowers are large, rapidly growing vines that cling with long tendrils. The large flowers (4 to 6 inches wide) are complex and quite striking. All types produce abundant three-lobed leaflets. You'll need a trellis or some other support to grow these vigorous plants. Give them plenty of space for maximum bloom.

P. caerulea has purple, white, and blue flowers in summer and autumn. *P. coccinea* has showy crimson flowers with protruding bright yellow stamens. *P. vitifolia* produces larger, bright red flowers and is almost never without blossoms. *P.* 'Incense' has fragrant, wavy, royal purple flowers in summer. *P. quadrangularis* is the popular passionfruit. Outdoors, in the South, it produces huge edible fruits. Indoors, you'll probably have to content yourself with fragrant white, pink, or violet flowers in the summer.

LIGHT: Intense.
WATER: Keep evenly moist.
HUMIDITY: High.
TEMPERATURE: Average.
FERTILIZER: All-purpose during growing period.
REPOTTING: As needed.
DIMENSIONS: Up to 30 feet tall, but can be maintained from 4 to 10 feet tall and 1 to 4 feet wide by pruning.
PROPAGATION: From stem cuttings or seed.
PROBLEMS: Will not bloom in low light. Spider mites, whiteflies, and scale insects are possible pests.
TIP: Prune just before the heavy blooming season, being careful not to remove flower buds.

Passiflora caerulea 'Blue Crown' produces its exotic flowers in summer and fall.

Pelargonium
pe lar-GON-ee-um

Pelargoniums are easy to care for in the proper environment. A sunny windowsill where it is fairly cool (never above 75°F) is ideal. Fertilize regularly and water when the soil is dry.

Pelargoniums add distinction to an indoor decor all year. They bloom in every season but are most appreciated in January and February when little else is in flower. Many get quite large and need plenty of room, but the most popular types come in miniature and dwarf varieties. And fancy-leaf pelargoniums have varicolored leaves, often in bronzes, scarlets, whites, and yellows.

Zonal geraniums *(P. ×hortorum)* often have a dark green or blackish ring on each leaf. Thousands of cultivars exist. They can have single flowers, double flowers, cactus flowers, and many other forms in red, salmon, apricot, tangerine, pink, or white. They are particularly easy to grow, indoors and out, and bloom all year long under good conditions (and sporadically even under poor conditions). Most of the fancy-leaf pelargoniums are also *P. ×hortorum* selections.

Martha Washington or regal geranium *(P. ×domesticum)* grows to about 2½ feet. It is most famous for its flowers, which are large and come in a wide range of striking colors, some brilliantly blotched. Leaves are dark green, solid-looking, with crinkled margins, and often lemon-scented. It tends to bloom in spring, after exposure to cool winter temperatures.

Ivy geraniums, hybrids of *P. peltatum*, bear leathery leaves with a shape similar to English ivy and sport many clusters of showy flowers, often veined with a darker shade of the overall color. They have weak, spreading stems and are excellent in hanging baskets.

Scented-leaf varieties are grown

GERANIUM

primarily for the sharp, evocative fragrances of their leaves. *P. crispum* smells like lemon; *P. graveolens* and others, like rose; *P. ×nervosum*, like lime; *P. odoratissimum*, like apple; and the list goes on and on. Most bloom uniquely in summer and only under intense light.

In addition to these well-known groups of geraniums, there are many species plants of all shapes and sizes, some with succulent stems.

LIGHT: Bright to intense.

WATER: Let potting mix dry slightly between waterings.

HUMIDITY: Average.

TEMPERATURE: Average. Some prefer cool to cold in winter.

FERTILIZER: All-purpose in spring; potassium-rich when in bloom.

DIMENSIONS: 6 to 36 inches tall and wide.

REPOTTING: As needed. Transplant seedlings as they grow.

PROPAGATION: From softwood cuttings. Use rooting hormone and do not cover. Geraniums can be grown from seed.

PROBLEMS: Low light causes spindly growth and poor bloom.

Overwatering leads to stem or root rot. Whiteflies are a common problem: Inspect and treat cuttings from outdoor plants before bringing them indoors.

TIPS: Pinch back stem tips of young or regrowing plants in autumn to improve form, being careful not to remove new flower buds. Remove faded blossoms.

Clockwise fom left: scented geraniums; 'American Violet'; ivy geranium.

PELLIONIA

Pellionia
pe-lee-ON-ee-a

Rainbow vine (*P. pulchra*, syn. *Elatostema repens* var. *pulchra*) has satiny, marbled leaves.

Pellionia's stems creep over the soil, then arch outward and trail downward over the pot's edge, and so are particularly attractive in hanging baskets. The nearly petiole-less leaves closely hug the creeping stems like shingles on a roof. They are somewhat irregular in shape, but most are generally heart- to lance-shaped with rounded tips and an oblique base.

P. daveauana is called trailing watermelon begonia, with brown-purple leaves overlaid with a patch of silver-green. The creeping, trailing stems are fleshy and pale pink. Mossy masses of tiny greenish flowers appear at the leaf axils.

P. pulchra, called satiny pellionia because of its texture, differs by its light green to grayish and abundant marbled leaves with a complex series of blackish or brownish veins above, reddish purple below. The stems are rose or purple.

LIGHT: Medium to bright.
WATER: Keep evenly moist.
HUMIDITY: High.
TEMPERATURE: Average to high year round. Avoid cold drafts.
FERTILIZER: All-purpose during growing period. Not a heavy feeder.
DIMENSIONS: 2 to 12 inches tall; can trail to 2 feet or so.
REPOTTING: As needed.
PROPAGATION: From stem cuttings.
PROBLEMS: Drafts or dry air cause leaf scorch. Soil that's too wet or too dry causes leaf drop. Mealybugs and scale insects are possible pests.
TIPS: Prune as needed to maintain the desired size and shape. Stick a few cuttings into pots of taller growing houseplants to make a wonderful small groundcover and hide the potting mix.

STAR FLOWER, EGYPTIAN STAR CLUSTER

Pentas lanceolata
PEN-tas lan-kee-o-LAH-ta

'New Look Pink' is a dwarf hybrid that blooms nonstop in a sunny window. Move it outdoors for the summer.

Pentas is a shrubby plant with elliptic or lance-shaped green leaves, slightly hairy and with sunken veins. Rounded clusters of small flowers are borne at the stem tips and, under good light, *Pentas* keeps blooming at least sporadically through the entire year, generally most abundantly in the spring and summer. Under appropriate artificial lighting, it may bloom nonstop.

The main species, *P. lanceolata*, with rose to red flowers, has been mostly superseded by a series of denser, dwarf hybrids in various shades of white, pink, magenta, purple, lilac, and red, most of which stay below 3 feet tall and wide (some only 12 inches) and require no staking. Several series are on the market, most in the full range of colors, such as the New Look series and the Galaxy series. If you can't find this plant in the houseplant section of your garden center, look among the annuals, as it is becoming a very popular outdoor garden plant.

LIGHT: Intense.
WATER: Keep evenly moist during the growing season.
HUMIDITY: Average.
TEMPERATURE: Average. Avoid cold drafts.
FERTILIZER: All-purpose during growing season.
DIMENSIONS: Up to 6 feet tall and 3 feet wide, but usually maintained below 3 feet.
REPOTTING: As needed.
PROPAGATION: From softwood cuttings or seed.
PROBLEMS: Low light causes spindly growth and poor bloom. Dry air causes leaf dieback. Spider mites and aphids are possible pests.
TIP: Prune or clip to desired height and shape at any time.

PEPEROMIA

Peperomia
peh-peh ROM-ee-a

Peperomia is an extremely varied genus, with more than 1,000 species in the wild and numerous cultivars and selections. It offers an astonishing variety of leaf forms, colors, and growth habits. Most peperomias are easy-to-grow, small plants ideally suited to windowsills and plant shelves. Under good conditions, they produce curious creamy white blooms the shape of mouse tails.

LIGHT: Medium to bright.
WATER: Let potting mix dry slightly between waterings.
HUMIDITY: Average. Thin-leaved species need high humidity.
TEMPERATURE: Average.
FERTILIZER: All-purpose during growing season.
REPOTTING: As needed.
DIMENSIONS: Depending on the variety, 5 to 15 inches tall and 6 to 24 inches wide.
PROPAGATION: From stem cuttings and by division; from leaf cuttings for some species.
PROBLEMS: Low light causes spindly growth. Overwatering leads to crown rot. Insects are rarely a problem.
TIPS: Remove yellowed leaves. Prune or pinch upright and trailing types as needed.

■ **Clumping peperomias** are made up of a mass of leaves on short stems that originate from a central point and form a rosette.

Watermelon begonia *(P. argyreia,* formerly known as *P. sandersii)* has thick, smooth, almost round leaves striped with green and silver.

Emerald ripple *(P. caperata)* has small, dark, heart-shaped leaves with a deeply corrugated surface. It has provided numerous cultivars in a wide variety of shades, including 'Tricolor', with milky green leaves bordered in creamy white and with contrasting red markings, as well as selections with crested flowers.

Silverleaf peperomia *(P. griseoargentea)* has a similarly corrugated surface but is silvery gray.

Princess Astrid peperomia *(P. orba)* is a dwarf plant with spoon-shaped, apple-green leaves covered with fine hairs.

■ **Trailing peperomias** have weak, pendant stems. The best-known is false-philodendron *(P. scandens* 'Variegata'), which bears 2-inch heart-shaped leaves with a broad cream edge on arching stems. It looks much like a variegated version of the heart-leaf philodendron.

Creeping buttons *(P. rotundifolia pilosior)* is very different; it produces thin, weak, zigzagging stems and tiny, round, domed leaves with green and silver markings.

■ **Upright peperomias** have visible stems that generally grow upward but often fall prostrate as they become heavier.

Baby rubber plant *(P. obtusifolia,* also called *P. magnoliifolia)* is the best known. It bears thick stems and waxy, rubbery, obtuse leaves of varying sizes. It has many cultivars with different forms of variegation, from light speckling to large zones of yellow or cream, or with red leaf margins, including 'Variegata', with broad, irregular variegation in yellow or creamy white, mostly along the edges.

Quite different is *P. verticillata,* with its shiny, pointed leaves in whorls of three to five along an upright, reddish stem.

Pelted peperomia *(P. incana)* is equally odd. It has thick, succulent stems like *P. obtusifolia,* but its thick, round leaves are covered in grayish fuzz.

Baby rubber plant *(P. obtusifolia)* is easy to grow on a windowsill. Many interesting cultivars are available.

Emerald ripple *(P. caperata)* produces unusual creamy white blooms.

Persea americana
PER-see-a a-me-ri-KAH-na

AVOCADO

Avocados are popular classroom and kitchen plants because the huge seeds germinate so readily. The best way to start an avocado is to carefully remove the seed from a fully mature fruit and half-bury it in a good growing mix, with the pointed end up. (You can remove the brown seed envelope before planting if you wish.) Within a few weeks, a sturdy green stem will grow straight upward, producing leaves as it grows. Pinch frequently or soon all you'll have is a single stem 10 feet tall with leaves only at the top. Avocados will not flower or set fruit indoors.

You also can start seeds in water. Stick four toothpicks into the sides of the seed at the same level all around so you can suspend it from

Children enjoy growing avocados because the seeds germinate quickly. The plants don't flower or fruit indoors.

the top of a glass or jar. Add water so the bottom of the seed is always moist. Pot it into growing mix when the roots are still small.

LIGHT: Intense. Tolerates medium light for long periods.
WATER: Keep evenly moist.
HUMIDITY: High.
TEMPERATURE: Average.
FERTILIZER: All-purpose during growing season.
DIMENSIONS: Easily maintained under 5 feet tall and 3 feet wide by pruning.
REPOTTING: As needed.
PROPAGATION: From seed.
PROBLEMS: Low light causes weak, spindly growth. Dry air causes leaf dieback. Overwatering leads to root rot. Thrips and mealybugs are possible pests.
TIPS: Pinch back stem tips routinely to encourage branching. Stake to keep plant upright. Compost the plant when it is no longer attractive.

Philodendron
fi-lo-DEN-dron

PHILODENDRON

No other group of plants is as widely used indoors as philodendrons. The great variety of sizes and growth habits, as well as the uniquely shaped glossy leaves, gives the indoor gardener many choices for almost any situation. Philodendrons are tough, tolerant plants that don't need a lot of sunlight. They are classified

according to their growth habit either as tree philodendrons, clump-forming philodendrons, or climbers.

The climbing species are the ones most commonly grown in the home. Under humid conditions, they can attach themselves to a support, especially if it has a rough surface, such as a bark slab or osmunda pole. Otherwise tie them to their support as they grow. Many of the climbing species also make great

Heart-leaf philodendron (left); 'Kaleidoscope' (above)

trailing plants for hanging baskets.

Tree philodendrons can become large plants 6 to 8 feet tall. Their leaves, of varying shapes, extend from self-supporting "trunks." Most produce aerial roots that reach down to the soil and help anchor the plant. You can cut those off but the plant may then need a stake to stay upright. Tree philodendrons are ideal for offices or large rooms with high ceilings.

Clump-forming philodendrons form ground-hugging rosettes that are often wider than tall. They rarely need staking and don't usually produce aerial roots. Some get lanky over time; just cut them back and they'll return to their original dense form. They make perfect floor or table plants for indoor locations with medium light.

LIGHT: Medium to bright. Some tolerate low light.
WATER: Keep evenly moist.

PHILODENDRON *(continued)*

HUMIDITY: Average; high for some.
TEMPERATURE: Average.
FERTILIZER: All-purpose during growing season. Do not fertilize plants in low light.
DIMENSIONS: Depending on type, from 1 to 10 feet tall and 1 to 8 feet wide.
REPOTTING: As needed.
PROPAGATION: From stem cuttings or by layering or air-layering.
PROBLEMS: Climbers become barren at the base with time. Spider mites, mealybugs, and scale insects are possible, but usually philodendrons are pest-free.
TIPS: Prune to keep climbing types to desired height and shape. Direct aerial roots to soil or remove them if they are unattractive. Clean the leaves periodically. All parts of the plant are toxic and the sap irritates the skin. Keep out of reach of children.

Lacy tree philodendron (*P. bipinnatifidum*) is a nonclimbing, cut-leaf species with a distinct trunk. It is often available as a small, immature plant with short petioles and arrow-shaped leaves. As it matures, the leaves become larger and more deeply cut, with long petioles. It tends to outgrow its allotted space quickly. The plant sold as *P. selloum* is now considered to be a *P. bipinnatifidum* with especially deeply cut leaves.

Spade-leaf philodendron (*P. domesticum*, also sold as *P. hastatum*) is a lush, evergreen, climbing vine with aerial roots. Deeply veined, bright green leaves take the shape of giant spearheads, 8 to 12 inches long. Keep it out of cold drafts.

Split-leaf philodendron (*P. pertusum*) is now classified as *Monstera deliciosa*. See page 168 for more information.

Red-leaf philodendron (*P. erubescens*) has red stems topped with bright green, yellow-veined,

Lacy-tree philodendron

spear-shaped leaves. It's a climber.

Heart-leaf philodendron (*P. scandens oxycardium*, also known as *P. cordatum*) has many glossy, deep green leaves. It is the most popular philodendron grown in North America. Because it's a vigorous climber, train it on a column, frame a window with it, or hang it from a beamed ceiling. This plant does fine in low light and is one of the easiest of all houseplants to grow. Limeleaf vine, *P. scandens* 'Aureum' ('Golden'), has lemon yellow new growth turning to lime green. *P. scandens micans* has plush, velvety bronze leaves that are red underneath, and 'Variegatum' has leaves splashed with gray, white, and dark green.

Hybrid philodendrons are usually clump-forming plants with attractive, glossy foliage. Many have some climbing genes in their background and will eventually produce stems that begin to clamber. You can either provide a support or cut them back to rekindle their juvenile habit. Those with colored leaves need bright light to perform well. 'Black Cardinal' has glossy, deep purple, nearly black leaves; new leaves are a coppery-bronze color when they first unfurl. 'Moonlight' has pointed

Red-leaf philodendron (*P. erubescens* 'Imperial Red')

***P. squamiferum* is one of the parents of *P.* 'Florida'.**

spade-shaped leaves in bright chartreuse green, darkening to lime green. 'Prince of Orange' has coppery-orange new leaves that fade to pale green. 'Xanadu' has arrow-shaped medium-green leaves with very regular lobes.

Philodendron 'Moonlight'

PILEA

Aluminum-plant (*P. cadierei* 'Minima') is a compact cultivar with silver markings.

More than 600 widely varied species belong to the genus *Pilea*. Most of those suitable for indoor gardening are small to moderately sized herbaceous plants, rarely more than a foot tall. They often have leaves with depressed veins, giving them a quilted appearance. The dark green leaves of many species are tinged with red, silver, or copper. Still others have a creeping or trailing habit that makes them particularly useful in hanging baskets. Some species produce inconspicuous flowers in summer.

Pileas are most attractive when young; prune them back severely or started anew from cuttings on a regular basis.

LIGHT: Bright.

WATER: Keep evenly moist.

HUMIDITY: High.

TEMPERATURE: Average to high. Avoid cold drafts.

FERTILIZER: All-purpose during growing period. Not a heavy feeder.

DIMENSIONS: 6 to 12 inches tall and 6 to 24 inches wide.

REPOTTING: Annually in late winter or early spring.

PROPAGATION: From stem cuttings. *P. microphylla* self-sows.

PROBLEMS: Low light causes spindly growth. Overwatering leads to crown rot. Cold air or cold water damages leaves; keep them warm at all times. Spider mites and mealybugs are possible pests.

TIPS: Start new plants to replace old specimens as they get weak. Prune to maintain desired size.

Aluminum-plant (*P. cadierei*) is one of the most popular species. Its wafered, green leaves look like they have been brushed with silver paint. *P. cadierei* 'Silver Tree' is similar, but has bronze leaves flushed silver.

Shiny creeping Charlie (*P. depressa*) is a low, creeping plant with small, rounded, dark green leaves and a smooth, hairless surface. It's a good choice for hanging baskets or for terrarium and dish gardens.

Panamiga or friendship-plant (*P. involucrata*) is like *P. cadierei*, but more compact, with thick clusters of broad leaves. They are yellow-green with a coppery sheen above, and they have a rich, velvety texture. *P. involucrata* 'Norfolk' has larger leaves in deep bronze and bright silver markings. *P. involucrata* 'Moon Valley' is taller and more upright, with larger, corrugated leaves. They are fresh green, with deep purple veins.

Artillery plant (*P. microphylla*) bears arching, upright, green stems and tiny, fleshy, apple-green leaves. It gets its common name from its tiny flowers that shoot out pollen within seconds after being watered. It self-sows abundantly when it is healthy and can even become an indoor weed. Dwarf, creeping, and variegated selections of this plant are available. *P. serpyllacea* is similar but has somewhat larger, more rounded leaves.

Chinese money plant (*P. peperomioides*) is an unusual pilea, looking much more like a peperomia, as the botanical name suggests. It produces thick, waxy, dark green, shieldlike leaves on a short, solid stem. It is more resistant to drought and cold temperatures than other pileas.

Hairy creeping Charlie (*P. nummulariifolia*) is much like *P. depressa* but with larger, paler green leaves and long creeping, trailing stems that cascade straight down over the pot edge 3 feet or more. It is best in a hanging basket.

The flowers of artillery plant (*P. microphylla*) shoot pollen.

***P. involucrata* 'Moon Valley' has large, textured leaves with purple veins.**

Pisonia umbellifera 'Variegata'
pis-OH-nee-a um-bel-LIF-er-a

In the wild, overly eager sparrows occasionally manage to work themselves in among the sticky, nutlike fruits of the birdcatcher tree and end up being trapped. Indoors, this plant produces neither its usual pale yellow or pink funnel-shaped flowers nor fruit.

Outdoors, birdcatcher tree grows very tall, but indoors it is grown as a shrub. It generally grows upward at first, then becomes more spreading. It branches abundantly if pinched occasionally.

Indoors, you'll want the variegated selection *P. umbellifera* 'Variegata' (syn. *Heimerliodendron brunoniana* 'Variegatum'). It bears large, whorled, elliptic to lance-shaped leaves that are medium green in the center but generously splashed and margined with creamy white. New leaves have a pinkish tinge that lasts for weeks.

BIRDCATCHER TREE

LIGHT: Bright to intense.
WATER: Keep evenly moist.
HUMIDITY: High.
TEMPERATURE: Average. Keep plants out of cold drafts.
FERTILIZER: All-purpose during growing period.
DIMENSIONS: Usually maintained under 3 feet tall and wide indoors.
REPOTTING: As needed.
PROPAGATION: From softwood or semi-ripe cuttings, with rooting hormone, or by air layering.
PROBLEMS: Dry air causes leaf dieback. Overwatering leads to root rot. Spider mites and scale insects are possible pests.
TIP: Prune as needed to keep the plant dense and compact.

Variegated birdcatcher tree won't catch anything but your attention with its dramatic foliage.

Pittosporum tobira
pi-TOS-po-rum to-BI-ra

Japanese pittosporum is a slow-growing woody shrub. Its primary attraction indoors comes from its glossy, leathery, whorled, dark green leaves that resemble those of a rhododendron. You can grow it uniquely as a foliage plant, but in late winter or early spring, it produces dense terminal clusters of flowers that are creamy white upon opening, then age to yellow. The blooms are highly fragrant, smelling much like orange blossoms. To obtain abundant blooms, though, keep it in a cool spot in the winter and in bright light year-round.

Although the species, with its solid green leaves, is occasionally available, *P. tobira* 'Variegata' is the cultivar most commonly sold as a houseplant. Its leaves are grayish green with a variable white margin. It blooms just as readily.

JAPANESE PITTOSPORUM, JAPANESE MOCK ORANGE

LIGHT: Bright, or medium if flowering is not a priority.
WATER: Let potting mix dry slightly between waterings.
HUMIDITY: Average.
TEMPERATURE: Cool to cold. Tolerates average temperatures but may fail to bloom.
FERTILIZER: All-purpose during growing period. Not a heavy feeder.
DIMENSIONS: Usually maintained under 3 feet tall and wide indoors.
REPOTTING: As needed.
PROPAGATION: From semi-ripe cuttings with rooting hormone, or by air layering.
PROBLEMS: Low light causes weak growth and poor bloom. Spider mites, mealybugs, and scale insects are possible pests.
TIPS: Prune after flowering to maintain the desired size and shape. Because it grows so slowly, always

purchase a large enough specimen for your current needs.

P. tobira 'Variegata' produces abundant early-spring flowers that smell like orange blossoms.

SWEDISH IVY

Plectranthus
plek-TRANTH-us

Pinch off Swedish ivy's flower spikes to keep the plant healthy.

P. coleoides 'Marginatus' has small leaves that smell minty when crushed.

Silver plectranthus (*P. argentatus*) is a larger-leaved, more erect species.

Most Swedish ivies grow upright at first, then lean over and eventually trail, making them ideal choices for hanging baskets. The stems are usually square and the leaves are often rounded or scalloped and may have a medicinal smell. Spikes of tiny two-lipped flowers, often white or pale mauve, appear occasionally. Pinch these off; blooming seems to weaken several species.

These striking plants are fairly tolerant and require a minimum of care. Place them in bright light and water regularly.

LIGHT: Medium to bright, with full sun in winter.

WATER: Keep evenly moist.

HUMIDITY: Average.

TEMPERATURE: Average.

FERTILIZER: All-purpose during growing season.

DIMENSIONS: Depending on species, 10 to 15 inches tall and 24 to 48 inches wide.

REPOTTING: As needed.

PROPAGATION: From stem cuttings or by layering.

PROBLEMS: Overwatering leads to stem rot. Spider mites and mealybugs are possible pests.

TIPS: Pinch back stem tips of young plants to improve form. Plants do not age gracefully; start new plants to replace old specimens when they become weak. Bring cuttings from container plants indoors for the winter.

P. amboinicus (syn. *Coleus amboinicus*) is often called Spanish thyme, Cuban oregano, Indian borage, or Mexican mint because of its use as a culinary plant in tropical countries. It has thick, succulent, hairy, grayish-green leaves that when stroked or crushed give off a scent like a mix of thyme and oregano. At least two variegated forms exist: one with white leaf margins sometimes tinted pink and one with a chartreuse splotch in the center of the leaf.

Silver plectranthus (*P. argentatus*) has a more upright, erect habit, often forming a single rosette. It produces much larger leaves than other Swedish ivies, up to 4½ inches long. They are entirely covered with white hairs, giving the plant a silvery, textured appearance. After producing its upright spikes of usually light purple flowers, the plant degrades considerably, so the flowers are usually removed. This species prefers intense light and is more drought-tolerant than most.

P. australis (syn. *P. nummularius*) is the old-fashioned Swedish ivy. It has waxy, leathery, bright green leaves and a trailing habit.

P. australis 'Variegatus' has leaves irregularly marbled white.

P. forsteri (syn. *P. coleoides*) has a shrubby habit at first, becoming trailing only at maturity, and fairly large, fuzzy, distinctly toothed leaves. Its cultivar 'Marginatus', with white margined leaves, is best known, but several other selections are available.

Mintleaf (*P. madgascariensis*) has a distinctly creeping habit and small leaves. In a hanging container, its stems cascade nearly straight down 4 or 5 feet. Its leaves give off a mintlike scent when crushed. Most common is *P. madgascariensis* 'Variegated Mintleaf' (syn. *P. coleoides* 'Marginatus'), which has bordered leaves.

Candle plant (*P. oertendahlii*) has scalloped, velvety green leaves with silver veins above and purple below. The narrow spikes of white to light blue flowers appear sporadically throughout the year, often in great numbers.

Plumbago auriculata
plum-BAH-go ow-rik-ew-LAH-ta

PLUMBAGO, CAPE LEADWORT

Plumbago (*Plumbago auriculata*, syn. *P. capensis*) is grown for its abundant pale blue flowers that can appear nonstop from spring through fall. Although a climber in the wild, in pots it is usually grown either as a shrub or a trailer.

The spoon shaped leaves are medium green or sometimes grayish, about 1½ to 3 inches long. The flowers are trumpet-shaped, with a flaring corolla of five petals and a distinctive sunken midvein. The flowers are similar to garden phlox (*Phlox paniculata*), borne in dense terminal clusters about 6 inches across. Buy a large plant if you want results the first year, as plumbago is very slow-growing.

P. auriculata alba, with pure white flowers, is a popular selection. If you find the pale blue flowers of the regular plumbago too washed out, try the cobalt blue selection 'Royal Cape'. A few other selections are available in various intensities of blue.

LIGHT: Intense.
WATER: Keep evenly moist; drier in winter.
HUMIDITY: High.
TEMPERATURE: Average; cool in winter.
FERTILIZER: All-purpose during growing season.
DIMENSIONS: Usually less than 3 feet tall and wide indoors.
REPOTTING: As needed.
PROPAGATION: From softwood cuttings with rooting hormone, or seed.
PROBLEMS: Low light causes spindly growth and poor bloom. Yellow leaves indicate a lack of manganese; apply a fertilizer with a complete range of trace elements. Spider mites, whiteflies, and mealybugs are possible pests.

TIP: Prune as needed to maintain desired size and shape.

Grow plumbago in a sunny, humid spot and you'll be rewarded with nonstop flowers from spring through fall.

Podocarpus macrophyllus 'Maki'
po-do-KAR-pus mak-ro-FIL-lus MAH-kee

BUDDHIST PINE, SOUTHERN YEW

Indoors this coniferous tree must be maintained as a shrub. Fortunately it reacts very well to pruning. Pinching the tips encourages branching and bushiness. It can even be maintained as a bonsai. The flowers and purple fruit are almost never produced indoors. The form usually grown is 'Maki'; it has a denser habit and shorter needles than the species. It's a slow-growing plant that does best with cool winters.

Its near relative, *P. gracilior*, also known as the African fern pine, produces graceful, arching to pendulous branches with narrow, glossy, blue-green needles. The best specimens have a structure that's similar to a small weeping willow. Look for plants that already show a weeping habit, as this characteristic is variable. It needs more light than a Buddhist pine.

When propagating *Podocarpus*, always take cuttings of an upright, terminal shoot. Side shoots produce plants with strictly horizontal growth.
LIGHT: Medium to intense.
WATER: Let potting mix dry slightly between waterings.
HUMIDITY: Average.
TEMPERATURE: Average; cool to cold in winter.
FERTILIZER: All-purpose during growing period. Not a heavy feeder.
DIMENSIONS: Depending on how much you prune, from 10 inches to 10 feet tall and wide.
REPOTTING: As needed.
PROPAGATION: Semi-ripe cuttings with rooting hormone, or seed.
PROBLEMS: Overwatering leads to stem rot. Leaves die back in dry air. Spider mites, whiteflies, mealybugs, and scale insects are possible pests.
TIPS: Prune as needed to maintain the desired size and shape. Because it grows so slowly, always purchase a large enough specimen for your current needs.

Pruning is the key to maintaining *Podocarpus* as an indoor plant. You also can use it as a bonsai subject.

ARALIA

Polyscias
po-LYE-skee-us

Polyscias are woody shrubs frequently grown indoors for their lacy, often variegated foliage and their treelike appearance even when small. In fact, Ming aralia is often used as an indoor bonsai.

Aralias grow large and bushy and are popular in commercial interiors. The leaves of some cultivars are aromatic when crushed or bruised. Give aralias plenty of room, and prune them frequently to achieve good form. Most achieve tree size outdoors and require pinching to maintain in the home. None of them is likely to bloom indoors.

Don't let their deeply cut, fernlike leaves fool you: They need bright light and potting mix that dries out a bit between waterings. They also require high humidity; if you find the leaves dropping off, try growing the plant on a humidity tray.

Ming aralia (*P. fruticosa*) has small, deeply cut, dense foliage. It needs bright light and high humidity.

LIGHT: Medium to bright.
WATER: Let the potting mix dry slightly between waterings.
HUMIDITY: High.
TEMPERATURE: Average.
FERTILIZER: All-purpose during growing period. Not a heavy feeder.
DIMENSIONS: 2 to 10 feet tall and 18 inches to 3 feet wide indoors.
REPOTTING: As needed.
PROPAGATION: From stem or root cuttings.
PROBLEMS: Low light causes spindly growth. Overwatering leads to stem rot. Dry air causes leaf drop and browning. Spider mites, mealybugs, and scale insects are possible pests.
TIP: Prune as needed to maintain desired size and shape.

Fern-leaf aralia (*P. filicifolia*) bears deeply cut olive-green leaves with purple midribs. It tends to form a single stem when young, although the leaves are so deeply cut and have so many leaflets that they pass for branches, giving the plant a fuller look. Pinch repeatedly to stimulate abundant stems or pot several plants in a single container. *P. filicifolia* 'Marginata' has leaves with white margins.

Ming aralia (*P. fruticosa*) has leaves much like those of fern-leaf aralia, only smaller and denser. It naturally looks so much like a small tree when young that it is often simply sold as a bonsai. Its cultivar 'Elegans' is smaller, with extremely dense foliage. It is often called parsley-aralia.

Roseleaf aralia (*P. guilfoylei*) gets its name from the way the leaves are cut. Each shiny medium-green leaflet is generally ovate with deep lobes, sharp cuts, and white margins. 'Laciniata' is more deeply cut, with white-margined, lance-shaped green leaflets. The variety usually sold, though, is 'Victoriae', lace aralia, with more deeply cut fernlike leaflets, also with white margins.

P. scutellaria differs from other aralias due to its rounded leaflets. They are glossy, dark green, and leathery, with distinctly sunken veins. The stems are glossy and bronzy with gray speckles. Most popular is *P. scutellaria* 'Balfourii' (*P. balfouriana*), with scalloped edges and a white margin. *P. scutellaria* 'Blackie' has smooth-edged leaflets in a very dark green, nearly purple-black shade. *P. scutellaria* 'Pennockii' is a highly variegated creamy white.

P. scutellaria 'Balfourii' (balfour aralia) has rounded leaves with scalloped, white-margined edges.

Primula
PREEM-ew-la

Though spectacular in bloom, primroses are not good long-term houseplants. Instead they are florist's plants, bought in bloom to decorate the home for a few weeks.

Primroses produce magnificent clusters of flowers above a rosette of light to medium green leaves in winter and early spring. For maximum bloom, choose healthy-looking plants with medium-green leaves and plenty of buds with only a few flowers open. Check under the leaves for signs of insects or diseases.

If you want to try growing them yourself, sow the fine seed on the surface of the soil and keep it moist and cool, even during germination. High humidity and cool temperatures are needed throughout the growing cycle. Pot seedlings into small individual pots, then repot to larger ones as they grow.

LIGHT: Bright, with full sun in winter.
WATER: Keep evenly moist.
HUMIDITY: High.
TEMPERATURE: Cool to cold.
FERTILIZER: No need to fertilize temporary plants. If you grow them from seed, use an all-purpose fertilizer.

PRIMROSE

DIMENSIONS: 6 to 18 inches tall and 6 to 20 inches wide.
REPOTTING: Not required for temporary plants. Pot seedlings into larger pots as needed.
PROPAGATION: From seed; *P. xpolyanthus* by division.
PROBLEMS: Dry air and heat cause leaf dieback and short-lived blooms. Excess mineral salts cause dieback. Spider mites can cause considerable damage, especially in dry air.
TIPS: Buy this plant in bloom and compost it when it has finished blooming. Only gardeners with cool to cold greenhouses should consider growing primroses from seed.

Fairy primrose (*P. malacoides*) bears star-shaped, scented flowers, single or double, usually in shades of white, lilac, pink, or red, in tiers on tall stalks up to 18 inches high. It forms a rosette of oval, softly downy, pale green leaves with lightly frilled margins.

German primrose (*P. obconica*), sometimes sold as *P. sinensis*, reaches a foot in height and blooms in white, lilac, crimson, or salmon. This small plant features delicate, ruffled flowers in a wide range of colors, including pink, lilac-blue, white, and red. The flowers are borne on thick, hairy stems over a rosette of rather coarse oval or heart-shaped medium-green leaves. Avoid handling this plant: The leaves contain primin, a skin-irritating substance to which some individuals are severely allergic. Or try primin-free strains, such as 'Libre'.

Polyanthus primrose (*P. xpolyanthus*) is a common garden perennial often offered as a gift plant in late winter or spring. It forms a rosette of heavily veined, strap-shaped leaves and bears dense clusters of colorful trumpet-shaped flowers on short stems. Flower colors include red, pink, white, yellow, orange, blue,

Fairy primrose (*P. malacoides*) holds its delicate, fragrant blooms on tall stalks above the foliage.

and purple, usually with a yellow eye. Unlike the other primroses, *P. xpolyanthus* can recuperate after blooming. After all danger of frost has passed, plant it in the garden in moist soil and partial shade.

German primrose (*P. obconica*) grows to a foot tall.

P. sinensis cultivars are among the earliest to bloom.

Pseuderanthemum
atropurpureum 'Tricolor'
soo-de-RANTH-uh-mum a-tro-pur-PEWR-ee-um

Purple false eranthemum has attractive flowers and even more spectacular marbled foliage.

PURPLE FALSE ERANTHEMUM

Purple false eranthemum is an open shrub that grows to 5 feet tall and fills out wonderfully when pinched occasionally. You can easily maintain it at less than half that size indoors. It is grown for its spectacularly colored foliage: The large elliptic leaves are a beautiful bronze-purple heavily splashed with slate green and pink. It has attractive spikes of tubular white flowers with purple spotting. These are borne in summer but don't stand out well against the colorful background of the foliage.

Other selections of this plant exist, including *Pseuderanthemum atropurpureum carruthersii*, with broad, metallic, deep purple leaves.

The gold vein shrub, *P. reticulatum*, is a close cousin, with similar blooms and narrower green leaves sporting showy yellow veins. *P. alatum* is the chocolate plant, a smaller plant that grows to about a foot tall (taller when in bloom), with winged petioles and heart-shaped leaves in a beautiful chocolate brown with silver blotches along the midrib.

LIGHT: Bright.

WATER: Keep evenly moist.

HUMIDITY: High.

TEMPERATURE: Average. Keep plants out of cold drafts.

FERTILIZER: All-purpose during growing period.

DIMENSIONS: 1 to 5 feet tall and 12 to 30 inches wide.

REPOTTING: As needed.

PROPAGATION: From semi-ripe cuttings.

PROBLEMS: Low light causes spindly growth. Dry air causes leaf dieback. Overwatering leads to stem rot. Spider mites and whiteflies are possible pests.

TIPS: Prune as needed to maintain the desired size and shape. Remove yellowed leaves and faded flowers.

Punica granatum nana
PEW-ni-ka gra-NAH-tum NA-na

Dwarf pomegranate is easy to grow and flowers and fruits indoors in intense light and high humidity.

DWARF POMEGRANATE

Dwarf pomegranate is a natural dwarf. It grows to 6 feet or more outdoors but with minimal pruning is easily kept at half that height indoors. It is popular as a bonsai subject because of its flowers and fruits that grow in proportion to the size of the plant.

Dwarf pomegranate has small, shiny, narrow dark green leaves. In early summer, but also sporadically throughout the year, it produces showy scarlet flowers with salmon calyxes that look a bit like fuchsia flowers. They form edible 2-inch reddish fruits. Stake any branches heavily laden with fruit, or they will bend over.

Several cultivars of dwarf pomegranate exist, with various flower colors or double blooms. In fact, you may find that the dwarf pomegranate sold to you is actually *P. granatum nana plena*, with double scarlet flowers.

For an edible fruit, dwarf pomegranate is surprisingly easy to grow indoors, although it does need very bright light and preferably full sun. It also makes an excellent patio plant for the container garden.

LIGHT: Intense.

WATER: Keep evenly moist; drier in winter.

HUMIDITY: High.

TEMPERATURE: Average; cool to cold in winter.

FERTILIZER: All-purpose during growing period.

DIMENSIONS: 12 to 40 inches tall and wide.

REPOTTING: Infrequently; blooms best when pot-bound.

PROPAGATION: From softwood cuttings or seed (single varieties).

PROBLEMS: Spider mites, whiteflies, mealybugs, and scale insects are possible pests.

TIPS: Prune as needed to maintain the desired size and shape. Leave faded flowers on the plant to produce fruit.

Radermachera sinica
rad-ur-mah-KEHR-uh SEE-nee-kuh

The shiny, bright green leaves of *R. sinica* are doubly compound, giving it a delicate, fernlike appearance. Each leaf measures up to 2 feet long and nearly as wide, with innumerable pointed leaflets, although young plants have much smaller, less abundantly divided leaves. Overall the leaves resemble the fronds of the holly fern (*Cyrtomium falcatum*), with a similar leathery, glossy appearance.

Although China doll is actually a tree, the plants usually sold are barely more than seedlings and don't even yet have woody stems, let alone branches. For a fuller appearance in the nursery, China doll is usually planted three to a pot. It is also treated with a growth retardant, which decreases the distance between the leaves, making the plant more compact. When the

CHINA DOLL

effect wears off, you'll have to begin pinching and pruning to stimulate branching. China doll does not bloom indoors.

LIGHT: Medium to bright.
WATER: Keep evenly moist.
HUMIDITY: Average to high.
TEMPERATURE: Average.
FERTILIZER: All-purpose during growing period. Not a heavy feeder.
DIMENSIONS: 8 inches to 5 feet tall and 8 inches to 4 feet wide.
REPOTTING: As needed.
PROPAGATION: From seed or cuttings, or by air layering.
PROBLEMS: Low light causes spindly growth. Dry air or overly dry soil causes leaf dieback. Overwatering leads to stem rot. Whiteflies, mealybugs and scale insects are possible pests.
TIPS: Remove yellowed leaves. Pinch regularly to maintain compact shape.

China doll is actually a tree, so it needs regular pinching and pruning to maintain its compact shape.

Rhododendron Indica hybrids
ro-do-DEN-dron IN-di-ka

Pot azaleas are usually sold in full bloom in a wide range of whites, pinks, salmons, reds, and bicolors. Their funnel-shaped flowers are usually semidouble or double. Unlike other azaleas, pot azaleas are evergreens, holding on to their small, thin, dark green leaves all year.

Pot azaleas were developed as gift plants. Usually winter-flowering, they are now offered all year long thanks to careful greenhouse culture. After flowering, some people simply toss them into the compost, but you can get them to bloom again. They need cold nights to initiate bloom, so put them outside in fall, bringing them indoors only when frost threatens. Better cultivars bloom through much of the winter; some bloom sporadically throughout the year.

LIGHT: Bright. Place temporary plants in any location.

POT AZALEA, BELGIAN AZALEA

WATER: Keep evenly moist.
HUMIDITY: High.
TEMPERATURE: Average; cooler in winter. Avoid cold drafts.
FERTILIZER: Acid-based with added trace elements.
DIMENSIONS: 6 inches to 4 feet tall and wide.
REPOTTING: Infrequently; does best if slightly pot-bound. Use a lime-free potting mix.
PROPAGATION: From softwood cuttings, with rooting hormone.
PROBLEMS: Low light causes spindly growth and poor bloom. Year-round warm temperatures prevent blooming. Dry air or soil causes leaf drop. Excess mineral salts cause leaf-tip burn and stem dieback, so leach frequently. Spider mites, aphids, mealybugs, and scale insects are possible pests.
TIP: Prune after flowering. The flowers of some plants are toxic, so keep away from children.

You can encourage a pot azalea to bloom again by moving it outdoors in the fall when nights are cool.

MINIATURE ROSE

Rosa
RO-sa

Grow miniature roses indoors as you would outside: in bright light and cool air with good circulation.

Usually thought of as outdoor plants, miniature roses also lend grace to your indoor decor. Delicate 1- to 1½-inch blooms are available in a wide range of colors. Grown as small bushes, climbers, or standards, they always make an appealing tabletop display.

Miniature roses are sold as gift plants, designed to be discarded after blooming or planted outdoors in the garden. But it is possible to grow and bloom miniature roses indoors. To succeed, give them the same care you would give them outdoors: abundant light and cool, well-circulated air. If possible, provide cold temperatures during the winter to replicate dormancy.

Spider mites are a major problem indoors, but rinsing miniature roses weekly under the faucet knocks the pests off before they can do any serious damage.

LIGHT: Intense.

WATER: Let the potting mix dry slightly between waterings.

HUMIDITY: High.

TEMPERATURE: Cool; cold in winter. Tolerates average temperatures.

FERTILIZER: All-purpose during growing season.

DIMENSIONS: 6 to 24 inches tall and 6 to 18 inches wide.

REPOTTING: In any season.

PROPAGATION: From softwood cuttings.

PROBLEMS: Poor light prevents blooming. Soil that's too wet or too dry causes leaf drop. Highly susceptible to spider mites, especially in dry air. Rinse plant weekly to prevent spider mites. Whiteflies, aphids, mealybugs, and scale insects are also common pests. Several leaf diseases are possible, although not as prevalent as on outdoor roses.

TIPS: Prune as needed to maintain the desired size and shape. Remove yellow leaves and faded flowers.

MONKEY-PLANT, TRAILING VELVET PLANT

Ruellia makoyana
roo-EL-ee-a ma-koy-AH-na

Monkey-plant blooms in fall and winter, but its foliage is attractive throughout the year, especially in hanging baskets.

The most commonly grown *Ruellia* for indoor use is *R. makoyana*, the monkey-plant. It's definitely a dual-purpose plant, enjoyed as much for its colorful foliage as for its bloom. This plant remains attractive throughout the year because of its thin, ovate leaves, which are silver-veined and velvety, olive green above and purple underneath. Blooms are numerous trumpet-shaped rose red flowers up to 2 inches in diameter, appearing during fall and winter.

Monkey-plant often has an open, airy habit, especially when in poor light, so you should pinch or prune it regularly to stimulate branching and denser growth. Trimming even helps improve flowering, as new growth produces blooms. You can form it into a small shrub or accentuate its trailing habit for use in a hanging basket.

Monkey-plant thrives indoors but does best in high humidity. Use a humidifier or a humidity tray if your house is dry.

LIGHT: Bright.

WATER: Keep evenly moist.

HUMIDITY: High.

TEMPERATURE: Average.

FERTILIZER: All-purpose during growing period.

DIMENSIONS: 10 to 24 inches tall and 10 to 18 inches wide.

REPOTTING: Annually.

PROPAGATION: From softwood cuttings.

PROBLEMS: Low light causes spindly growth and poor bloom. Overwatering leads to stem rot. Spider mites, whiteflies, mealybugs, and scale insects are possible pests.

TIPS: Pinch back regularly for full growth. Prune after flowering. Start anew from cuttings or seed when older plants' health goes downhill.

Saintpaulia ionantha
saynt-PAWL-ee-a ee-on-AN-tha

No other plant can match African violet's ability to thrive and bloom indoors for months on end. Its compact size makes it perfect for windowsills or small tabletop arrangements, and it fits wonderfully into light gardens.

Typical plants produce a single rosette of velvety leaves on short petioles and bear clusters of single, semidouble or double flowers in white or shades of pink, red, violet, purple, or blue, and even lime green, pale yellow, and bicolors. Petals can be ruffled, rounded, or fringed, star- or bell-shaped. Foliage is likewise quite variable. Leaves are usually hairy and spoon-shaped but can be smooth or ruffled, medium to dark green, with varying degrees of white, cream, yellow, or pink variegation.

Standard varieties form rosettes 8 inches or more in diameter. Semiminiatures range from 6 to 8 inches; miniatures, from 3 to 6 inches; and microminiatures, less than 3 inches in diameter.

Trailing African violets come in all sizes, most resulting from crosses with other *Saintpaulia* species. Instead of a single rosette, they bear numerous stems that arch outward and hang down. They look best in hanging baskets.

African violets have a reputation for being temperamental but that isn't true. Plenty of bright, indirect light is the key to constant bloom. Supplement with artificial light in winter. Evenly moist soil, warm temperatures, high humidity, and light but regular applications of fertilizer are the other important factors for growth. Except for trailing types, plants will flower best with only one crown per pot.

LIGHT: Bright.
WATER: Keep evenly moist. Avoid wetting foliage.
HUMIDITY: High.

AFRICAN VIOLET

TEMPERATURE: Average. Avoid sudden changes in temperature.
FERTILIZER: All-purpose during growing season.
DIMENSIONS: 2 to 10 inches tall and 2 to 24 inches wide.
REPOTTING: Does best when slightly pot-bound. Use a pot about half the width of the plant.
PROPAGATION: From leaf cuttings, or from suckers or offsets from flower stems. Can be grown from seed.
PROBLEMS: Mushy, brown blooms and buds indicate botrytis blight. Remove diseased parts, provide good air circulation, avoid excess humidity and use fertilizer with less nitrogen. Cold water that touches foliage causes yellow rings on leaf surfaces. Streaked, misshapen leaves with irregular yellow spots are infected by a virus. No cure exists, so discard the plant. Sudden wilting indicates crown rot, resulting from erratic watering. Do not allow the soil to dry out between waterings. Severe temperature changes also cause crown rot. Thrips, aphids, cyclamen mites, and mealybugs are possible pests.
TIPS: Remove all dead leaves and flowers promptly. Shape by removing side shoots, except on trailing cultivars.

'Vermont'

'Connecticut'

'Maine'

'Kazuko'

Sanchezia speciosa
san-KAYZ-ee-a spee-see-OH-sa

Although sanchezia is grown primarily for its spectacular foliage, the vivid flower spikes are beautiful too.

SANCHEZIA, SHRUBBY WHITEVEIN

Sanchezia (*S. speciosa*, syn. *S. glaucophylla*, *S. nobilis*, and *S. spectabilis*) is a large, shrubby plant grown especially for its dramatic foliage. The smooth, bright green stems bear large, glossy, dark green, elliptic leaves up to 12 inches long, with spectacular veining. Both the midrib and the main veins are brilliantly colored white or yellow, depending on the amount of light the plant gets. The flowers are stunning terminal spikes made of up small red bracts from among which shoot bright yellow blooms. They appear in summer and can last over a month.

Sanchezia needs occasional pruning. It reaches up to 7 feet tall and 5 feet wide, but you can keep it under 3 feet tall and wide by pinching and trimming it. Prune anytime after flowering until late winter. Any later and you risk removing the summer's flower buds.

LIGHT: Bright.
WATER: Keep evenly moist.
HUMIDITY: High.
TEMPERATURE: Average.
FERTILIZER: All-purpose during growing period.
DIMENSIONS: 3 to 7 feet tall and 2 to 5 feet wide.
REPOTTING: As needed.
PROPAGATION: From softwood and semi-rooted cuttings, with rooting hormone.
PROBLEMS: Low light causes spindly growth and poor bloom. Dry air causes leaf dieback. Overwatering leads to stem rot. Spider mites and scale insects are possible pests.
TIPS: Remove faded flowers. Wash leaves occasionally with a soft, moist, soapy cloth to remove grime and dust, or give the plant a shower.

Sansevieria trifasciata
san-sev-ee-ER-ee-a try-fas-ee-AH-ta

Grow *Sansevieria* in bright light and it may send up a stalk of tubular flowers that are fragrant at night.

SNAKE PLANT, MOTHER-IN-LAW'S TONGUE

Legendary for their ability to tolerate low light, burning heat, and even months of total neglect, snake plants actually don't grow well in dark corners and total aridity. They do much better with proper care, a bright location, and regular watering as soon as the soil becomes dry.

Sansevieria trifasciata produces erect, leathery, strap-shaped leaves, horizontally banded dark and light green in a snakeskin pattern. Colonies of separate plants accumulate in the original pot. Under bright light, snake plant eventually produces a tall stalk of tubular greenish flowers that give off a heavenly scent at night.

S. trifasciata 'Laurentii', with yellow stripes along the leaf edges, is a popular cultivar. *S. trifasciata* 'Hahnii' is a dwarf snake plant that forms dense rosettes of broad, dark green leaves less than 10 inches tall.

S. trifasciata 'Golden Hahnii' has creamy yellow stripes.
LIGHT: Medium to bright. Tolerates low light for extended periods.
WATER: Let the potting mix dry slightly between waterings. Water sparingly in winter.
HUMIDITY: Low to average.
TEMPERATURE: Average.
FERTILIZER: All-purpose during growing period. Not a heavy feeder.
DIMENSIONS: 4 feet tall and 20 inches wide.
REPOTTING: Repot infrequently in a well-drained growing mix.
PROPAGATION: By division, or from leaf cuttings or leaf section cuttings of nonvariegated types.
PROBLEMS: Leaves become floppy under low light. Leaves break easily. Overwatering leads to root rot. Spider mites and mealybugs are possible pests.
TIP: Remove flower stalks after blooming has stopped.

Saxifraga stolonifera
saks-IF-ra-ga sto-lo-NI-fe-ra

Strawberry begonia is a ground-hugging, rosette-forming plant with rounded, dark green leaves. It is marked with silver along the veins and covered with reddish hairs underneath. In the summer, it may produce airy stalks of lopsided white flowers. The flowers are not particularly showy and many gardeners simply cut them off.

Strawberry begonia's real draw is its numerous runners. Thin and stringy, they produce plantlets at their tips, exactly like the runners of strawberries do. Outdoors these runners arch out over the surface of the soil, allowing the plantlets to root elsewhere. Indoors strawberry begonia is usually displayed in hanging baskets.

S. stolonifera 'Tricolor' is a variegated cultivar with an attractive pink to white leaf margin It does

STRAWBERRY BEGONIA, STRAWBERRY GERANIUM, MOTHER OF THOUSANDS

best in a terrarium or greenhouse.

LIGHT: Bright.

WATER: Let the potting mix dry slightly between waterings.

HUMIDITY: Average; high for *S. stolonifera* 'Tricolor'.

TEMPERATURE: Cool to cold. Tolerates average temperatures.

FERTILIZER: All-purpose during growing period. Not a heavy feeder.

DIMENSIONS: 1 foot tall and wide.

REPOTTING: Annually, when flowering ceases.

PROPAGATION: By division or layering, or from offsets.

PROBLEMS: Low light causes spindly growth and poor bloom. Excess mineral salts cause leaf-tip burn and stem dieback, so leach frequently. Dry air and hot temperatures cause leaf dieback. Spider mites, whiteflies, mealybugs, and scale insects are possible pests.

TIP: Flower stalks can be removed to improve the plant's appearance.

Strawbery begonia is best displayed in a hanging basket, so its delicate runners can sway gently.

Scadoxus multiflorus
skay-DAHKS-us mul-tee-FLOOR-us

Blood-lily (*S. multiflorus*, syn. *Haemanthus multiflorus*) is a tender bulb ideal for indoor growing. It sends up broad, lance-shaped to oval, nearly stemless leaves that form an arching rosette, followed by a thick, leafless flower stalk often marbled with maroon spots. At the tip forms a large ball of bright red flowers up to 6 inches across. Although each bloom has six colorful petals, the flower is dominated by the long, scarlet stamens, giving the entire flower head the appearance of a giant red powderpuff. After blooming, the leaves remain on the plant throughout the summer, then fade as the plant enters winter dormancy.

Blood-lily requires a winter rest in dry soil, if possible at cooler temperatures. Cut off the faded foliage and store bulbs, still in their

BLOOD-LILY

pots, in a cool basement or other similar spot.

LIGHT: Bright. Keep in darkness when dormant.

WATER: Keep evenly moist; keep dry during dormancy.

HUMIDITY: High.

TEMPERATURE: Cool to average; cool to cold when dormant.

FERTILIZER: All-purpose during growing period.

REPOTTING: Infrequently; pot-bound plants bloom more profusely. Plant with the tip of the bulb protruding from the soil.

DIMENSIONS: 18 to 24 inches tall and 12 to 18 inches wide.

PROPAGATION: From offsets or seed.

PROBLEMS: Dry soil or excess mineral salts may damage roots, causing dieback. Otherwise, few significant problems.

TIPS: Remove old leaves as plants go dormant. Give plants plenty of room.

S. multiflorus katherinae, sometimes called Catherine wheel, has huge flowerheads.

Schefflera
shef-LER-a

Use multiple stems of schefflera for a bushier appearance.

Common schefflera (*S. actinophylla,* syn. *Brassaia actinophylla*) is often sold several small seedlings to a pot, each with only three to five pointed, toothed, bright green leaflets and thin stems. It matures rapidly into a plant with much larger, darker green leaves a foot or more across, made up of seven to 16 smooth-edged leaflets spreading out like the

Some shiny-leaved scheffleras are more resistant to spider mites.

SCHEFFLERA

sections of an umbrella on thick, sturdy stems.

Common schefflera grows upright indoors and is not inclined to branch, so it is better to buy pots with several stems: They guarantee a fuller appearance over time. It is normally susceptible to spider mites, but some cultivars, such as *S. actinophylla* 'Amate', with particularly shiny leaves, were chosen for mite resistance. It is slow to root from cuttings and is usually propagated by seed or, for cultivars, by tissue culture or air layering.

Dwarf or miniature schefflera (*S. arboricola* syn. *Heptapleurum arboricola*) is only smaller than the common schefflera in leaf size; it can easily reach over 6 feet in height and diameter. Fortunately, unlike the common schefflera, it branches readily and you can keep it in check by pruning regularly. The compound leaves are up to 7 inches across and dark green. Several named cultivars exist, including some with yellow variegation or notched leaves, such as 'Gold Capella', with creamy yellow leaflets surrounded by green, and 'Trinette', with more irregular gold variegation. This species is easy to root from cuttings.

S. elegantissima is far better known by its old name, *Dizygotheca elegantissima.* Even its common name reflects no link with the schefflera clan: It's called false aralia. In its youth, it doesn't look at all like a schefflera, with thin, dark brownish green leaves with lighter veins that spread into nine fingers with saw-toothed edges. However, at maturity it changes its appearance completely and produces bigger leaves with broad, medium-green leaflets that better show its schefflera nature. Like the common schefflera, it is difficult to propagate from cuttings but air layering works well.

Several different cultivars of false-

A young false-aralia (*S. elegantissima*) looks different from its mature form.

aralia are available, such as 'Galaxy', with broader and less numerous segments than the species, and 'Galaxy Variegated', a variant of 'Galaxy' with similar leaves edged in cream.

LIGHT: Medium to bright. Tolerates low light for short periods.

WATER: Let potting mix dry slightly between waterings.

HUMIDITY: Average.

TEMPERATURE: Average.

FERTILIZER: All-purpose during growing period. Not a heavy feeder.

DIMENSIONS: 2 to 10 feet tall and 1 to 4 feet wide.

REPOTTING: Infrequently.

PROPAGATION: By air layering, or from seed. Use rooting hormone with cuttings.

PROBLEMS: Low light causes spindly growth. Overwatering leads to root rot or leaf loss. Leaves may also drop if the air is too dry. Spider mites, thrips, mealybugs, and scale insects are possible pests.

TIPS: Remove yellow leaves promptly. Prune as needed to maintain the desired size and shape.

Selaginella
se-lah-gi-NEL-la

Moss-Fern, Spike-Moss, Sweat-Plant, Spreading Club-Moss

The genus *Selaginella* is a group of primitive, mosslike plants related to ferns. They are popular terrarium plants that don't do well in the open air, as they need high humidity and moist soil at all times.

Trailing spike moss (*S. kraussiana*) is the most popular species. It forms spreading mats of trailing stems with bright green foliage. Its cultivar 'Aurea' is similar, but in chartreuse green. Tiny *S. kraussiana* 'Brownii' forms a dense cushion of green only 2 inches tall but up to 6 inches wide. It is a particularly good choice for terrariums, as it doesn't wander.

The most unusual species is the so-called resurrection fern (*S. lepidophylla*). It is usually sold as a rolled-up ball of apparently dead foliage. Soak it in water, though, and the ball unfurls to reveal a flattened rosette of green, scale-covered stems.

It makes an interesting curiosity but is harder to maintain than the others because it prefers alkaline soils.

LIGHT: Medium to bright.
WATER: Keep evenly moist.
HUMIDITY: High to very high.
TEMPERATURE: Average. Keep plants out of cold drafts.
FERTILIZER: All-purpose during growing period. Not a heavy feeder.
DIMENSIONS: 2 to 6 inches tall and 4 to 8 inches wide.
REPOTTING: As needed.
PROPAGATION: From stem cuttings. Simply press the stems into moist sphagnum moss or soil and maintain high humidity. Most self-layer and can be divided.
PROBLEMS: Dry air causes leaf dieback.
TIP: Trim any overgrown sections.

Trailing spike-moss (*S. kraussiana*) is a popular terrarium plant. It needs high humidity and constantly moist soil.

Senecio ×*hybridus*
se-NAY-kee-oh HIB-ri-dus

Florist's Cineraria

Cinerarias (also known by the name *S. cruentus* and perhaps more correctly as *Pericallis* ×*hybrida*) are popular winter-blooming florist plants. They form a rosette of heart-shaped medium to dark green leaves that is sometimes entirely covered with masses of small, daisy-like flowers in shades of pink, red, white, blue, purple, and bicolors. For longest bloom, keep them as cool as possible, down to 50°F, especially at night. Since they are annuals, toss them into the compost pile after they finish flowering.

You can grow florist's cinerarias from seed as long as you can keep them cool during the whole process, even during germination. Give the plants plenty of light before flowering so they will not become leggy. Start seeds in mid-July for late winter or early spring blooms.

LIGHT: Bright.
WATER: Keep evenly moist.
HUMIDITY: Average.
TEMPERATURE: Cool to cold. Tolerates average temperatures for a short time. Avoid cold drafts.
FERTILIZER: No need to fertilize temporary plants. Give seedlings all-purpose fertilizer as they grow.
DIMENSIONS: 18 to 24 inches tall and 10 to 24 inches wide.
REPOTTING: Not necessary for temporary plants. Transplant seedlings several times.
PROPAGATION: From seed.
PROBLEMS: Avoid wetting leaves to prevent leaf spots. Dry air causes leaf dieback. Plants quickly wilt and die when dry; keep evenly moist. Spider mites, whiteflies, and aphids are possible pests. Susceptible to powdery mildew.
TIPS: When purchasing, choose plants with plenty of flowers yet to open; plants in full bloom will soon be on the decline. Discard the plants after flowering.

Florist's cinerarias are annuals that bloom colorfully in late winter. Discard them when they finish flowering.

SERISSA, SNOW-ROSE

Bonsai enthusiasts are credited with having introduced this attractive plant to indoor growers. Dwarf in all respects, serissa makes an attractive miniature tree or shrub, rarely reaching over 2 feet tall and easily maintained at half that. Left on its own, it becomes a bushy, domed shrub. It supports pruning well, allowing it to be trained into topiary or bonsai forms.

The tiny, leathery leaves are elliptic and dark green. Many cultivars have variegated foliage with cream or yellow markings. The flowers, borne most heavily in spring and summer, are barely ¼ inch in diameter and can be pink or white and single or double, depending on the clone. Plants with plain green leaves tend to flower more heavily

Serissa is often grown as a bonsai tree but also makes a good small shrub. Plants with plain leaves bloom heavily.

than those with variegated leaves.

Popular cultivars include 'Flore Pleno', with smaller, fully double white flowers and 'Variegated Pink', with cream-edged green leaves and pink flowers.

LIGHT: Bright to intense.

WATER: Keep evenly moist.

HUMIDITY: Average.

TEMPERATURE: Average to cold. Avoid cold drafts.

FERTILIZER: All-purpose during growing period.

DIMENSIONS: 10 to 24 inches tall and 10 to 30 inches wide.

REPOTTING: Annually in late winter or early spring.

PROPAGATION: From stem cuttings and by air layering.

PROBLEMS: Low light causes spindly growth and poor bloom. Overwatering leads to root rot. Spider mites and scale insects are possible pests.

TIP: Prune as needed.

Florist's gloxinias (*S. speciosa*) thrive for many years when given a dormant period between flowerings.

SINNINGIA

Sinningias usually have hairy, elliptical leaves and tubular or bell-shaped flowers, but their tubers help distinguish them from other gesneriads, most of which have fibrous roots or rhizomes.

Plants with tubers usually go dormant after they bloom, and that is true of many sinningias in the wild. In culture, though, if you cut the old stems back after they have finished blooming, most of them start a new cycle right away.

To induce dormancy, simply stop watering, and when the foliage has died back, cut or pull it off. You can then store the tuber, still in its pot, in a cool, out-of-the way spot. When new sprouts appear, usually three to five months later, repot and start watering again.

LIGHT: Bright. Miniatures tolerate medium. No light needed during dormancy.

WATER: Keep evenly moist.

Withhold water to induce dormancy.

HUMIDITY: Average to high. Very high for microminiatures.

TEMPERATURE: Average; cool during dormancy.

FERTILIZER: Rich in phosphorous.

DIMENSIONS: Vary according to species.

REPOTTING: After dormancy, when growth resumes.

PROPAGATION: From seed or from leaf or stem cuttings.

PROBLEMS: Too much moisture causes crown rot. Poor light prevents bloom. Excess mineral salts cause leaf-tip burn and stem dieback, so leach frequently. Flower buds fail to open when air is too dry. Cyclamen mites, thrips, aphids, whiteflies, and mealybugs are possible pests.

TIP: Remove faded growth after flowering.

Miniature sinningias (*Sinningia* spp.) bear tubular flowers with flared tips on short-stemmed rosettes rarely

SINNINGIA *(continued)*

Cardinal flower *(S. cardinalis)* bears long-lasting bright red or white tubular flowers on upright stems in fall or winter.

more than 8 inches in diameter and often less than 2 inches. The flowers come in a wide variety of colors, including purples, pinks, reds, salmons, whites, and bicolors.

Miniature sinningias produce new shoots even before the previous ones have faded, thus providing blooms throughout the year. Some of the most popular ones include 'Cherry Chips', with red flowers bearing small dots in a white throat, and 'Cindy-Ella', with a purple tube and upper lobes and white lower lobes spotted black. Both reach about 3 inches tall and wide and have rounded, scalloped, somewhat downy, dark green leaves.

S. pusilla is a one of the aptly labeled microminiatures: tiny 1- by 1-inch plants that form mini-rosettes of downy dark olive green leaves rarely more than an inch in diameter. It produces a constant flow of tiny tubular lilac flowers with white throats throughout the year and rarely goes dormant. 'White Sprite' is a popular selection with white flowers. Both plants self-sow abundantly in terrarium environments.

In general, miniature sinningias need higher humidity than larger species and do best on a humidity tray. They also tolerate lower light than larger sinningias. Microminiatures need extra-high humidity and are best grown in a terrarium.

Cardinal flower *(Sinningia cardinalis*, formerly called *Rechsteineria cardinalis)* is an upright grower that produces one or more stems of bright green, hairy leaves from a large woody tuber that is usually left partly exposed. It grows 12 to 24 inches tall and 12 inches wide and produces brilliant red tubular flowers with a distinct hood over a long period, usually in fall or winter. You can also find white-flowered cultivars, such as 'Innocence'.

Brazilian edelweiss *(Sinningia canescens)* produces whorls of 6-inch obovate leaves on a short, stocky stem rising from a large, woody, partly exposed tuber. The plant grows to 1 foot tall and wide. Both the stem and the leaves are abundantly covered with silvery white hairs, giving the whole plant a silver appearance. Tubular red flowers bloom in clusters directly over the leaves but are so covered with silvery hairs that they appear pink. This plant does not enter into dormancy right after blooming; pull off the faded flowers and enjoy the beautiful foliage for months. When the leaves dry up, stop watering and store the plant dry until new growth appears.

Florist's gloxinia *(Sinningia speciosa),* originally from Brazil, has large, velvety leaves encircling bell-shaped single or double flowers, often with ruffled edges. The blooms, either upright or slipper-shaped, are borne well above the foliage and come in purple, red, pink, and white, often with a white margin or abundant speckling. It is

commonly sold in full bloom as a gift plant, about 1 foot tall and wide. To grow well and last for many years, florist's gloxinias need humidity and bright light. If fading foliage is removed, they can bloom three or four times in succession. Then give them several months of dormancy before starting a new growth cycle.

Miniature sinningias bloom continuously throughout the year.

Solanum pseudocapsicum
so-LAH-num soo-do-KAP-si-kum

Move Jerusalem cherry outdoors in summer or pollinate it by shaking it when it blooms so it will set fruit.

JERUSALEM CHERRY

Jerusalem cherry is often confused with ornamental pepper *(Capsicum annuum,* page 128). It derives its common name from its colorful round, orange-red fruits that usually mature in December and continue through much of the winter. It's an erect, bushy evergreen shrub with small white flowers.

S. pseudocapsicum needs an abundance of light to bloom and set fruit properly, and the flowers have to be pollinated. That's why many gardeners often start seedlings indoors in early spring, put them outdoors for the summer, then bring them back indoors in September after they have been pollinated. If you grow them indoors, pollinate the blooms simply by gently shaking the plant daily when it is in flower.

Jerusalem cherries are usually treated as annuals and discarded after blooming, but they can be kept from year to year if trimmed back harshly. They also grow readily from seed.

LIGHT: Bright to intense.
WATER: Keep evenly moist.
HUMIDITY: High.
TEMPERATURE: Average.
FERTILIZER: All-purpose during growing period.
DIMENSIONS: 12 to 18 inches tall and wide.
REPOTTING: As needed.
PROPAGATION: From seed. Semi-ripened cuttings don't develop as vigorous a plant as seed.
PROBLEMS: Low light causes spindly growth and poor bloom. Overwatering leads to stem rot. Flowers must be pollinated to set fruit. Spider mites, whiteflies, aphids, and mealybugs are possible pests.
TIPS: Be careful not to remove flower buds when pruning. Discard a plant that is too leggy. Fruits and leaves are somewhat toxic; keep out of reach of children and pets.

Soleirolia soleirolii
so-lay-ROL-ee-a so-lay-ROL-ee-eye

Corsican mint smells delightful when crushed. It thrives in high humidity and continuously moist potting mix.

BABY'S TEARS, CORSICAN MINT

Baby's tears is a tiny creeping groundcover with thin stems and tiny round leaves. It can spread indefinitely as long as it can find open, moist soil, rooting as it grows.

Baby's tears makes a good terrarium groundcover as it thrives in high humidity. It is, however, highly invasive and may need to be pruned back every few weeks or so. It also makes an interesting trailing plant for a small hanging basket, as its stems cascade beautifully over the edges of its pot.

Baby's tears does not tolerate drought. Make sure the soil is always at least moist. You can even leave its pot permanently sitting in a saucer of water.

The green form is most common, but you'll also find 'Aurea', with golden-green leaves, and 'Variegata', with silver-variegated leaves.
LIGHT: Medium to bright.
WATER: Keep evenly to very moist at all times. Can stand in water.
HUMIDITY: High to very high.
TEMPERATURE: Cool to cold; tolerates average.
FERTILIZER: All-purpose during growing season.
DIMENSIONS: 2 inches tall and indefinite in width.
REPOTTING: In any season.
PROPAGATION: By division or from cuttings. Simply press the stems into moist rooting mix.
PROBLEMS: Low light causes spindly growth. Dry soil or excess mineral salts damage roots, causing dieback. Aphids are possible pests.
TIPS: Prune as needed to maintain the desired size and shape. Keep the pot in a saucer of water to ensure constant moisture.

COLEUS, FLAME NETTLE, PAINTED NETTLE

Solenostemon scutellarioides
soh-len-AH-steh-muhn
skoo-tel-ayr-ree-OY-dees

This old-fashioned houseplant is back in style and has a new name (it used to be known as *Coleus ×hybridus* or *Coleus blumei*). This is certainly one of the most colorful of all houseplants, entirely due to its variably colored leaves. It easily replaces a flowering plant in decors that need a bit of pizzazz.

Coleus is a fast-growing, tropical shrub. It produces square stems that are usually upright but sometimes creeping or trailing. Old-fashioned cultivars tended to produce a single stem unless pinched regularly, but most modern selections are self-branching.

It is fairly easy to train a coleus to become a standard (indoor tree). Simply pinch out side branches until it reaches the desired "trunk" height, then begin to pinch the upper stems to encourage the plant to produce masses of foliage-covered stems at the top of the trunk. Make sure you stake it, as the stem can be fragile.

The velvety, oval, scalloped leaves taper to a point and come in a multitude of colors, with toothed or fringed margins, depending on the variety. Some cultivars have deeply cut leaves or even lacy ones. Dark blue or white flowers form in late summer or fall on narrow spikes. They are usually pruned off.

Leaf color in coleus is remarkably varied. Leaves can be combinations of red, pink, white, green, orange, or dark purple and may be unicolored, bicolored, multicolored, or splashed with contrasting colors. Pale-colored plants, like bright yellows, tend to burn in too much sun. Dark shades, like some deep purples that are nearly black, need lots of light and some direct sun.

Old-fashioned cultivars were usually grown from seed and tended to produce unwanted flowers with annoying frequency. Modern selections, though, are usually cutting-propagated and have been selected from among plants that rarely bloom.

Literally thousands of cultivars of coleus exist, and none is universally available. Visit a nursery or obtain a mail-order catalog and buy the ones that strike your fancy.

LIGHT: Bright to intense.
WATER: Keep evenly moist.
HUMIDITY: Average.
TEMPERATURE: Average.
FERTILIZER: All-purpose during growing period.
DIMENSIONS: 10 to 36 inches tall and wide.
REPOTTING: Repot annually, in any season.
PROPAGATION: From softwood cuttings. Easy to grow from seed but not all varieties grow true to species.
PROBLEMS: Low light causes spindly growth. Tends to decline in beauty and vigor after blooming. Dry air causes leaf dieback. Whiteflies, mealybugs, and scale insects are possible pests.
TIPS: Prune at any season. Pinch back the stem tips of young or regrowing plants to improve their form. Remove flower spikes as they appear to encourage foliage.

'Jack of Diamonds'

'Big Chief'

'Newcomber'

'Black Velvet'

'Defiance'

Spathiphyllum wallisii
spath-i-FIL-lum wa-LIS-ee-eye

Peace lily blooms in medium to bright light, sometimes sporadically throughout the year.

PEACE LILY

The peace lily gets its common name from its distinctive flower. The spathe is a pure white bract that forms a softly curved backdrop for the central column (spadix) of tiny, closely set true flowers. The blooms are often deliciously scented but sometimes only at night.

Broad but pointed to lance-shaped leaves on arching stems form a rosette around the flower. The leaves are so attractive that even when not in flower, the peace lily makes an appealing foliage plant. With time, a single plant slowly produces offsets, creating an attractive full pot of foliage. To mimic this effect, nurseries often sell peace lilies several to a pot.

Peace lilies generally bloom in spring and sometimes in autumn. Some flower sporadically throughout the year. Dozens of cultivars exist in a variety of sizes; choose according to the size of the plant you need.

LIGHT: Medium to bright. Peace lily survives in low light but probably won't bloom.
WATER: Keep very moist during periods of growth and flowering; let dry slightly between waterings at other times.
HUMIDITY: Average.
TEMPERATURE: Average to high. Avoid cold drafts.
FERTILIZER: All-purpose during growing period. Not a heavy feeder.
DIMENSIONS: 6 inches to 5 feet tall and wide.
REPOTTING: Infrequently.
PROPAGATION: By division.
PROBLEMS: Poor bloom in low light. Overwatering leads to stem rot. Spider mites, whiteflies, mealybugs, and scale insects are possible pests.
TIPS: Remove yellowed leaves. Wash foliage occasionally.

Stephanotis floribunda
ste-fa-NO-tis flo-ri-BUN-da

Grow stephanotis on a trellis in a cool, sunny window and enjoy its fragrant, long-lasting flowers.

STEPHANOTIS, BRIDAL WREATH, MADAGASCAR JASMINE

Stephanotis is a climbing plant that grows quite large. It has thick, ropelike stems and fleshy, leathery, dark green, elliptic leaves similar to those of wax plants (*Hoya* spp.). The flowers are traditionally used in wedding bouquets, as they make great, long-lasting cut flowers. They are thick, waxy, white and extremely fragrant. Stephanotis blooms in spring and summer and sporadically most of the year if given enough light. Allow the plant to rest during winter, as cool temperatures and reduced watering help it bloom.

Train stephanotis up a trellis or around a hoop. Unlike many climbing plants, though, it does not do well in a hanging basket.

Stephanotis belongs to a family of poisonous plants. However, there is no known case of poisoning specifically from stephanotis.

LIGHT: Intense.
WATER: Keep evenly moist during active growth, then let the soil dry slightly between waterings.
HUMIDITY: Average.
TEMPERATURE: Average; cool in winter.
FERTILIZER: All-purpose during growing period.
DIMENSIONS: Can be maintained at any height or width desired.
REPOTTING: Infrequently. Plants bloom best when pot-bound.
PROPAGATION: Softwood cuttings.
PROBLEMS: Low light or excessively warm temperature causes poor bloom. Mealybugs and scale insects are possible pests.
TIPS: Pinch back stem tips of young or regrowing plants to improve form. Prune after flowering. Be careful not to remove flower buds.

Streptocarpus
strep-to-KAR-pus

Streptocarpus subgenus *Streptocarpus*, called Cape primrose, produces arching flower stalks directly from the stemless, narrow leaves. The leaves grow up to 12 inches long. Colorful flowers in white, pink, red, violet, or blue are available, often with contrasting veins and a yellow throat. They prefer cool winter temperatures. If the leaves go limp yet the potting mix is still moist, the plant is suffering from overwatering or excess heat. Keep the plant drier than usual and place it in a shady spot until it has recovered.

S. subgenus *Streptocarpella* produces arching stems of small, thick leaves. Flowers are small but numerous, especially during the summer months. Colors range from pale lavender to deep purple.
LIGHT: Bright.

STREPTOCARPUS, CAPE PRIMROSE

WATER: Keep evenly moist during growth and flowering; otherwise, allow to dry between waterings.
HUMIDITY: High.
TEMPERATURE: Average.
FERTILIZER: All-purpose during growing period.
REPOTTING: As needed.
DIMENSIONS: Cape primrose is 8 to 14 inches tall and 10 to 30 inches wide. *Streptocarpella* is 6 to 12 inches tall and 18 to 24 inches wide.
PROPAGATION: Cape primrose by division or from seed, leaf cuttings, or leaf section cuttings; *Streptocarpella* by division or from stem cuttings or seeds.
PROBLEMS: Overwatering or excess heat causes wilting. Will not bloom at high temperatures or in low light. Aphids, thrips, and mealybugs are possible pests.
TIPS: Remove yellowed leaves and trim back those with brown tips. Remove flower stalks after blooming.

Cape primrose 'Sandra' has pink blooms with contrasting dark red veins.

Strobilanthes dyerianus
stro-bi-LANTH-eez dye-er-ee-AN-us

Here's a plant with color galore. The narrow, lance-shaped, quilted leaves of Persian shield are heavily marbled with rich purple and highlighted with iridescent silvery pink markings above and deep wine red below.

Once considered strictly a houseplant or a shade plant for tropical climates, Persian shield is becoming popular as a cutting-grown annual for the summer garden and containers. If you do put it outside for the summer, give it no more than half-sun. In early fall, take cuttings and start new plants to overwinter indoors.

Persian shield is a fast-growing shrub; it may need pinching or pruning to prevent lankiness. Leaves are less colorful in early autumn, a sign that the plant is leaving its juvenile stage behind. It produces

PERSIAN SHIELD

long-lasting, pale blue, funnel-shaped flowers just before it goes into decline. To prevent this, many people pinch off the flower buds before they open.
LIGHT: Bright.
WATER: Let potting mix dry slightly between waterings. Water sparingly in winter.
HUMIDITY: High.
TEMPERATURE: Average.
FERTILIZER: All-purpose during growing period. Not a heavy feeder.
REPOTTING: As needed.
DIMENSIONS: 1 to 4 feet tall and 1 to 3 feet wide.
PROPAGATION: From softwood cuttings.
PROBLEMS: Dry air causes leaf dieback. Spider mites are possible.
TIPS: Prune as needed to maintain the desired size and shape. Older specimens tend to weaken over time; start over with fresh cuttings.

Persian shield grows quickly and becomes less colorful as it ages, so take frequent cuttings for new plants.

SUCCULENTS

Succulents have learned to store water in their stems, leaves, or thick roots in order to adapt to arid climates. In the course of developing such special talents, these plants evolved into unique and wonderful shapes, colors, and textures.

Succulents are generally easy to care for and are a good starting point for beginning gardeners. Despite their variety, they require the same basic care. To grow well, they need a porous, fast-draining soil, plenty of sunlight, good air circulation, and plenty of water. During the winter, they prefer to go dormant in a cool, dry environment. Many succulents need this rest time in order to bloom the following season. In summer, revitalize the plants by moving them outdoors. For more information on succulents, see "Growing Cacti and Succulents" on pages 86–87.

LIGHT: Bright to intense.

WATER: Let potting mix dry slightly between waterings. Water sparingly in winter.

HUMIDITY: Dry. Tolerates humid air.

TEMPERATURE: Average to high; cool to cold temperatures in winter.

FERTILIZER: All-purpose during growing period. Not heavy feeders.

REPOTTING: Annually for young plants. Mature plants do better when pot-bound. Use a shallow pot and a very porous soil (see page 45).

DIMENSIONS: Depending on type, 3 inches to 10 feet tall and 3 inches to 5 feet wide.

PROPAGATION: From stem cuttings and offsets, and from leaf cuttings of some species.

PROBLEMS: Overwatering leads to root rot. Stem and leaf rot are caused by cool, damp air. Leaves wilt and discolor from too much water, especially in winter. Underwatering causes brown, dry spots. Mealybugs and scale insects are possible pests.

TIP: Cut off flower stalks as the blooms age.

■ **Adenium** (*Adenium*) takes rather strange forms, each one creating its own sculptural design. The fleshy stem varies from gray to pale brown; the leaves are a shiny green but not produced in abundance. They generally drop off during dormancy. Flowers are brilliant red to pink with pale centers and appear in clusters at the branch tips during the summer. *A. obesum* (desert-rose) is a popular variety with pink flowers.

■ **Adromischus** (*Adromischus*)— called pretty-pebbles, sea-shells, plover-eggs, leopard's-spots, and crinkleleaf, among many other common names—are stout-stemmed succulents that grow in clumps and look best in a shallow, broad container. Many have crinkled or egg-shaped leaves with speckles or spots. The plants will grow in indirect light but develop better leaf color in bright light.

■ **Pinwheel-plants** (*Aeonium*) produce rosettes, some on tall stems, others hugging the ground. The spoon-shaped leaves vary from apple-green to a deep maroon-tinged red. The flowers are usually small and yellow and bloom in profusion. Stems die after blooming.

■ **Agaves** (*Agave*) are large plants with thick, pointed leaves. Several of the smaller types, such as *A. victoriae-reginae* (painted century plant), are particularly suitable for indoor gardening, although *A. americana* and its various variegated clones are also popular indoor plants, despite their large size. After a plant matures it may produce a tall flower spike but will die after producing seed.

■ **Aloe** (*Aloe*) is another genus of great diversity, but all species produce rosettes of spiny leaves. *A. vera* (also known as *A. barbadensis*) is the best known. It is commonly called medicine-plant or burn aloe, since it is most widely known for the healing properties of its sap. Many people use the liquid from a broken leaf to treat minor burns. It is a stemless plant with green leaves and yellow flowers, but blooms rarely.

Living stones (*Lithops*)

Zebra haworthia (*Haworthia fasciata*)

Echeveria elegans

Burro's tail (Sedum morganianum)

Aloe vera (A. barbadensis)

Rosary vine (Ceropegia woodii) looks best in a hanging basket or on a windowsill where its stems can dangle.

■ **Rosary vine** *(Ceropegia)*, also called hearts-entangled, produces long, purple runners with tiny, heart-shaped leaves. The leaves, borne in pairs at regular intervals along the vine, are patterned with silver on top and purple beneath. To start new plants, you can remove and root the tiny tubers that form at the leaf joints as the plant matures.

■ **Silver crown** *(Cotyledon)* is a large and diverse genus. The plants are shrubby, and their mature size ranges from a few inches to several feet. Most species have persistent succulent leaves in varying colors from yellow-green to blue-gray and bell-shaped yellow to red flowers on long stems held above the leaves during spring and summer. *C. orbiculata* has red-margined leaves and red flowers; *C. undulata* is large, with wavy-edged leaves.

■ **Jade plant** *(Crassula)* forms a widely diversified plant group, characterized by unusual and varied leaf forms, arrangements, and colors. Most are easy to grow. Common names include airplane-plant, baby jade, moss crassula, rattail crassula, rattlesnake, scarlet-paintbrush, and silver jade plant.

■ **Hen and chicks** *(Echeveria)* and other echeverias all have a common rosette form. Their greatly varied leaf color ranges from pale green through deep purple. They can be smooth-leaved or hairy, with stemless rosettes, or they can grow on a stalk.

■ **Euphorbia** *(Euphorbia)* is too diverse a genus to allow more than a few generalizations. Common names include African-milkbarrel, corkscrew, cow's-horn, crown-of-thorns, and living-baseball. All species have a toxic or at least irritating milky sap. Mature sizes range from a few inches to many feet. The leaves are generally insignificant and deciduous. Many species have spines. The flowers are usually quite small, often yellow or greenish yellow. Euphorbias are propagated most easily from cuttings. The cut end must be immersed in cold water or powdered charcoal and allowed to form a callus before rooting.

■ **Tiger's-jaws** *(Faucaria)*, a popular short-stemmed succulent, takes its name from its triangular leaves, which have small teeth along their margins. The leaves are often

spotted and grow in small, low clumps, ranging in color from green to olive green. Their yellow blooms resemble dandelions.

■ **Ox-tongue** *(Gasteria)* has leaves that form fans, one on top of another, or spirals. They are thick and usually dark green with variously colored dark or light spots. In summer, tubular reddish-orange flowers appear on a long stalk, which may dip or arch. These plants tolerate slightly less light than other succulents.

Euphorbia milii, Crown-of-thorns

Panda plant *(Kalanchoe tomentosa)*

Silver squill *(Ledebouria socialis)*

■ **Mother-of-pearl plant**
(Graptopetalum) bears lovely
rosettes of thick leaves on long
stems. The leaves are a luminous
white with pink-purple tones. Mature
rosettes measure approximately
3 inches in diameter. The bell-shaped
flowers are straw-colored with
maroon markings. *Graptopetalum*
is easy to grow and especially suited
to hanging baskets.

■ **Haworthias** *(Haworthia)* come
in many forms, and all are excellent
indoors. Although they grow in
moderate light, bright indirect light
improves their foliage color and
texture. The leaves of most species
are thick and form rosettes on
stemless plants. They flower at
different times, depending on the
species. The flowers are small and
borne in clusters on long stems.
After flowering, the plants may go
dormant and will need repotting.

■ **Kalanchoes** *(Kalanchoe)* are
popular succulents grown for both
their flowers and their foliage. *K.*

blossfeldiana (Christmas kalanchoe)
produces heads of brilliant scarlet,
orange, or yellow flowers on thin
stems 15 inches tall. Its shiny, oval
green leaves are tinged with red. It
blooms only if it receives short days
(nights of over 14 hours) in winter.
K. tomentosa (panda plant) grows
to 15 inches. Plump leaves covered
with silvery hairs branch from a
central stem. The pointed leaves
are tipped with rust brown bumps.
K. daigremontiana, like some other
species, has plantlets on its leaves.

■ **Silver squill** *(Ledebouria socialis)*,
usually sold under its old name,
Scilla violacea, is a small plant
ideally suited for windowsills.
Its fleshy, pointed olive green leaves
are splotched silvery gray, with wine
red undersides. The leaves are 2 to
4 inches long. The purple bulb grows
above the soil. Clusters of tiny green
flowers are produced in spring.

■ **Living stones** *(Conophytum,
Dinteranthus, Fenestraria, Lapidaria,
Lithops, Pleiospilos*, and others) are
perhaps the most interesting of all
succulents. As the name implies,
these plants resemble small rocks.
Because their cultural needs can
be complex, living stones are
recommended only for advanced

gardeners. They need minimal
watering during their nonflowering
periods, which for some occur in
summer months. They are usually
best propagated from seed.

■ **Pachyphytum** *(Pachyphytum)*,
or thick-plant, has fat, rounded
leaves that form attractive rosettes
on long stems. Leaf color varies from
a dusty gray-pink to a bluish gray.
Rosettes can be up to 8 inches
across, depending on the species.
Small, bell-shaped flowers range
from white to orange to red or pink.
Thick-plants need plenty of bright,
but not too hot, light to bring out
their maximum foliar color. They are
a good choice for hanging baskets.

■ **Madagascar palm**
(Pachypodium) is a widely varied
genus that includes plants that are
shrubby and plants that are
columnar and covered with thorns.
Most species have long, thick,
leathery dark green foliage. The
flowers range from white to yellow
to red. The star-shaped blooms are
borne at the tips of the branches in
spring. Pachypodiums go through
a leafless winter dormancy, during
which you should withhold water.
P. lamerei has spiny, gray-green,
thick stems and long, narrow leaves.

■ **Variegated devil's backbone**
(*Pedilanthes tithymaloides*
'Variegatus') gets its name from its
fleshy gray-green stems that zigzag
upward. They bear waxy, pale green
leaves that are beautifully variegated
and edged white with a carmine-red
tinge. The spurred, bracted
inflorescences are red and look
like birds' heads.

■ **Elephant bush** (*Portulacaria*) is
a shrub with a reddish-brown trunk
and stems and small green leaves.
This plant is very easy to grow, and
the attractive stems and shrubby
habit make it ideal for bonsai
gardens. *P. afra* 'Variegata' has light
green and creamy white variegated
foliage.

■ **Sedums** (*Sedum*) are another
varied genus that includes species
easy to grow and maintain indoors.
S. morganianum (donkey's tail,
burro's tail) is a trailing, slow-
growing succulent. Its light gray to
blue-green leaves are ½ to 1 inch
long, oval, and plump. The 3- to
4-foot trailing stems, densely covered
with leaves, create a braid or rope
effect. This plant is ideal for hanging
containers. *S. ×rubrotinctum*
(jellybeans) has rosy-tipped, bean-
shaped leaves on upright stems
and yellow flowers that bloom
in late winter.

■ **Senecio** is a large and widely
varied genus that includes small
succulents, hanging or climbing
vines, and large shrubs. The stems
of all the succulent species are
spineless, supporting leaves that
are spherical and thick, or flat and
elongated. The flowers are daisy-like
but not as interesting as the foliage.
S. herreianus (gooseberry-kleinia)
is an excellent hanging plant with
elliptical green leaves. String-of-
beads plant (*S. rowleyanus*) has
hanging stems that bear unusual,
½-inch, spherical leaves. The leaves
look like light green beads with
pointed tips and a single translucent
band across them.

■ **Carrion-flowers** (*Stapelia*) have
leafless green stems and large star-
shaped flowers that are notable for
their lurid colors, odor, and size.
The flowers are generally in shades
of yellow or red with maroon
spotting and are borne along the
stems in late summer and fall.
Sometimes they have an extremely
unpleasant scent like decaying meat.
S. gigantea (giant toadplant) has
flowers that are large even for the
genus; they are yellow with red
ridges and grow to 12 inches.
S. nobilis has flowers of
a darker yellow and are lightly
covered with thick, purple fuzz.

■ **African milkbush** (*Synadenium
grantii* 'Rubra') makes an attractive,
fast-growing indoor tree or shrub.
The stem is thick, and the leaves
are spoon-shaped, measuring 4 to
6 inches long. The leaves are
irregularly splashed with dull red,
sometimes to the point where the
whole leaf is burgundy. This is an
extremely adaptable plant; it
tolerates just about all indoor
conditions. Be careful, though,
of its toxic sap.

■ **Yuccas** (*Yucca*) bear thick,
swordlike leaves with sharp tips.
Mature plants have a canelike trunk
with whorls of foliage at the end.
Side shoots form occasionally.
Y. elephantipes has wide, dark
green leaves 4 feet long that are
particularly effective for a dramatic
setting; *Y. elephantipes* 'Variegata' is
a variegated cultivar. Both are often
sold in the form of recently rooted
canes taken from large stock plants,
each with a rosette or two.

Pedilanthus tithymaloides 'Variegatus'
has upright stems and red bracts.

String-of-beads (S. rowleyanus) is
named for its unusual elliptic leaves.

Yucca elephantipes has sharp, pointed
leaves with saw-tooth edges.

Syngonium podophyllum
sin-GON-ee-um po-do-FIL-lum

Prune out climbing stems to maintain arrowhead vine's variegated, arrow-shaped leaves.

ARROWHEAD VINE

Arrowhead vine is unusual because of a change that occurs in the leaf shape as the plant ages. Young plants are stemless and compact, producing arrow-shaped leaves at the ends of erect stalks. They are usually dark green and may have bold, silvery white variegation. With age, though, the leaves become lobed and the stems begin to climb. Eventually the variegation disappears, and each leaf fans into several leaflets. Older leaves may have as many as 11 leaflets.

To retain the juvenile leaf form and variegation, prune back the climbing stems as they appear. New growth will appear at the plant's base with the compact habit and arrow-shaped leaves of young plants.

Arrowhead vines are very tolerant plants, able to put up with most indoor environments. Older climbing stems require support.

Popular cultivars include 'Emerald Gem', with green leaves attractively quilted; 'White Butterfly', with a white overlay on a green background; and 'Pink Allusion', with attractive metallic pink highlights.

LIGHT: Medium to bright. Can tolerate low light but won't thrive.
WATER: Keep evenly moist; slightly drier in low light.
HUMIDITY: Average.
TEMPERATURE: Average. Keep plants out of cold drafts.
FERTILIZER: All-purpose during growing period. Not a heavy feeder.
REPOTTING: As needed.
DIMENSIONS: 1 to 10 feet tall and 1 to 4 feet wide.
PROPAGATION: From stem cuttings in any season.
PROBLEMS: Overwatering leads to stem rot. Spider mites, aphids, mealybugs, and scale insects are possible pests.
TIP: Toxic; keep away from children.

Tolmiea menziesii
tol-MEE-a men-ZEEZ-ee-eye

Plantlets sprout on top of the leaves of piggyback plant, pulling the foliage downward for a trailing effect.

PIGGYBACK PLANT, YOUTH-ON-AGE

Piggyback plants are popular with indoor gardeners because of their plantlets, which sprout on top of the foliage, causing the leaves to arch downward. The trailing leaves quickly produce a large plant suitable for a hanging basket or a plant pedestal.

Piggyback plant forms a clump of hairy, lobed, medium-green leaves that look much like maple leaves. It readily produces upright, open stalks of tiny brownish flowers, but they're of little ornamental value and are usually cut off.

Besides the medium-green piggyback plant, there is also a variegated form, *T. menziesii* 'Taff's Gold' *(T. menziesii* 'Maculata'), which has paler green leaves mottled with cream and pale yellow.

LIGHT: Bright.
WATER: Keep evenly moist; water sparingly in winter.
HUMIDITY: High.
TEMPERATURE: Cool; cold in winter.
FERTILIZER: All-purpose during growing period. Not a heavy feeder.
REPOTTING: Annually in any season.
DIMENSIONS: 1 to 2 feet tall and 3 feet wide.
PROPAGATION: Remove plantlets and press them into moist soil to root. Or layer by pegging leaves into potting mix, then potting the plants individually when rooted.
PROBLEMS: Leaves scorch if the plant is in a draft or dry air. Dry soil or excess mineral salts can damage roots, causing the plant to die back and making it prone to infestations of spider mites. Mealybugs are another possible pest.
TIP: Older plants do not age gracefully, so start new ones from plantlets.

SPIDERWORT, WANDERING JEW, INCH-PLANT

Tradescantia
tra-des-KANT-ee-a

Not so long ago, several different genera of spiderworts existed—*Rhoeo, Setcreasea, Zebrina,* etc.—but many of these have since been incorporated into the genus *Tradescantia.* In general, it's a genus of plants that share such similar needs and growth habits that they are best grouped together.

Typically spiderworts have boat-shaped leaves of varying lengths borne alternately along trailing stems. All of them flower seasonally, with small, three-sepaled blooms, but most are grown strictly for their colorful or variegated foliage. They are used as groundcovers, in hanging baskets, or as trailing plants on shelves. Pinch back the stem tips and remove old, unattractive stems frequently to prevent legginess or a spindly appearance. They are renowned for their ease of care; in fact, many are pass-along plants that have been shared among neighbors, family, and friends for generations.

LIGHT: Bright.

WATER: Keep evenly moist.
HUMIDITY: Average to high. A humidifier or a humidity tray might be necessary for those with smooth leaves; those with hairy leaves tolerate drier air.
TEMPERATURE: Average.
FERTILIZER: All-purpose during growing period. Not heavy feeders.
REPOTTING: As needed.
DIMENSIONS: Depending on variety, 8 to 16 inches tall and 10 to 36 inches wide.
PROPAGATION: From stem cuttings in any season.
PROBLEMS: Low light causes spindly growth. Dry soil or excess mineral salts can damage roots, causing dieback. Variegated leaves sometimes revert to an all-green form; remove these. Spider mites and aphids are possible pests.
TIPS: Cut back overly long stems to stimulate regrowth from base. Pinch stem tips frequently. Remove dried leaves. Spiderworts do not age

Purple wandering Jew

gracefully; start new plants from stem cuttings.

The following are some of the most popular spiderworts for indoor growing. Although botanists put them in various genera, most home gardeners instantly recognize them as spiderworts.

Striped inch-plant (*Callisia elegans,* syn. *Setcreasea elegans*) is very similar to *Tradescantia* and shares the same common name. The leaves are olive green with white lengthwise stripes, purple underneath, and silky to the touch. The flowers are white and appear in clusters at the stem ends in winter.

The trailing stems of *Tradescantia albiflora* 'Albovitata' are best displayed in a hanging basket.

Teddy-bear plant (*Cyanotis kewensis*) is a smaller creeper with a fleshy brown stem and triangular, somewhat succulent leaves that are olive green above and reddish below. It is entirely covered with fuzzy brown hair, giving it a huggable, teddy-bear appearance. It may produce pink-purple flowers in summer.

Teddy-bear plant (Cyanotis kewensis)

Tahitian bridal-veil (Gibasis geniculata)

Seersucker plant (*Geogenanthus undatus*) is a prostrate plant that creeps but doesn't trail. It has shiny leaves, broader than those of most other spiderworts. They are dark metallic green with gray pinstripes and a red reverse, but the plant's main attraction is the beautiful quilting of the leaves. The flowers are blue-purple, but it rarely blooms.

Tahitian bridal-veil (*Gibasis geniculata*) is a hanging plant with small, pointed leaves—green above, purple below—borne oppositely along trailing stems. Given enough light, the plant bears a profusion of tiny, delicate, white flowers on thin stalks above the foliage. This is where the name bridal-veil comes from. The plant is particularly sensitive to dry air and dry soil. It has several botanical synonyms: *Tradescantia geniculata*, *T. multiflora*, and *Tripogandra multiflora*.

Brown spiderwort, or bear ears (*Siderasis fuscata*), is one of the rare spiderworts that doesn't trail but forms clustering rosettes of broad, oblong, olive green leaves with a silvery central band and a purple reverse. The whole plant is covered with copper brown hairs. It bears large, lavender-blue flowers in clusters from the center of the plant.

Because it produces no visible stems, it can't be multiplied from cuttings, only by division.

Flowering inch-plant (*Tradescantia cerinthoides*, syn. *T. blossfeldiana*) has larger leaves than most spiderworts, up to 6 inches long, green and hairless above and purple with fuzzy white hairs below. It produces white flowers intermittently throughout the year. *T. cerinthoides* 'Variegata' (syn. *T. blossfeldiana* 'Variegata') has creamy stripes and is purplish below. It is more common in culture than the species.

Striped inch-plant, or wandering Jew (*Tradescantia fluminensis*), is a trailing plant with light green over purple leaves that occasionally produces white flowers. Better known than the species, though, are its variegated varieties: *T. fluminensis* 'Albovittata', with very broadly white-striped leaves and *T. fluminensis* 'Variegata' (syn. *T. albiflora* 'Variegata'), with creamy stripes.

Purple-heart (*Tradescantia pallida* 'Purpurea', syn. *T. pallida* 'Purple Heart') was long known as *Setcreasea purpurea*. It is slower growing than most spiderworts, has longer purple leaves and requires less pinching. It needs more light to bring out the attractive deep purple that gives it its name. It is upward-growing at first but eventually trails. The bright pink flowers are short-lived but nonetheless very attractive.

Silver wandering Jew (*Tradescantia pendula*, now *T. zebrina*) is a long-popular trailing plant with shiny green leaves with broad, iridescent silver bands and purple undersides. Better known is *Zebrina pendula*. Among the various variegated forms, *T. pendula* 'Quadricolor' is the most colorful; it's heavily striped with white and pink.

White velvet (*Tradescantia sillamontana*) is one of the hairiest spiderworts. Its green leaves are densely covered in woolly, white hair. It has shorter, more densely covered stems than most others in its group and tends to grow upright at first but does become trailing. The magenta-pink flowers are spectacular in summer.

The common names for *Tradescantia spathacea* (long known as *Rhoeo spathacea*) come from the odd way it bears flowers. At the base of the terminal leaves on the shoots, small white blooms appear within cupped bracts like a small boat or a swaddled baby; thus it is called boat-

Bear ears *(Siderasis fuscata)* is one spiderwort that does not have trailing stems.

lily and Moses-in-the-cradle. The foliage is striking: green on top and deep purple or maroon beneath. The yellow-striped cultivar *T. spathacea* 'Vitatta' is especially noteworthy. The plant has cane stems that trail as they get older,

so it is generally grown in a hanging basket. Fertilize lightly, and leach the potting mix occasionally to keep the older leaves from dropping. Unlike most spiderworts, Moses-in-the-cradle is not propagated by cuttings but by division.

Boat-lily *(Tradescantia spathacea)*

Zamioculcas zamiifolia
zam-ee-o-KUL-kas zam-ee-eye-FO-lee-a

AROID PALM, AROID FERN, ZEEZEE PLANT

Although its botanical name means "with leaves like *Zamia*," a reference to one of the cycads, this plant is actually in the aroid family, a group better known for plants like the philodendron.

The plant forms a rosette of thick, fleshy leaf stalks that radiate upward and outward. They bear pinnately arranged glossy, elliptic leaflets, creating the effect of a palm leaf. The whole plant is dark green. With time, it produces offsets and fills up its pot with foliage.

It is better to let the soil dry out somewhat between waterings. It can go for long periods without any water at all, eventually losing its leaflets. If it still gets no water, the petioles start to dry out, too, but not before producing small tubers along

Aroid palm is a philodendron relative that tolerates average household conditions and some neglect.

their length, where the leaflets used to be.

LIGHT: Medium to bright. Tolerates low light for long periods.
WATER: Let the potting mix dry slightly between waterings. Tolerates long periods of drought.
HUMIDITY: Average.
TEMPERATURE: Average.
FERTILIZER: All-purpose during growing period. Not a heavy feeder.
DIMENSIONS: 2 to 4 feet tall and 2 to 5 feet wide.
REPOTTING: As needed.
PROPAGATION: By division of suckers. Aroid palm may also produce bulblets from its leaves.
PROBLEMS: Overwatering leads to stem rot. Mealybugs and scale insects are possible pests.
TIPS: Remove faded leaves as they appear. Purchase a large-enough specimen for your current indoor needs. The plant is toxic, so keep it away from children.

Zantedeschia
zan-te-DIS-kee-a

CALLA, CALLA LILY

The elegant flower of the calla lily, actually a colored leaf called a spathe that curls around a fragrant, yellow column of true flowers, needs no introduction. Most people recognize it on sight. Besides being a popular cut flower, calla lily also makes a good houseplant.

The best-known calla lily is the largest: *Z. aethiopica*. It bears creamy white spathes, 5 to 10 inches long, on top of wide, glossy, arrow- or heart-shaped leaves. It can reach 4 feet or more in height when in flower, but some cultivars are much smaller. Other species include *Z. eliottiana* (golden calla), which has white-spotted, arrow-shaped leaves, and *Z. rehmannii* (pink calla), with strap-shaped leaves often covered with white dots. Hybrid callas in shades of white, pink, yellow, orange, and red are becoming increasingly popular.

Keep moist, even wet, during

Hybrid calla lilies are a colorful change from the original white. They're available in shades of pink, yellow, orange, and red.

growth; when blooms fade, reduce watering. During dormancy, keep the rhizome nearly dry, watering it only enough to keep it from shriveling. Divide if necessary before starting a new growth cycle.

LIGHT: Bright.
WATER: Keep thoroughly moist but allow to dry during dormancy.
HUMIDITY: High.
TEMPERATURE: Average; cool to cold during dormancy.
FERTILIZER: All-purpose during growing period.
DIMENSIONS: 1 to 3 feet tall and 6 to 24 inches wide.
REPOTTING: At the end of dormancy.
PROPAGATION: By division or from rhizome sections.
PROBLEMS: Low light causes spindly growth and poor bloom. Dry air causes leaf dieback. Spider mites are possible pests in dry air.
TIPS: Pick off yellowed leaves. Cut faded flower stalks.

Resources

Please call nurseries and greenhouses before planning a visit, some are open by appointment only and many are not open to the public every day of the week. Note: Canadian nurseries cannot ship plants to the United States.

Plants

Alannah's Greenhouses
Box 1342
Grand Forks, BC V0H 1H0
Canada
250/442-2552
www.alannahs.com
African violets, gesneriads, specialty geraniums, and assorted flowering tropical houseplants

Davidson-Wilson Greenhouses
3147 E. Ladoga Rd.
Crawfordsville, IN 47933 USA
877/723-6834
www.davidson-wilson.com
Unusual houseplants; specialty geraniums

Florida Plants Online
www.floridaplants.com/
interior.htm
Indoor plants and supplies

Glasshouse Works
Church St., P.O. Box 97
Stewart, OH 45778 USA
740/662-2142
Orders: 800/837-2142
www.glasshouseworks.com
Tropical and rare plants

Harborcrest Gardens
1581-II Hillside Ave.,
Suite 230
Victoria, BC V8T 2C1 Canada
250/642-7309
www.harborcrestgardens.com
Tropical flowering and foliage plants and African violets

Hobbs Farm & Greenery
979 Barnestown Rd
Hope, ME 04847 USA
207/763-4746
www.hobbsfarm.com
Houseplants; ivies

Kartuz Greenhouses,
Sunset Island Exotics
1408 Sunset Dr.
Vista, CA 92085 USA
760/941-3613
www.kartuz.com
Gesneriads, begonias, flowering tropicals, subtropicals, vines

Lauray of Salisbury
432 Undermountain Rd.,
Rte. 41
Salisbury, CT 06068 USA
860/435-2263
www.lauray.com
Cacti, orchids, begonias, gesneriads, succulents

Logee's Greenhouses
141 North St.
Danielson, CT 06239 USA
888/330-8038
www.logees.com
Tropicals and subtropicals

Lyndon Lyon Greenhouses
P.O. Box 249
14 Mutchler St.
Dolgeville, NY 13329 USA
315/429-8291
www.lyndonlyon.com
African violets and orchids

McKinney's Glasshouse
P.O. Box 782282
Wichita, KS 67278 USA
316/686-9438
Gesneriads, rare and exotic tropicals, supplies

Northridge Gardens
9821 White Oak Ave.
Northridge, CA 91325 USA
818/349-9798
Succulents, hard-to-find items

Oak Hill Gardens
P.O. Box 25
37W 550 Binnie Rd.
Dundee, IL 60118 USA
847/428-8500
www.oakhillgardens.com
Specialty plants, orchids, and supplies

Packer Nursery
P.O. Box 4056
Kailua-Kona, HI 96745 USA
888/345-5566
www.alohapalms.com
Palms and tropicals

P. & J. Greenhouses
20265 82nd Ave.
Langley, BC V2Y 2A9 Canada
604/888-3274
www.geranium-
greenhouses.com
Geraniums and fuchsias

Rainbow Gardens Nursery &
Bookshop
1444 E. Taylor St.
Vista, CA 92084 USA
760/758-4290
www.rainbowgardensbookshop.com
Plants and books

Rhapis Gardens
P.O. Box 287
Gregory, TX 78359 USA
361/643-2061
www.rhapisgardens.com
Lady and sago palms, grape ivy, ming aralias

Stokes Tropicals
4806 W. Old Spanish Trail
Jeanerette, LA 70544 USA
337/365-6998
Orders: 800/624-9706
www.stokestropicals.com

Sunrise Nursery
13105 Canyon View
Leander, TX 78641 USA
512/267-0023
www.sunrisenursery.com
Succulents, cacti

Resources

(continued)

Tiki Nursery
P.O. Box 187
Fairview, NC 28730 USA
828/628-2212
Gesneriads (African violets)

Supplies

Eco Enterprises
1240 N.E. 175th St., Suite B
Shoreline, WA 98155 USA
800/426-6937
www.ecogrow.com
Growing supplies, lighting

Charley's Greenhouse &
   Garden
17979 State Route 536
Mount Vernon, WA 98273 USA
800/322-4707
www.charleysgreenhouse.com
Growing supplies, ornaments,
   greenhouses, lighting

Diamond Lights
1701 4th St.
San Rafael, CA 94901 USA
888/331-3994
www.diamondlights.com
High intensity lighting, indoor
   growing supplies

Digital Raingardens
5922 Shadow Wood Dr.
Corpus Christi TX 78415 USA
361/852-5063
www.raingardens.com
Houseplant seeds

Gardener's Supply Co.
128 Intervale Rd.
Burlington, VT 05401 USA
800/955-3370
www.gardeners.com
Seed-starting supplies, organic
   fertilizers and pest controls,
   hand tools, and watering
   systems

Hydro-Farm
755 Southpoint Blvd.
Petaluma, CA 94954 USA
707/765-9990
www.hydrofarm.com
High-intensity lighting and
   indoor growing supplies

Indoor Gardening Supplies
P.O. Box 527
Dexter, MI 48130 USA
800/823-5740
www.indoorgardensupplies.com
Growing supplies

The Scotts Company
800/225-2883
www.scotts.com
www.ortho.com
www.miracle-gro.com
Fertilizers, mulches, and pest
   controls

Seedlings.com
15 Valley Farms
Fairfield, ME 0493 USA
www.seedlings.com/seeds/
   houseplants/
Houseplant seeds

William Dam Seeds
P.O. Box 8400
279 Hwy. 8 (Flamborough)
Dundas, ON L9H 6M1
Canada
905/628-6641
www.damseeds.com

Windowbox.com
3821 S. Santa Fe Ave.
Vernon, CA 90058 USA
888/427-3362
323/277-1137
www.windowbox.com
Container gardening supplies

METRIC CONVERSIONS

U.S. Units to Metric Equivalents			Metric Units to U.S. Equivalents		
To Convert From	**Multiply By**	**To Get**	**To Convert From**	**Multiply By**	**To Get**
Inches	25.4	Millimeters	Millimeters	0.0394	Inches
Inches	2.54	Centimeters	Centimeters	0.3937	Inches
Feet	30.48	Centimeters	Centimeters	0.0328	Feet
Feet	0.3048	Meters	Meters	3.2808	Feet
Yards	0.9144	Meters	Meters	1.0936	Yards
Square inches	6.4516	Square centimeters	Square centimeters	0.1550	Square inches
Square feet	0.0929	Square meters	Square meters	10.764	Square feet
Square yards	0.8361	Square meters	Square meters	1.1960	Square yards
Acres	0.4047	Hectares	Hectares	2.4711	Acres
Cubic inches	16.387	Cubic centimeters	Cubic centimeters	0.0610	Cubic inches
Cubic feet	0.0283	Cubic meters	Cubic meters	35.315	Cubic feet
Cubic feet	28.316	Liters	Liters	0.0353	Cubic feet
Cubic yards	0.7646	Cubic meters	Cubic meters	1.308	Cubic yards
Cubic yards	764.55	Liters	Liters	0.0013	Cubic yards

To convert from degrees Fahrenheit (F) to degrees Celsius (C), first subtract 32, then multiply by $\frac{5}{9}$.

To convert from degrees Celsius to degrees Fahrenheit, multiply by $\frac{9}{5}$, then add 32.

Index

Note: Page numbers in **boldface type** indicate Gallery entries. Page numbers in **_bold italic type_** indicate photographs.

Ortho Complete Guide to Houseplants
Project Editor: Elsa F. Kramer
Editor: Denny Schrock
Contributing Writer: Larry Hodgson
Senior Associate Design Director: Tom Wegner
Assistant Editor: Harijs Priekulis
Copy Chief: Terri Fredrickson
Copy and Production Editor: Victoria Forlini
Photographers: Marty Baldwin, Jay Wilde
Editorial Operations Manager: Karen Schirm
Managers, Book Production: Pam Kvitne,
  Marjorie J. Schenkelberg, Rick von Holdt
Contributing Copy Editor: Kim Catanzarite
Technical Consultants: Deborah Brown, Michael D. Smith
Contributing Proofreaders: Julie Cahalan, Terri Krueger,
  Elise Marton
Contributing Map Illustrator: Jana Fothergill
Contributing Prop/Photo Stylists: Susan Strelecki,
  Diane Witosky
Indexer: Kathleen Poole
Editorial and Design Assistants: Kathleen Stevens,
  Karen McFadden

**Additional Editorial Contributions from
Art Rep Services**
Director: Chip Nadeau
Designers: lk Design
Illustrator: Shawn Wallace

Meredith® Books
Editor in Chief: Linda Raglan Cunningham
Design Director: Matt Strelecki
Executive Editor, Gardening and Home Improvement:
  Benjamin W. Allen
Executive Editor, Gardening: Michael McKinley

Publisher: James D. Blume
Executive Director, Marketing: Jeffrey Myers
Executive Director, New Business Development:
  Todd M. Davis
Executive Director, Sales: Ken Zagor
Director, Operations: George A. Susral
Director, Production: Douglas M. Johnston
Business Director: Jim Leonard

Vice President and General Manager: Douglas J. Guendel

Meredith Publishing Group
President, Publishing Group: Stephen M. Lacy
Vice President-Publishing Director: Bob Mate

Meredith Corporation
Chairman and Chief Executive Officer: William T. Kerr

In Memoriam: E.T. Meredith III (1933–2003)

Note to the Readers: Due to differing conditions, tools, and individual skills, Meredith Corporation assumes no responsibility for any damages, injuries suffered, or losses incurred as a result of following the information published in this book. Before beginning any project, review the instructions carefully, and if any doubts or questions remain, consult local experts or authorities. Because codes and regulations vary greatly, you always should check with authorities to ensure that your project complies with all applicable local codes and regulations. Always read and observe all of the safety precautions provided by manufacturers of any tools, equipment, or supplies, and follow all accepted safety procedures.

Thanks to
Janet Anderson, Rosemary Kautzky, Mary Irene Swartz

Photographers
(Photographers credited may retain copyright ©
  to the listed photographs.)
L = Left, R = Right, C = Center, B = Bottom, T = Top

Lynne Brotchie/Garden Picture Library: 76; **Pat Bruno/Positive Images:** 188T; **Karen Bussolini/Positive Images:** 162B; **David Cavagnaro:** 114TR, 117T, 118B, 120T, 126BL, 126BR, 128B, 132L, 134TR, 136T, 138B, 146TR, 163B, 165T, 169T, 175R, 177T, 179B, 181T, 185B, 203BL, 203T, 203TRC, 203BR, 207L; **Walter Chandoha:** 78TL, 78TR, 140T; **Alan & Linda Detrick:** 8TL, 80, 95T, 97B, 175L, 186BR, 193B, 194T, 200B; **Derek Fell:** 11T, 39, 105B, 115T, 122R, 129T, 144TC, 149TR, 164B, 168T, 174R, 180T, 185CR, 198TR, 198B, 199T, 201B, 206BR, 207R, 211B, 213T, 214CL; **Bisser Georgiev/Hermann Engelmann Greenhouses Inc.:** 167B; **John Glover:** 25, 119L, 126BC, 128T, 135B, 137B, 153T, 155T, 158B, 161T, 162T, 163C, 164T, 173L, 188B, 199B, 204B, 214BL, 214R; **John Glover/Positive Images:** 109BL; **Jessie M. Harris:** 163T; **Larry Hodgson/Horticom Inc.:** 187T; **Jacqui Hurst/Garden Picture Library:** 75B; **Bill Johnson:** 13BL, 93C, 104B, 108B, 135T, 145T, 153B, 156T, 166T, 181BL, 182B, 194B, 203BRC, 205B; **Dency Kane:** 184BR; **Rosemary Kautzky:** 2-3, 24, 85, 95B, 96T, 96C, 102B, 105T, 111, 124B, 129B, 136B, 151T, 157B, 173R, 176T, 189T, 192, 196T, 202T, 209R, back cover BL; **Noel Kavanagh/Garden Picture Library:** 77T; **Kent's Bromeliad Nursery Inc.:** 1, cover, cover spine; **Lamontagne/Garden Picture Library:** 141B; **Scott Leonhart/Positive Images:** 155B; **Lee Lockwood/Positive Images:** 144BC; **Marilynn McAra:** 144B, 146TL, 170B; **Jerry Pavia:** 23R, 106BR, 119R, 126T, 130B, 131BC, 131B, 138C, 139T, 145B, 146B, 149BL, 156B, 161B, 168B, 186T, 197B, 209L, 210C, 213B, 214T; **Ben Phillips/Positive Images:** 107TL, 109BR, 165B; **Howard Rice/Garden Picture Library:** 103T, 131TC, 171B; **Kenneth Rice:** 47; **J.S. Sira/Garden Picture Library:** 167T, 201T, 205T; **Alberg Squillace/Positive Images:** 5, 100; **Friedrich Strauss/Garden Picture Library:** 8TR, 8BL, 74, 77B, 102T, 132R, 147T, 171T, 172R, 177B, 191; **Michael S. Thompson:** 13T, 13BR, 14, 79B, 106BL, 110B, 120B, 123, 124T, 133T, 140B, 147B, 148BR, 149BR, 152B, 158T, 159T, 160R, 169B, 170T, 172L, 174L, 176B, 180B, 182T, 185TL, 187B, 188C, 189B, 190T, 200T, 208R, 212, back cover BC; **Ron West:** 89T, 90T, 92T; **Steven Wooster/Garden Picture Library:** 107TR, 183B, 185TR, 208L

All of us at Meredith® Books are dedicated to providing you with the information and ideas you need to enhance your home and garden. We welcome your comments and suggestions about this book. Write to us at:
  Meredith Corporation
  Meredith Gardening Books
  1716 Locust St.
  Des Moines, IA 50309–3023

If you would like to purchase any of our gardening, home improvement, cooking, crafts, or home decorating and design books, check wherever quality books are sold. Or visit us at: meredithbooks.com

If you would like more information on other Ortho products, call 800/225-2883 or visit us at: www.ortho.com